ALTHUSSER, THE INFINITE FAREWELL

ALTHUSSER,

Translated by Gavin Arnall   With a foreword by Étienne Balibar

EMILIO DE ÍPOLA

THE INFINITE FAREWELL

Duke University Press   Durham and London   2018

© 2018 DUKE UNIVERSITY PRESS. ALL RIGHTS RESERVED.

Printed in the United States of America on acid-free paper ∞
Text designed by Courtney Leigh Baker
Cover designed by Matthew Tauch
Typeset in Whitman by Copperline Book Services

Library of Congress Cataloging-in-Publication Data to come
Names: De Ipola, Emilio, author. | Arnall, Gavin, [date–]
translator. | Balibar, Étienne, [date–] writer of foreword.
Title: Althusser, the infinite farewell / Emilio de Ípola ;
translated by Gavin Arnall ; with a foreword by Étienne Balibar.
Other titles: Althusser, el infinito adiós.
EnglishDescription: Durham : Duke University Press, 2018. |
Includes bibliographical references and index.
Identifiers: LCCN 2017049282 (print) | LCCN 2017054711 (ebook)
ISBN 9780822372141 (ebook)
ISBN 9780822370246 (hardcover : alk. paper)
ISBN 9780822370154 (pbk. : alk. paper)
Subjects: LCSH: Althusser, Louis, 1918–1990—Criticism and
interpretation.
Classification: LCC B2430.A474 (ebook) |
LCC B2430.A474 D413 2018 (print) | DDC 194—dc23
LC record available at https://lccn.loc.gov/2017049282

COVER ART: Photograph by José Luis Barcia Fernández

To Claudia   To Julia and Miguel

CONTENTS

Translator's Acknowledgments ix
Translator's Note on References xi
Foreword by Étienne Balibar xiii

PROLOGUE. **ALTHUSSER?** 1

ONE. **THE PAST, THAT STRANGE LAND** 10

TWO. **THE "CLASSIC" ALTHUSSER AND HIS SLIPS** 29

THREE. **THE TRAPS OF IDEOLOGY** 64

FOUR. **THE SOLITARY HOUR** 82

CONCLUSION. **ALTHUSSER'S LAST LESSON** 103

Notes 111
Bibliography 141
Index 149

TRANSLATOR'S ACKNOWLEDGMENTS

First and foremost, I would like to express my gratitude to Emilio de Ípola for affording me the opportunity to translate *Althusser, el infinito adiós*. His infinite encouragement, humor, and support converted the typically solitary task of translation into a lively conversation and exchange. I would also like to thank Étienne Balibar, who was the first to discuss this translation project with me when we met a number of years ago. Since that encounter, I have benefitted greatly from his intellectual generosity and kindness.

I am grateful to Michael Arnall, Bruno Bosteels, Katie Chenoweth, Sabrina de Luca, Susana Draper, Jacques Lezra, and Anna Kazumi Stahl for contributing in different ways to this translation and its publication. I also wish to acknowledge Courtney Berger, Sandra Korn, two anonymous reviewers, and the other editors at Duke University Press, Presses Universitaires de France, and Siglo XXI who made the publication of this book possible. Ana Sabau deserves special recognition for patiently helping me work through the most complicated passages of the text, sometimes more than once. I dedicate this translation to her.

Gavin Arnall
Ann Arbor, Michigan
May 2017

TRANSLATOR'S NOTE ON REFERENCES

Whenever possible, I cite existing English translations of original sources. If a text is cited that has not yet been translated, I provide my own translation and cite the original. Sometimes both the existing translation and the original source are cited if the latter provides relevant information to the reader or plays a role in the book's argument.

FOREWORD ÉTIENNE BALIBAR

A philosopher's purgatory can last for more or less time. In Althusser's case, it will have been thirty years. There is no shortage of reasons to explain this fact, and they should not be obscured. Certain signs suggest, however, that this purgatory may be coming to an end. How long will the current renewal of interest last, and what reassessment will it yield? How will it transform the intellectual image of the author of *For Marx* or the way we philosophize? It is likely too early to say. It is possible, however, to get an idea of the questions that will form the heart of the discussion.

Emilio de Ípola's book is one of the striking testaments to this reversal of fortune, perhaps the most original one to date.[1] This book combines three of the elements that have, in a general way, contributed to the unanticipated rise of "Althusserian" studies: the return to the intellectual context of the 1960s to 1980s by one of its active participants; the use of posthumous publications (which exceed in volume, and often in interest, that which appeared during Althusser's lifetime), in order to reexamine what motivated his "project," as well as the internal tensions that marked it; and the relation of this project to a political critique whose points of reference have changed but whose urgency is greater than ever. I do not hesitate to recommend it to both new and old enthusiasts of "theoretical practice."[2]

Emilio de Ípola's book is written in the first person, and I will ask permission to do the same in the hopes that, rather than leading to sentimentalism, it will more candidly reveal "where I'm speaking from," as one used to say. Having been (along with others) the student, collaborator, and friend of the man designated here as the "classic Althusser," I cannot claim any detachment from what is discussed in these pages. I will not conceal, then, that I read de Ípola's book with much emotion and much pleasure, but also with much interest and, before long, much surprise. He brought me the book one evening when I was in Buenos Aires, lending my support to a teaching program that is striving to maintain a long tradition of Franco-Argentinian exchanges. Emilio is not the kind of person who broadcasts the importance of his work to sing his own praises. He is one of the most authentic dandies I've ever had the fortune to meet, a man you might see up on the barricades with a cigar between his teeth, someone whom generations of students have revered, while he insists he was just trying to pass along a few concepts. "You'll see," he told me, "I went back to those old debates from our youth using the files at IMEC.[3] Maybe some of my *porteño* ideas will move you to laughter or tears." That's putting it mildly. I spent all night devouring it. Then I reread it pen in hand, determined to make this work accessible to a non-Hispanophone readership.

Before getting into the substance of the book and describing what I believe to be the contribution of de Ípola's analysis, it would be fitting to say a few words about the very particular relationship that Althusser maintained with Latin American intellectual revolutionaries during the 1960s and 1970s. In France and the rest of Europe, and elsewhere still, everyone had an opinion about his "intervention." There were Althusserians and anti-Althusserians, attempts at application or extrapolation, virulent critiques, and reversals of attitude dictated by reflection, emotion, or political stances, not to mention Althusser's own palinodes. But between Buenos Aires, Santiago de Chile, São Paulo, Bogotá, Mexico City, and even Havana, at least for a few years, in the period between the guerrillas and the dictatorships—as what Régis Debray called "the revolution in the revolution" was finding its way among the "paths" of Fidel Castro, Che Guevara, and Salvador Allende—the situation was altogether different: there was a general conviction not only that Marxism was *alive*, but that it was being *reborn*, in the strict sense of the term.[4] Effacing decades of dogmatism and revisionism to undertake the "return to Marx," going inside his laboratory of thought and reassessing all the old assumptions from a different perspective, which allowed for an absolute fidelity to what the author of *Capital* intended and, at the same time, the victorious overcoming of the obstacles that had tripped up "Marxists" in his wake. The Marxism "recommenced" by Althusser would have been, as in a Jorge Luis Borges story (but now with stakes that were in direct contact with history), at once *identical* to itself and yet *entirely other*;[5] Marxism's own empirical history would, in retrospect, have represented a deviation or "drift [*dérive*]."[6] In this way, the figure of Althusser managed, incredibly, to become distinct from the interpreter or critic, without transforming into the political leader; instead, he came to resemble a "double."

There would be room, of course, to interrogate the historical, cultural, psychological, and geopolitical reasons for this representation, which was fashioned out of desire and the imaginary, but also out of demand and intractability.[7] Some other time, if I can muster the courage, I will describe the devastating effects that this representation ultimately had on Althusser himself—who was unable to bear the position of master, even at a distance. But here we are discussing something more cheerful. After coming to terms with the hope of witnessing the return of truth incarnate, after regaining freedom in the face of both nostalgia and resentment, after effectively measuring the distance between two worlds that are in some sense each other's doubles—which for this very reason can neither divide nor intersect—reflection can take its rightful place. This book, *The Infinite Farewell*, which presents itself as an anamnesis provoked by the shock of the encounter with Althusser's posthumous works, is not just a portrait—the likeness of which we will discuss later on—but also a veritable conversation with him, a conversation in which the irreducible multiplicity of his faces mitigates to some extent his actual absence. In the absence of the ability to summon him to respond, it is still possible to set up the discussion he must have had with himself (or should have had) and to intervene as a third party. What results is a powerful and original construction that is anything but mere commentary. It owes as much to the concerns, knowledge, and thought of its author as it does to the formulations of *Reading Capital* and *Machiavelli and Us*. Others may, if they wish, enter into this work themselves and seek to inflect it. I think it would be time well spent.

Let us now look at how this book breaks new ground in its reading and discussion of Althusser. It will be helpful to follow the order of the three main chapters. In chapter 2, de Ípola offers an entirely updated interpretation of Althusser's relation to structuralism, based essentially on the reconstruction of his so-called *différend* with Lévi-Strauss, the difference between his attitude and Lacan's, and the importance of Badiou's and Miller's interventions in this domain. This interpretation is not archaeological or anecdotal. We will see that it is a key to arguments about the much-discussed "theoreticism." The approach de Ípola has chosen imparts the full weight of a philosophical problem as profound as it is difficult—that of "structural causality"—that has not yet, perhaps, revealed all its dimensions.

I can attest to the fact that the dispute between Sartre and Lévi-Strauss in the early 1960s over the articulation of symbolic structures and the different regimes of historicity (following the nearly simultaneous publication of *Critique of Dialectical Reason* and *The Savage Mind*) indeed sparked numerous theoretical projects (in Marxism, epistemology, and applied psychoanalysis, as well as anthropology and politics, in the history of philosophy), which the group provisionally assembled around Althusser was attempting to combine.[8] I also think de Ípola is right to propose a symptomatic reading of the denials contained in the double movement of imitation and rejection that marked our attitude toward the idea of "structure" as Lévi-Strauss understood it, both before and after *Reading Capital* was put together. Some minor individual differences aside, Althusser and the rest of us were all much closer than we ever wanted to admit to the question posed by the idea of symbolic efficacy (one need only look closely, as de Ípola does here, at the analogies between the problematic of the lacking signification [*signification manquante*] in Lévi-Strauss and that of the absent cause in Althusser to be convinced of this fact) and, on the other hand, not attentive enough to its implications with respect to the question of the "supposition of the subject," to the extent that structure reveals itself to be essentially incomplete, marked by a constitutive lack. By the same token, I think he is right to suggest that in this ambivalent relation to structuralism (which combined a systematic attempt to take structuralism beyond its own formulations and a retreat before its "idealist" philosophical consequences) there resides one of the keys—if not *the* key—to the uncertainties and inconsistencies that mark Althusser's theoretical project: either one attributes these to the internal, subterranean pressure of another philosophy that is contradictory with the first and betrays itself in the form of a "Freudian slip," or else one attributes them to the external pressure of politics and its organizational demands. The implications of this complex would also be the point of departure for revisiting what, precisely, is *theoretical* in Althusser's *theoreticist* ambition (which we shared with him) to rectify the course of revolutionary politics by starting from an "epistemological break," which was understood as tantamount to a revolution in the field of "science."

As a matter of fact, this work, which brings up to date fine conceptual figures and surprising relationships between texts, is not lacking in contemporary relevance; it goes beyond a rewriting of Althusser's self-critique that would restore to him what he *did not say* or said insufficiently.[9] Indeed, now is the time to reread the structuralist debate and to reassess the roles that different representatives of the "philosophical moment" of the 1960s played in that debate.[10] And this rereading must not limit itself to discussions about the legitimacy of applying the "linguistic model" to anthropology, literature, the history of religion, and psychoanalysis, or (to use Milner's terminology)[11] the relation between a "research program" and a "structuralist *doxa*," or the possibility or impossibility, in general, of relegating questions of knowledge and practice (even those of affectivity and "life") to one or more *orders of discourse*, to an *instance of the letter*, as Lacan, Foucault, and Derrida debated. This rereading must address above all the relation between the *idea of structure* as such and the category of the *subject*, which governs the entirety of classical philosophy (potentially under other names, in particular, that of *praxis*). As I have argued elsewhere, this relation cannot be reduced to a reciprocal exclusion (such that a coherent structuralism would constitute the archetype of a philosophy "without a subject," and the condition for thinking subjectivity would be to "do away with structure"), yet it necessarily entails a certain contradiction. In recreating—"inventing," in the literal sense—the debates of Lévi-Strauss and Althusser on this topic, de Ípola does not just reconstruct the backdrop of contemporaneous developments (the most ambitious expression of which was probably the Lacanian notion of the *barred subject*, which Jacques-Alain Miller related to the *function of misrecognition* that Althusser said was shared by Marx's and Freud's critiques of humanism); he also brings to light a singular chiasm [*chassé-croisé*]. It is unquestionably true that adopting the structural point of view should block the path to any conception of any *constituting subject* (be it in thought or in history), at the risk of seriously troubling any political philosophy that takes on the task of recognizing in history the collective subject capable of "transforming the world." But, as it so happens, the incessantly renewed questioning into the properties and modalities of the *constituted subject* (for Althusser, the subject constituted by "ideology," which is itself considered to be the representative "instance" in which the material "last instance" is recognized and misrecognized) confers on Lévi-Strauss's work a remarkable relevance after the fact. What de Ípola diagnoses in Althusser is a wavering between a return to the themes of philosophies of praxis (Sartre, Gramsci, even Lukács) to reestablish the possibility of a *transformation* of social relations and the existing state of things, and (the more interesting option, in his view) the ambiguous opening (in the form of things that spring to mind in a premonitory way, or Freudian slips) onto another problematic (by way of "conjuncture," "singularity," and "overdetermination"). One can see that he also took cues from Lévi-Strauss himself as to the relations between culture and individual psychical processes, which form the very site of variation and, more profoundly, of anthropological *deviation*.

I will say no more about that. But one can see, I think, that de Ípola's analysis harbors the seeds of a *general* questioning (concentrated here on two authors) of what, in the work of structuralists—those who claim that label or repudiate it, those whose work is of greater or lesser significance—makes it possible to revolutionize the question of the subject, starting with a critique of its ideological and metaphysical inheritance, but also to clear the way for a new position, one that is still uncertain, in which indetermination and efficacy could be in question simultaneously. This allows us to glimpse the fact that, from a philosophical perspective, the great frontier that must be recognized is the problematic of *modalities* (classically: reality, contingency, necessity). Such would indeed be the heart of the inquiries undertaken by the "last Althusser," which de Ípola, in a Straussian vein, dubs *esoteric*.[12] But prior to this, we must go through and take seriously, whether we want to or not, the privileged lens through which Althusser, nearly from start to finish, undertook to treat (and rectify) the philosophy of the subject: his problematic of *ideology*, which he attempted to think "for Marx and against Marx."

Let us move on, then, to the second trouble spot identified by de Ípola (in chapter 3). One might ask oneself, ultimately, given both the problems it encompasses (precisely those having to do with the *constitution of the subject*) and the method it unceasingly applies (which is always characterized, at bottom, by the search for a *double inscription of the ideological*, at once "within" and "without" the existing social formation, or knowledge, thus at the point where these are made and undone), whether ideology for Althusser is not another name for structure. I am tempted to think so, retrospectively, and to draw from this an argument in favor of the idea that, in his search for a "philosophy for Marxism" that would not be the existing "Marxist philosophy" (the centerpiece of which has always been the development of the *materialist concept of ideology*, which Marx named but immediately gave up in favor of considerations grounded in the search for the "language of real life" and in the power of the "ideas of the dominant class"), Althusser was destined sooner or later to run into a contradiction with his own "theoreticism," insofar as it actually represented less an epistemology than a politics.

Assisted by some of his students, Althusser of course made great efforts to find a common language for dialectical materialism, the history of sciences focused on the "formation of concepts," and the analysis of discourse and unconscious formations (whether individual or collective), the horizon of which was represented (initially) by an "idea of science" applicable to the theories of Frege, Husserl, Lenin, and Freud. First developed around 1900, but only recognized as a conceptual unit after the fact and in a different geophilosophical location (Paris), this idea certainly owed nothing to Hegel, whom it suspected of mysticism and sophistry; it sought rather to extend an "applied" rationalism (Bachelard) of formalization and experimentation, adapted to what would later be called "complexity" (rather than "life"), beyond the field of natural sciences. But in Althusser's version (which de Ípola here calls a "Kautskyian" *theory*, which will require younger readers to do some archaeological digging),[13] on account of his political objectives, rationalism focuses on results that one could call "pedagogical" in the broadest sense. The watchword was not just *theory* but *theoretical training [formation]*. The dominant ideology is "inculcated" by State ideological apparatuses (such as school and family, but also political parties), all the more effectively because it happens unconsciously, by way of material practices or behaviors, if you will, imposed on individuals by institutions, rituals, and disciplines that always already "think" for them. How to *undo* this conditioning, which is as necessary to individuals as the air they breathe? By "fighting," of course, but first (and to be able to fight) by "understanding" and "analyzing" the mechanism that forms you and makes you think the way you do. . . . *Sed intelligere*, wrote Spinoza.[14]

I believe that in chapter 3 of his book de Ípola uncovers, in an altogether illuminating way, why it is that the idea of "the interpellation of individuals [as] subjects"—an idea that even today drives interest in Althusser for disciples of "critical theory" in much of the world[15]—*displaces this pedagogism* by revealing its incompatibility with an effective materialism (all the more flagrant given that, from the start, Althusser was ardently opposed to the Platonic or Kantian notion of a relation of knowledge to ideology that would be modeled on the antithetical pairing of truth and error, or illusion, even a transcendental one). But he also shows why it *gives rise to internal contradiction* in the concept of ideology, in a form that is no longer epistemological (or is no longer dominated by epistemology), but that is thoroughly political (and historico-political). To move quickly (since the readers must go to the text and form their own opinion), I think de Ípola is absolutely right to insist on the idea that two theories Althusser articulated successively[16]—one that accounts for the "reproduction of relations of production" by the fact that ideological apparatuses recruit individuals to serve as carriers of these same relations, and one that accounts for the effect of subjectivity by the way in which subjects "recognize" themselves in the figure and injunctions of an (imaginary) Subject to which they are "subjected"—are logically contradictory. He is likewise absolutely right to interpret, once again as a symptom, the way in which, in his attempt to overcome his readers' confusion, Althusser ends up having recourse to the very idea he had argued against as "historicist," "Hegelian" (and Lukacsian), etc.—namely, the idea that the *abstraction* of mechanisms of "ideology in general," which allows them to function "in the mode of eternity," is *the product of forms of individuality*, themselves *abstract* and reified, imposed by capitalism on its carriers in order to incorporate their labor force.[17]

What is worth asking oneself, however, is why Althusser was not able to give up on the idea that there is a *class function* of ideology (in "class societies"—but what other kinds of societies are there?), or the idea that subjectivization entails *in general* an effect of misrecognition (or alienation, not in the Feuerbachian sense, but rather in the Lacanian sense, thus in the final analysis still a Hegelian sense). And what is interesting about these ideas is that *they are both political*, albeit in radically incompatible senses. One is political because it attacks a social, collective domination that distributes power among groups and submits individuals en masse to an expropriation of the very conditions of their own lives, and the other is political because it sets the internal limits of what each individual can effectively grasp of the conditions and motivations of her actions or her participation in a process of emancipation. These are the two sides, which it is tempting to call "objective" and "subjective," of what constitutes a relation in a structuralist sense. But a relation is, precisely, not an "individual," and there is no pineal gland or psychophysiological parallelism that connects these two sides in an immediate way. In order to make this hold water theoretically, one would have to admit that the revolutionary struggle itself represents a form of ideological subjection (as, precisely, interpellation by a Subject—a Subject that could very well be Revolution or Communism) (and all of Althusser's work was likely haunted, without his admitting it, by the question of the alienation of revolutionary political action itself, and what distinguishes this form of alienation—or does not distinguish it—from imprisonment within the framework of the dominant ideology).[18] But how can we concede this last thesis (in view of "ideology in general," which "will have no end," as Althusser announced from the start, and in view of his analogy, even his identification of ideology "in the last instance" with the mechanism of the unconscious) without *negating* the difference in efficacy, in historical significance, and even in ethical value (where does one get the idea that Althusser overlooked this dimension?) between multiple ways of *being subjected*, which may very well be formally identical, but which do not in any way entail, in *given conditions*, the same conservative or transformative effects on the "world"?

It seems that, no matter what, the analysis of ideological mechanisms always winds up in an all-or-nothing aporia: *either* a liberation that is "absolute" or "total," extracting individuals and their collective movements from the very limits of ideology (which, for Althusser, is a myth), *or* no liberation at all, because all subjection is the flip side of a reproduction of "domination." Unless we consider that not only is there contingency, variability, or ambivalence to the effects of subjection, but, perhaps, that there is no ideological formation—monotheism, rights of man, social revolution, what have you—that is conservative or transformative *in itself*, but there are only *effects of conservation, resistance, or transgression* of ideology, of which the figure of interpellation is never the only explanation. Here we approach the famous "labyrinth of freedom" that Leibniz speaks of, and it is understandable that Althusser would have gotten caught in it, given the double pressure of a philosophical context dominated by Spinozism (to which he himself had made a significant contribution) and a political situation dominated by the swaying movements of the idea of revolution (which he had made his life's work), as de Ípola demonstrates relentlessly.[19] But I would suggest that we not rush to declare these aporias unproductive or unimportant or to believe that we have at our disposal the guarantee of escaping them once and for all.

This brings us to the third part of de Ípola's argument, the "solitary hour" of a thought taken to "extremes" that it had always foreseen but had never arrived at naming as such, as the title of chapter 4 suggests in a wonderful turn of Althusser's famous formulation of the inaccessible "last instance" of historical analysis. In other words, in a series of texts that are unfinished, uneven, intentionally provocative, and resolutely indifferent to the conventions of pedagogical and dialectical exposition, texts that are sometimes a bit mad, but that suddenly allow us to reread in another way everything that came before, the uncovering of a long-repressed "esoteric" philosophy, or better, one that was prevented from growing by the joint effect of (structuralist, rationalist) theoreticism and (Marxist, revolutionary) practicism: this is what one calls the philosophy of the "last Althusser," which is contained essentially in two posthumous texts and marked by the repeated (some are tempted to say *incantatory*) use of formulations like "aleatory materialism" or "materialism of the encounter," which evoke explicitly or implicitly the Epicurean and Lucretian model of the *clinamen* as a beyond (or a below) of the metaphysical opposition between determinism and freedom, and which suggest, within the field of history, a resolute *primacy* of the "conjuncture" (of cases, of singular situations) over "structure" (or better still, the erasure of the opposition between structure and conjuncture, the latter being only the spare change of the former, according to the preference clearly affirmed by all of the structuralists).[20] What I find particularly interesting here is not only de Ípola's effort to demonstrate the *reversal* that took place in Althusser's priorities, causing what previously seemed to need lengthy theoretical construction or deduction to enter a state of primitive "materialist fact" (like the fall or rain of atoms in the void). It is not even simply the way he elucidates the virtual coherence of this philosophy to come (which a whole subset of Althusser's current readers, both young and older, are choosing to work on today). It is two characteristics particular to de Ípola's reading, starting from the end.

First of all, there is the fact that de Ípola (drawing in part on the remarkable work of his former student Francisco Naishtat and playing liberally on analogies with both Sartre and more recent essays in political sociology) inscribes the question of aleatory materialism within the perspective of *collective action*, which entails both discursive (performative) and nondiscursive elements. Twisting a phrase of Badiou's (a great Sartrean if ever there was one), de Ípola speaks of "subjectivity without a subject," an oxymoron that marks the necessity of twisting traditional philosophical perspectives in order to analyze the forms and stages of political action (or agency, or organization).[21] The "encounter" Althusser spoke of and the "swerve" [*déviation*] he situated at its origin (not a punctual origin, but an origin that is virtual, always available) here takes on a more concrete and historical meaning, far removed from the naturalism of habitual Lucretian references and yet alien to any dialectic of the subject of history as an "I that is we and we that is I" (Hegel).[22] The encounter is the *crystallization of collective units* (themselves contextual, aleatory, contradictory, but not at all indeterminate as a pure "multitude" would be) that *cause situations to deviate* from their internal instability, or from "counter-tendencies" inherent in their tendencies (de Ípola very rightly points out how far back this preoccupation with counter-tendencies goes in Althusser, and that they go from being a precaution against a naturalist positivism of the laws of history to an ontological characteristic of processes, or historical eventalism). This way of reading Althusser's indications from a resolutely political perspective (and not *metapolitical*, as a whole set of contemporary readings have a tendency to do, particularly those who locate in Althusser's turn against his own organizational "Leninism" arguments for assigning him a metaphysics of spontaneity) is already, it seems to me, very elucidating with respect to the referent of the "last Althusser," which was constituted more than ever by the field of class struggles and questioning into the *alternative to capitalism* as a "material possibility" (or a possibility *in fact*) of its very movement.

But there is more still. By referring extensively to Althusser's "Machiavelli and Us" (an unpublished work that largely dates, let us not forget, from 1972, and that thus illustrates in a striking way the idea that there exists a "subterranean" Althusser that permanently shadows his public writing, a work of which I have elsewhere said that, precisely in its imperfect state, is perhaps the most perfect thing Althusser ever wrote),[23] de Ípola also introduces another idea: that of the profound identity between the thought of *encounter* (or conjuncture) and that of *conflict* (or struggle). As you will see, tying together the disjointed threads of different texts leads de Ípola to assign a strategic value to Althusser's "thesis" (first articulated as a reaction against Marxist sociologism and economism) according to which "classes" would not precede their own struggle, but on the contrary, would *result from* the modes, vicissitudes, and degrees of intensity of that struggle.[24] Pushed a bit further, this hypothesis leads to the idea that "classes" (an essentially *relational* notion, or whose existence "for itself" is only ever the objective and subjective effect of a "for the other," as Sartre would have said) only form *within a historical conjuncture* (temporarily and locally—though this does not mean they are short-lived or have no future) through the convergent action of those who are mobilized in the resistance of these classes and recognize themselves in their struggle. It seems to me that we come very close here to the possibility of moving beyond the obstacle Althusser believed could not be overcome when he was contemplating—in a fairly scholastic way, it must be said—classes and masses (not to mention heads), which explains, among other reasons, his reticence to "finish" the *Machiavelli* text and make it public. I wonder if we haven't come right back to the aporia I mentioned previously, with an "ideology" the effects of which are transformative but whose mechanism is, as such, conservative. This would likely not be de Ípola's own thesis, given that he tends (along with Naishtat, Cefaï, or even Badiou) to posit the logic of *action* against that of *subjection* (or ideology), and probably understands the expression "subjectivity without a subject" in this way, as a final nod to the "first Althusser." But the discussion is just beginning (again).

I hope that with the foregoing remarks, by setting out certain necessary steps and reversals, I have not overly encroached upon an author's right to himself present his own thought, in his own language. If this is the case, I beg his forgiveness; we shall place our faith in the reader's ability to distinguish between what he actually demonstrates and what I've just attributed to him—shaking up some of his formulations a bit, just as he himself does with those of Althusser. I've done this because I found it necessary to explain why an old Althusserian might find himself at once destabilized and moved to revisit his earliest lines of inquiry by a reading as thought-provoking as that of *Althusser, The Infinite Farewell*. I've done it, in fact, because I glimpse in this text the possibility of rejoining the ranks, if not handing over the reins once and for all to other interpreters, others who are taking up the pieces of analysis scattered across Althusser's troubled "career," others who may or may not be "Marxists," but for whom the double demand—the double intransigence—of the concept (which is theoretical, whether we like it or not) and of transformation (of "ourselves," as Foucault would say, and thus of the relations that constitute us) will always be meaningful. I think that this is what Emilio de Ípola had in mind when, with an audacity none of us could have mustered, he conceived of this book and brought it to fruition. Which is an altogether effective way of remaking the exoteric—in other words, the common—out of the esoteric: the involuntary secret of a man who thought he was "alone."

Irvine, California, February 2012
Translated by Katie Chenoweth

Althusserianism (what a word!).
—LOUIS ALTHUSSER, *Lettres à Franca*

PROLOGUE. **ALTHUSSER?**

I initially conceived of this work as a brief presentation of the philosophy of the "last" Althusser. For obvious reasons, it was supposed to focus on the works that the French philosopher produced during the last years of his life, or more precisely on the texts written and published late in Althusser's life or released after his death.[1]

I nevertheless stumbled upon a difficulty not long after beginning that revealed itself to be resistant to any solution, despite my best efforts to the contrary (and some objectionable tricks of the trade). The object that I had decided to investigate and that I thought would be possible to grasp without too much trouble was becoming more and more complicated and intangible, as if it insisted treacherously on deterring my efforts to contain it, on demonstrating that it was—at least for me—completely elusive.

Some formulations that the last Althusser employs, for example, seemed entirely novel at first glance, such that it was possible to view them as signs of a profound philosophical rupture with the "classic" Althusser.[2] After a second reading, however, either because of some passing reference or a sudden experience of déjà vu compelling me to return to earlier texts, it became clear that what had seemed like the discovery of something novel was not actually that novel, that the extent of its novelty was more limited than initially presumed. Or perhaps its alleged originality, to reveal itself as such, required an arduous labor of reinterpretation and revision of Althusser's earlier texts, which seemed, at least partially, to anticipate later formulations. The frequent irruption of difficulties such as these eroded the idea that something like a clearly perceptible and analyzable philosophy of the "last Althusser" existed. I accordingly had to either abandon writing the book or reconsider and amplify the bounds of its object of study.

This sort of "retrospective" demand, by virtue of which the originally pared-down object of study called for an unanticipated return to earlier texts, generated a second, complementary demand, anticipatory in nature. Indeed, to make matters even more complicated, I noted after a while that my object of study stretched not only back toward the past but also forward into the future.[3] This future was one that Althusser, who died in 1990, would not witness, a future that would have as its protagonists other authors, some of them Althusser's former disciples, and others affiliated with his thought. The former group consists of philosophers such as Étienne Balibar, Alain Badiou, Jacques Rancière,[4] and Jacques Bidet, while the latter group includes, among others, Slavoj Žižek and Ernesto Laclau. It is likely that some of these authors did not have access until very recently to Althusser's unpublished works. In those texts, they might have discovered that Althusser, during his solitary journey lasting almost a decade, explored the same philosophical terrain that each of them, in their own way, has traversed since then.[5] There was, accordingly, continuity that stretched into the future and that challenged the thesis of a sui generis philosophy with no ties to the past and no anticipatory projection, a closed philosophy, if you will, of the "last Althusser."[6] My initial object of study, as the saying goes, thus "melted into air." This is not the entire story, however, and to clarify this point, please permit me a detour. It does not give me pleasure to warn the reader that this detour will not be the last.

I AM CONSCIOUS OF the fact that, given the author under consideration and the current intellectual climate, it is inevitable to run into an obvious and pertinent objection: why return to Althusser today? Who could be interested in his work?[7] Despite the commotion and renewed interest provoked by the publication of his autobiography and some other unpublished writings, it would be dishonest not to recognize that this interest is still limited and is even considered by some, typically sociologists and political scientists, to be incomprehensibly anachronistic. There is furthermore no shortage of people who still to this day brand Althusser's work as the most thorough verification of the terminal crisis of Marxism.

But the passing of time improves vision and opens up new perspectives with which to approach and evaluate the work of a formerly celebrated author. It even makes possible the correction of certain oversights (some of which, as I will show, are a bit suspicious) and calls attention to some blind spots in the criticism that targeted Althusser's work when it was already past its prime.[8]

The first complete edition of Althusser's autobiography was published in 1992 with the title *The Future Lasts Forever*.[9] Its author had died two years earlier after sinking into such profound oblivion that it had appeared definitive. In Argentina, the youngest generations ignored his existence and even forgot his name, while many among those who remembered him did so only to insistently advocate for the need to forget him. With the appearance of his autobiography, however, things began to change. The book stirred up old memories among those who had known him, and those who had discovered him through this work read it with interest. This commotion and interest grew as new posthumously published texts progressively came to light.

The publication of *The Future Lasts Forever* troubled many, making them feel almost remorseful. There was no shortage of individuals who declared, after decades of bitter attacks, that they had discovered an "other" Althusser. Of course, psychologists and psychoanalysts of all theoretical tendencies and geographical locations also jubilantly welcomed this *morceau de roi* with which they were unexpectedly provided. They did not hesitate in celebrating it with lavish banquets.[10]

Additionally, the Institut Mémoirs de L'édition Contemporaines (IMEC), in coordination with the *Fondation Althusser*, took on the task of methodically publishing the vast collection of unpublished manuscripts that Althusser had produced between 1947 and 1986 and that the *Fondation* had entrusted to IMEC. This effort is still currently underway.

Knowledge of these unpublished texts, many of them recently released or soon to be released, provoked, among other things, the emergence of a renewed interest in Althusser's classic works. Since the 1990s, a considerable number of monographs and essays have appeared that analyze from different angles the relationship between the classic works and those of the last Althusser. Not all of them have been celebratory, of course, but none of them have been devastating critiques. Time has tempered certain passions and dissolved the partisan fervor of certain polemics. Althusser has accordingly been slowly and unevenly reintroduced into contemporary philosophical and political debates, a process that, at least for the moment, is still taking place.

This account may help clarify the insurmountable difficulties experienced while attempting to delimit the object of study and confine it to the last Althusser. Yet, as I previously mentioned, this was not the entire story. I quickly discovered in fact that there was something personal underlying my reasons for writing about Althusser, something that incited me to expand my object of study and opt for an interpretation of the whole. It happens to be the case that I was myself an Althusserian enthusiast starting in the early 1960s and, as was required, occasionally also a critic of some of Althusser's theoretical positions. In all honesty, I did not yet realize that those two characteristics were the trademark of all good Althusserians (it was not accidental that our principal referent was, after Althusser himself, the young philosopher Alain Badiou, who more than satisfied both criteria).

Since the mid-1970s, Althusser "had fallen out of favor [*cayó en desuso*]," to apply Salvador Giner's formulation.[11] I accepted this situation, which coincided with what had generally been referred to as the "crisis of Marxism," neither happily nor with surprise. In October of 1980, I thought, along with the grand majority, that beyond the famous psychopathological or criminal story appearing in the media, no one would continue to care about the work of Althusser, not even to subject it to the most ferocious of critiques. I was prey, although less so than others, to what Oscar Terán called "the moment of aversion to Marxism," which affected so many intellectuals of the Left during the early 1980s.[12] It was an intense, although transient, collective passion. Not long thereafter, someone took up the gauntlet, and that someone was in fact Althusser himself with the release of his unpublished texts. Reading those "unforeseen" texts revived interest in his work. The storm had already passed by then, and the time that had elapsed permitted me to see things more objectively and with better judgment than I did in the 1980s.

Without a doubt, this revival of interest in Althusser's philosophy was and *is* partial. This is in part because Althusser was the last Marxist thinker who, as he himself would have said, "usurped" the heaven of philosophical and theoretico-political ideas during the 1960s. Even worse, he was a philosopher who presented his opinions with a seductive and, at the same time, deliberately lofty turn of phrase. He was an intellectual tailor-made for the iconoclasts of Marxist symbols that we all aspired to be—and were—during those years. Apprehension toward his work partly endured, along with a resistance to revisiting it.

For that reason, even though Althusser has become interesting again—and not only because of the tragedy of his personal life—this new interest is not the same as before. It is more philosophical than political, more theoretical, let's say, than militant. The anachronism that still affects Althusser's thought could no doubt be partially transmitted to this book. If so, I will have simply added more untimeliness to the untimeliness that, for many people, definitively stigmatizes the work of Althusser.

In this way, I quickly discovered the appeal of reviewing the global itinerary of Althusser's thought. Above all, it would permit me, or rather oblige me, to review and perhaps take stock of my own theoretical itinerary. While satisfying, this conclusion also comes with a proviso that I have tried with great effort to respect—namely, that of inhibiting my personal background from surreptitiously occupying center stage, even if only intermittently or unobtrusively. In chapter 1, I felt obligated to refer to the intellectual climate of the moment and to how students and young leftists, myself included, were affected by Althusser while at the same time contributing to his own formation.[13] But there is nothing further from my intent than to force upon the unknowing reader a covert autobiography.

The preceding observation clarifies the specific and singular objective of this text. My aim, simply put, is to give an account of Althusser's philosophical itinerary and especially of the conceptual and political tensions and conflicts that unsettled, like a kind of silent but constant turbulence, the unfolding of his entire oeuvre. These tensions and conflicts—at least this is my hypothesis—tended to partially dissipate and lead to a way out in the texts produced during the last years of Althusser's life, but not without the price of injurious revisions. To provide an emblematic date, I am referring to the texts published by Althusser or posthumously disseminated by others after *Positions* (1976).[14] It should be noted, of course, that *The Future Lasts Forever* (1992) and the volume titled *Lettres à Franca* (1998) shall not be excluded from the inventory of works considered.

But it should also be clear that my focus is *not* on the life or the narration of the life of Althusser the individual. It is even less my goal to "explicate" his writings and his philosophical itinerary through the interpretation of the avatars of his personal life. The Lacanian psychoanalyst Gérard Pommier, among others, has already attempted this, and it has resulted in an obvious failure, not counting the interest awakened by the intrigues of private life and the tragedy of others.[15] While a modest inventory of reconstructed memories and of the alleged trickery that the "play of the Signifier" inflicted on the "victim" may perhaps maintain appearances,[16] it contributes nothing to psychoanalysis or to our knowledge of an author's work.[17] My objective is of an exclusively theoretical and philosophico-political nature. Occasionally, and for reasons that the reader will have to understand, this study will adopt the form of a story, but I have sought to abstain entirely from meddling with Althusser's personal history.[18]

It is well known that Althusser addressed the issue of reading and discussed it with striking insistence, even to the point of engaging in polemics with himself on the matter. He expressed one of his recurring concerns with the similarly recurring formulation: *to see clearly in Marx*.[19] Yet to see clearly in Marx required having available the basic elements for a theory of reading. Althusser forged these basic elements out of an acute critique of standpoints that conceive of knowledge as a form of vision. Clearly tracing a line of continuity with the theory of analytic listening, Althusser proposed his own theory of "symptomatic" reading. Although inspired by Freud and Lacan, this theory had as its immediate referent an essay written by Jean Laplanche and Serge Leclaire titled "The Unconscious: A Psychoanalytic Study."[20] Althusser understood this kind of reading to be comparable to what psychoanalysts call, in reference to analytic listening, the principle of "free-floating attention," which is to say the guideline that recommends remaining alert and attentive to lacunas, questions without answers, answers without questions, turns of phrase and the twisting of words, repetitions, metaphors, and in general the rhetoric of a determinate discourse *at every level*.[21] This guideline also advises paying special attention to what is forgotten, to contradictions, to slips, and to open-ended conclusions in the text being read. The analogy with analytic listening does of course have its limits. From this point of view, a text is always (im)patient, it slowly but surely reveals its certainties and doubts, and, as Plato once said, it does not respond to the questions that are posed to it but rather continually insists on its positions, ignoring its own silences and disregarding the queries of the reader.

Today I think that the outline of this symptomatic theory constituted a necessary but insufficient step toward a form of reading that does not want to lose itself in the quagmire of commentary or justification. Althusser's own practice tried to be faithful to the symptomatic theory, but, despite achieving some noticeable results,[22] his fidelity was merely sporadic, and had he truly adhered to it, he would have encountered certain limits that would have impeded the free unfolding of his own thought. For this reason, the imagination, intuitions, and above all ex ante conclusions prevailed in the Althusserian reading of Marx (as in the reading of other authors). With his pen, Althusser converted the works of Marx, Engels, and Lenin into an infinitely moldable material, malleable to his previously held theoretical convictions, to his shifts in philosophical direction, and, on occasion, to his righteous indignation (something that—far from opposing—I am inclined to celebrate).[23]

Accordingly, what I am interested in analyzing here—and I insist on this point—is the path of Althusserian thought and not the path of his readings or of the "lessons" that Althusser believed he could extract from these readings. This is nevertheless where I run into problems, specifically the problems of *my* reading.

If, as noted earlier, my intention is to explore and discuss the trajectory of Althusser's thought as a whole (and not only that of the "posthumous" Althusser), this is because in the very course of my investigation I glimpsed, despite appearances, how Althusser's thought does not lend itself to being divided into clearly demarcated stages. On this issue, I am contradicting the widely held opinion that such stages do in fact exist. It has thus been said that there was initially a "classic" Althusser, the Althusser of the 1960s, who was habitually and not arbitrarily associated with the structuralist tendency. Later on, there would be the intermediate period during which Althusser would deploy in multiple ways what he called his "self-critique." This self-critique focused on two points: (a) forgetting about the class struggle in his classic writings and (b) his theoreticism (linked in diverse ways to the prior issue). Toward the late 1970s, an unknown and somewhat unpredictable Althusser began to emerge, an Althusser who at first only gained expression through allusions, ironies, and criticisms—such as, for example, by adopting an attitude increasingly less complaisant toward Marx (as well as toward Engels and Lenin). A bit later, this Althusser became plainly visible in his last philosophical works, those published after his death, on "aleatory materialism" or "materialism of the encounter."

I will nonetheless try to demonstrate during the course of this book that these chronological demarcations, despite offering valid and useful points of reference, are ultimately inadequate. The way in which Althusser's thought and writing evolves, oftentimes despite the author himself, is more complicated, more "twisted" [*retorcido*], to use an unscholarly word. In Althusser's work, there are changes in position, core thematic ideas that appear and disappear without explanation, and a burdensome doubleness [*duplicidad*] in the economy of his thought, a doubleness located at the center of his work's aporias but also at the center of the interest that his work arouses. I believe that the key to understanding the Althusserian itinerary as well as the eventual *actuality* of his thought can be found in this doubleness, which needs to be broken down in what follows. It can be found at least there where Althusser manages to transcend the conditioning of the historical moment in which he lived, and especially there where he manages to break out of the "long-term prisons" in which some of his own theoretical positions had enclosed him.

If this is the case, then the periodization of Althusser's thought into "stages" ignores something of fundamental importance: that *already in his first well-known writings—the book on Montesquieu, for example—there are unexpected statements, incongruent with the logic of the argument, and observations that slip by as though the author decided to let them pass unnoticed.*[24] *It is already possible at that moment, I repeat, to detect traces, which would become more and more frequent later on, of other thought, not so much different from the thought that Althusser develops in explicit terms as incommensurable with it.* But let's not get ahead of ourselves.

Before concluding this prologue, I would like to note that during the month of February 2005, with the intention of writing this book along with other publications already in circulation, I had the opportunity to consult Althusser's unpublished manuscripts in the library of the Ardenne Abbey (Normandy) at IMEC, where I was received and lodged with generous hospitality. I was accordingly able to access some extremely valuable sources of information. For that reason, I want to express my sincerest gratitude to Mme. Eliane Vernouillet and the Comité de Accueil of the abbey for their hospitality, and to IMEC's director, M. José Ruiz-Funes, for his helpful cooperation. Without this disinterested collaboration, without the mild calm of the mountains and of the afternoons in Saint-Germain-la-Blanche-Herbe, where the Ardenne Abbey is located (and where the cruel devastation of the Nazi bombers of 1944 can still be felt), without the amicable silence of the library, it would have been very difficult for me to write this manuscript.

I would also like to express my profound gratitude to María Elena Qués and Carlos Altamirano, who read this text and who made suggestions that were softened by well-chosen compliments to facilitate my acceptance of said suggestions, constantly encouraging me, insisting that the work was worth publishing.

I would of course also like to recognize the decisive intellectual and affective support of my wife, Claudia Hilb, the best possible reader, a critic so intelligent that even her objections felt like praise, a generous collaborator in resolving the technical problems that my inexperience multiplied. I also want to recognize the support of my son, Miguel, who has given me the breath of his music, and of my daughter, Julia, happy that she could finally be the one to tell me with loving seriousness that it was time to finish my "homework." But I feel thankful above all for something much simpler and easier to say: because they are here, by my side.

Emilio de Ípola
Buenos Aires, fall 2007

> The past is a foreign country: they do things
> differently there. —L. P. HARTLEY, *The Go-Between*

> We are discussing living water which has not yet flowed away.
> —LOUIS ALTHUSSER, *Reading Capital*

ONE. THE PAST, THAT STRANGE LAND

In the prologue, I alluded to some anticipatory traces of the thought of the final Althusser, of the "subterranean" Althusser, traces that almost imperceptibly slipped in behind the beautiful exposition and carefully crafted prose of Althusser's most well-known works. Among other examples, I noted that already in Althusser's first book, *Montesquieu, la politique et l'histoire*, glimpses appeared every so often of the "subterranean current" that silently flowed below the exoteric work, although still outside of the main channel and not yet exhibiting the force with which it would rise to the surface many years later.[1] I also suggested that after reading Althusser's first book I had begun to suspect that the essential idea was already there from the beginning. The reflections that Althusser shared with Franca Madonia in May of 1963 are therefore telling:

> [I]n every beginning [*commencement*], Philosophy is there, completely whole. [. . .] This is why its beginning haunts it, until it recognizes

itself as nothing more than that beginning itself. [. . .] To begin is its own absolute. To reach this absolute it is therefore enough for Philosophy to begin; to begin with those silhouettes that Theaetetus could not make out in the fog of night; to begin with those hats that, before Cartier-Bresson, during their first theoretical stage, Descartes and Comte saw slowly float by on the waterways of a street, toward the meeting of a crossroads; to begin, at last, with that flame shared without a word, simply, freely, between two beings, in spite of carrying the world with their gestures: the cigarette of a street worker that Sartre lights with his lighter; to begin with Aron's mangled ticket, punched at the entrance to the *Métro* in order to enter into the circulation of man; to begin with the round moon on the horizon, filled with trees, shadows, and dreams; to begin with the land overwhelmed by light where a madman painted his night. It is enough to begin.[2]

Althusser wrote these words at the beginning of May 1963. According to the editor of his posthumous volume *Écrits philosophiques et politiques*, Althusser sent this note along with a letter to Madonia on May 6, 1963; the note was supposed to be included as part of the introduction to a book that was never written. With slight variations, these formulations would reappear often in Althusser's work, always leaving open, as in this first statement, the implicit question being posed.

Only in a much later text on Machiavelli does this tacit question receive an answer that is at least conclusive, if not exactly clear: "To the question that has forever haunted philosophy, and always will—with what should one *begin?*—Machiavelli replies quite non-philosophically, but with theses not lacking in philosophical resonance: one should begin at the beginning. The beginning is ultimately nothing. [. . .] It is necessary to begin with nothing—not with 'nothingness' but with the void."[3] The individual who reasons in this way is not a novice thinker unfamiliar with the most arcane realms of philosophy. He is, on the contrary, a thinker of noted prestige who, in the 1960s, renewed and gave fresh strength to a Marxism that was theoretically exhausted and politically innocuous. He is a philosopher whose writings have been recognized, commended, and discussed by the entire world. He is an individual who has forged his thought and elaborated his writings with the (sometimes scorching) heat of imperishable works, chiefly though not solely those of Marx.[4]

And nevertheless, he knows—he always knew—that he cannot rely on the knowledge of such masters to give birth to his own philosophy, or, more precisely, that these masters converge around the common teaching that there are no footholds, no given certainties, no luminous truths to which one can turn. One begins to philosophize in solitude, from the void.

There will of course be no shortage of individuals who think that such ideas are the fruit of fatigue or skepticism, or perhaps ramblings born out of the aftermath of the tragedy of 1980, the last convulsions, in short, of the last Althusser. However, the note attached to the letter for Madonia dates from 1963, which is to say from the beginning. Many years separate that letter and the text on Machiavelli, difficult years during which Althusser, struggling with insistent doubts and problems, produced his principal works and with them gave life to his philosophical and political program. The drama of 1980 seemed to mark the end of his public life as a thinker and intellectual. Nevertheless, slowly and at great costs, Althusser managed to recover and recuperate, at least in part, his capacity to think and to write. He could then return, not without great effort, to philosophy, or, to say the same thing with his words, to go back to the beginning.

IT IS A COMMONPLACE to refer to Althusser's "philosophical and political project." It was initially my intention, once the object of study had been redefined in the aforementioned terms, to clarify the meaning of that project. But I quickly realized that such a task assumed that many questions had already been answered and that many enigmas had already been resolved. I will clarify this point before continuing.

It is certain that an explicit philosophical and political program exists in Althusser's work, a *declared* project that, in agreement with the majority of his interpreters, would have been for better or for worse his sole contribution. Nonetheless, by going a bit deeper and without preconceptions into the details of Althusser's analysis and the subtle weaving of his writing, one discovers, not without growing confusion, the unexpected presence of certain dissonances, the intermittent yet systematic irruption of certain atypical declarations, and occasionally of certain incoherencies in the logic of the argument, all of which encourages doubt regarding the univocal character of Althusser's program.

One reasonable and possible reaction to these anomalies would be to propose the hypothesis that the "disobedient" statements indicate the existence of an *other* project, more radical but also more complicated, underlying Althusser's *declared* project. At stake for both, for the theses of the declared project as much as for the tenor of the discordant formulations, would be the relationship between philosophy and politics. Although divergent, these projects would intersect and coincide at certain points, blurring the borders that separate the one from the other, which could disorient the reader more than once and could possibly even mislead the author himself on occasions. This was the response that I had initially adopted, calling Althusser's first project *declared* and provisionally calling his second project *subterranean*.

As I will attempt to demonstrate, these terms should nevertheless be used with caution. If, through these terms, I deliberately make use of the philosophical commonplace that distinguishes the superficial from the profound and confers ontological primacy to the latter—something that, at first glance, could be conceded to me—I believe that to qualify the subterranean dimension of Althusser's work as a "project" would be both limiting and excessive. It would be limiting because, given the modalities under which the subterranean dimension gradually came to manifest itself, its aim appeared to be from the start to function as a base or ground for the declared project, to which it would confer a firm philosophical foundation and therefore a formal validity that would transcend the conjunctural problematic in which it was formulated. It would moreover be excessive to call the subterranean dimension of Althusser's work a "project" because it persistently stayed in an embryonic state and never achieved clear expression, except for in the final moments of Althusser's oeuvre. When that finally occurred, some obstacles (and perhaps a lack of time) blocked the development of some points and impeded, in particular, the sustained unfolding of the theses Althusser articulated. Although the essential was said, a completed exposition of the new philosophy was missing.

By contrast, what I have called the *declared* project, besides its explicit character, appears to be much more developed and coherent, particularly if the aforementioned "transgressions" are omitted. The project also appears in a certain sense as more "true," since it faithfully expresses that which almost everyone, including Althusser himself, has always understood by Althusserianism. The declared project is, of course, not without problems and unresolved questions, but, beyond the criticism and self-criticism of which it was repeatedly the object, its proposal is clear and its development is continuous and reasoned.

The subterranean "project," on the other hand, abounds with forward movements and reversals, with absences, with vacillations, with sudden boldness, and with confused formulations. As I signaled earlier, this "project" at the beginning could only be seen sporadically in certain formulations that Althusser elusively and intermittently dropped into his first writings. Nonetheless, these formulations gradually became more abundant and vivid such that the contours of the "project" began to take shape and definition. The formulations became, as it were, *recognizable*, as if Althusser himself had suddenly noticed their quiet presence and had cautiously brought their basic axioms to light. Although, as I have also suggested, this "project" never reached the same level of development and clarity as the first one, there lies in the unfinished formulations that Althusser left us, whether in the impact of a phrase or in the brilliance of a new concept, flashes of a more profound philosophical inquiry, of an inquiry more penetrating and more far-reaching than that of the declared project.

It is nevertheless important to elaborate upon a point mentioned in passing earlier—namely, that the declared project and the subterranean "project" are not necessarily always contradictory, even if only because they have not been conceived of as antagonistic instances. Of course, the unexpected irruption of "out of place" statements in the middle of the elaboration of this or that aspect of the declared project generates a kind of tension, even a kind of enmity, between the developed thought and the "transgressor" statement that emerges abruptly out of nowhere. But in Althusser's work there are also zones in which the positions of both the declared and the subterranean are juxtaposed without hostility. Sometimes their coexistence generates baffling effects: ambiguous reasoning, the cohabitation of contradictory—or rather unintelligible—theses, unjustified leaps in the argument, and even *diktats* that sharply and arbitrarily put an end to a latent dispute. In any case, as I will have the opportunity to demonstrate later, the effort to untangle this web is not without interest and is often rewarding. It is, moreover, unavoidable.

I PREVIOUSLY SUGGESTED that our theoretical and philosophico-political trajectory would occasionally adopt the form of a story. This is one of those occasions. I am choosing this path for two very simple reasons: first, because the history that I will narrate, especially during its "triumphant" stage, forms part of my own personal history. I know that being present at the birth and subsequent peak of Althusserianism does not in itself place me in an advantageous position over those who did not live through the same experience. But I also know that a narrative approach is the best approach for someone who has directly experienced an event, even if only partially, and who seeks to return to it years later. Second, the "story" form lends itself better than other forms to the presentation and discussion of a work that is marked by fluctuations, disjointed trajectories and arguments, and unexpected divergences and convergences, to which must be added, particularly starting in 1970, an accumulation of revisions, self-critiques, and additions that were not always assimilable into a reasonably coherent whole.

The history to which I am referring happened more than four decades ago. It is, moreover, a brief, agitated, and in many ways nostalgic history, laden with the illusions, deceptions, and exaltations of the 1960s. From the start of that period, and more forcefully after the publication of *For Marx* and *Reading Capital* in 1965, the work of Althusser had become the obligatory reference point for what Perry Anderson would call "Western Marxism." Leaving aside that whole polemic, one had to salute the renewal that took place at the heart of a rather weak Marxism, a Marxism that was left almost unarmed before the critiques directed against it.[5]

In what follows, I have had to refer to myself on occasions. This is something that makes me uncomfortable and impels me to apologize to the reader. I refer to myself, in any event, so as to "typify" my experience and present it as one example among many (since that is indeed what it was) of someone who unexpectedly but also willingly, after becoming better informed, found himself all of a sudden inserted into an intellectual climate composed of the many innovatory schools of thought that flourished in those years; someone who, after a kind of passive resistance, enthusiastically adhered to the Althusserianism that was thriving at that moment: an Argentine who had obtained a scholarship from the French government in 1964 and became a doctorate student in Paris, which permitted him from the beginning to follow the evolution of the French cultural world in that period. I am also referring to my experience because it was not an isolated one but rather one that many French, but also South American, students shared. This fact bestows some generality on my situation and, for that reason, perhaps also some interest. And finally, I refer to my own experience because, by returning to the theoretical milestones that mark that experience, I have found multiple anticipations of the philosophy of the last Althusser, as if that philosophy had already been present, although hidden and perhaps unknown to the author, from the very beginning of his oeuvre.

After setting up in Paris, a friend told me that what was most interesting in France those days was "Althusser's stuff." This exchange occurred toward the beginning of 1965. On my friend's recommendation, I promptly read, partly seduced and partly scandalized (I was, like many others, *still* a Sartrean), almost all the texts Althusser had published up to that point. A little later, *For Marx* and the two volumes of *Reading Capital* appeared simultaneously.

Every so often, Althusser met with a group of Latin American students from the École Normale Superieure—a group of which I was a part—and conversed with us there, showing signs of great modesty, great intellectual generosity, and great frankness.[6] It was in this way that I quickly converted to Althusserianism, or more precisely to its *declared* project.[7]

That project began to take shape at the end of the 1950s and achieved full expression in the 1960s. It explicitly presented itself as a strategy aimed at accomplishing a leftist transformation of the French Communist Party line through a theoretical labor of renewal and development of Marx's thought. Althusser and his disciples believed that this transformation was possible. They were furthermore of the opinion or felt that there was no possible political alternative outside of the Communist Party, the Party of French workers par excellence, despite its intellectual mediocrity, its servile obedience to the Soviet Union, and its total absence of revolutionary spirit. Some of my Latin American colleagues and I were skeptical of this position once we examined our own communist parties, which were dogmatic, mediocre, authoritarian, and proud of their sectarian ineptitude. But the project of returning to Marx with the aim of discovering in his works the inspiration and the materials necessary for the forging of a truly revolutionary leftist politics seemed to us both legitimate and very appealing.

We thought that it was worth a shot, that it would be possible to take advantage of the new atmosphere of relative freedom open to Marxist investigation due to the crisis of Stalinism that followed the Twentieth Congress of the Communist Party of the Soviet Union. We also believed that a path existed beyond the endpoint of the Stalinist legacy that did not lead to either *theoretical eclecticism* (of which the French Communist Party was already showing symptomatic signs, such as, for example, in the religious humanism of Roger Garaudy) or to *practical reformism*, a reformism that, incidentally, was also able to garner support during the tolerant climate of that period.[8] The return to Marx, the recuperation of his thought, would provide the scientific basis for the correct framing and discussion of the political problems of the present.

As Jacques Rancière has suggested, it was possible at that time to once again talk about Marx, to analyze his work, to move past the recitation of the famous passages.[9] It was possible to seek out and discover a solid foundation in Marx's scientific production, or in Lenin's political practice, or in Mao's philosophical writings and interpretation of political practice. From this solid foundation, it would be possible to think through and resolve old and new political problems while also providing, above all, the means necessary for such a process of thinking and of resolution. The task to be carried out was explicitly formulated as a "theoretical detour" that would define and develop Marxist politics in its specificity.[10]

The time in which we lived seemed auspicious. It was in fact a time filled with enthusiasm, with feverish agitation, with adventurous hopes. Those who were a part of that generation remember it with an indissoluble veneer of nostalgia. Sometimes, despite myself, I faintly hear the happy echoes of those years and evoke with melancholy those illusions that are definitively lost today.

The preoccupation that led to politics through theoretical reflection was indelibly yet clearly inscribed in one of Althusser's first key texts: "Contradiction and Overdetermination."[11] In that text, Althusser contraposed the schematic reductionism of his colleagues with the necessity to reflect on the complex unity of a *plurality* of contradictions that defined the "current moment [*momento actual*]," the place of political intervention. In contrast to the mere discussion of ideas, which was a product of the theoretical destitution of French Marxism, Althusser also considered the reality and the political logic of revolutions in China and Cuba that were in full swing at that time. In that essay, as in another entitled, "On the Materialist Dialectic,"[12] there were some malicious provocations directed toward the party—in particular, the frank and clearly celebratory exegesis of Mao's text on contradiction during the height of the Sino-Soviet conflict, in response to which the leadership of the French Communist Party had already pronounced with habitual clarity its support of the Soviet Union.

But "Contradiction and Overdetermination" was not only about combating the reductionism, dogmatism, and poverty of French Marxism. It was also about restoring Marxist philosophy and theory to its rightful place, in opposition to the ideological, anti-Marxist offensive that, as Althusser maintained with some sensationalism, began to flourish in those years in France. He insisted that the essay had to do with a complex theoretical struggle, above all against the anti-Marxism of the right (that of Raymond

Aron and his acolytes) and the anti-Marxism disguised as orthodox Marxism that was located at the heart of the French Communist Party (that of Roger Garaudy and Gilbert Mury, among others). But it was also aimed at the professedly pro-Marxist or Marxian tendencies of thinkers like Lucien Goldmann, Henri Lefebvre, and Jean-Paul Sartre, the latter of whom Althusser nevertheless always treated with great consideration and respect in his published work.

Althusser, finally, had to face off against an adversary of a different kind, one that held implications for the very core of Althusserianism. This adversary was all the more frightening because of his not unfounded association with Althusserianism. I am referring to Claude Lévi-Strauss. *This is a point that I consider to be fundamental.* In 1962, Lévi-Strauss entered into a polemic for the first time with Sartre, and in contrast to a philosophy based on consciousness and the primacy of individual *praxis*, Lévi-Strauss proposed the efficacy of the unconscious, the incoercible power of structures, their determining character with respect to human action and thought. Although Althusser and his group seemed to share—and in truth did share—much in common with Lévi-Strauss's theses, and even though they utilized concepts and carried out analyses inspired by these theses, they appeared to be no less interested in distancing themselves from the thinker. To put it briefly and therefore schematically, Althusserianism viewed as incompatible with its project an inquiry like that of Lévi-Strauss's, one that was completely given over to structures (e.g., kinship, mythological structures), that, in Lévi-Strauss's own words, should bow before "the power and the inanity of the event" and that exiled history and politics from its horizon of investigation.[13]

Nevertheless, in the theoretical terms with which it was formulated, such an incompatibility was purely declarative and, one could say, "pragmatic." As I will attempt to demonstrate, despite what Althusser and his disciplines insisted on asserting ex post, this was not simply a matter of terminology, nor was it merely an instance of colluding with what was intellectually fashionable at the time.

This issue is of particular importance because it points to one of the book's principal theses. Here I will only allude to it, for its presentation and development will in fact constitute the primary material of the next chapter. In my opinion, the structuralist turn that has been rightly attributed to Althusserianism was undoubtedly one of the key aspects of Althusser's enterprise. But this was the case not for the reasons that are habitually given, but for other reasons. These other reasons are more profound and more generalizable insofar as they transcend the case of Althusserianism, even if it was above all Althusser and later Jacques Lacan, via Althusser's former student Jacques-Alain Miller, who recognized and were responsible for structuralism's relevance. These reasons will not be found in the beautiful and symmetrical exposition of the structures (of circulation) among kinship relations or of the structures (of signification) among myths. They must be located precisely in some of Lévi-Strauss's early intuitions, formulated in some of the (older) writings included in *Structural Anthropology* and in the famous *Introduction to the Work of Marcel Mauss*. These texts are of course very well known and well circulated; however, with the exception of a few cases, they have been associated only tangentially with the philosophical climate of the 1960s and, as a result, have been disassociated with Althusserian thought and the theoretical and philosophical problems that it struggled to clarify and resolve beyond what appeared at the surface.

I am coming to the end of my story. Regarding the debates in which Althusser participated and the economy of his theorization, it is important to consider two conflicting characters that played a decisive role in the Althusserian *dispositif*, as much for their defensive maneuvers as for their offensive theoretical positions. I am of course referring to the opposition "science vs. ideology." Althusser will not only affirm this opposition from the start but will also make it the main target of theoretical debate. From the beginning, Althusser abruptly affirmed without qualification his positions and his divergences with the orthodoxy of the French Communist Party and its acolytes. In a defiant key, he addressed his critics, pointing out that if there was something upon which they could all agree, something that was as important for his critics as for himself, it was on the matter of upholding the positions of Science against Ideology, or more broadly against the ideologies that threatened and denatured Science. In "On the Materialist Dialectic," Althusser deployed a series of categories (theory, Theory, 'theory,' theoretical practice) and demanded that his critics grasp their precise meaning. Althusser instructed his critics, in the event that no valid objections were leveled against these categories, to take them on as their own. He instructed them to do so, I would add, with a hint of contempt and overconfidence.

During that militant and almost triumphant moment of the Althusserian project, the party adhered in theory to the position that Althusser sought to present and sustain, but it did not uphold his position in practice, nor did it believe in the position. Let us call this position "Kautskyian," since it was Karl Kautsky, as can be seen in Lenin's *What Is to be Done?*, who first formulated it. According to this perspective, scientific theory and socialist politics were not, nor could they be, the product of the working class, which was incapable of overcoming its reformism due to its limited knowledge and its experience of the struggle. Instead, scientific theory and socialist politics were the products of intellectuals and scientists endowed with great culture and great freedom of investigation. It was their duty to "import" theory into the working class so that the working class could shed its reformist skin and adopt new, revolutionary positions.

The political bureau of the party could not contradict a sacred thesis of the international communist movement, but it obviously did not have the slightest interest in a group of pretentious philosophers with diplomas proceeding to rummage through Marxist theory and to develop, without oversight, who knows what kind of theories to promote who knows what kind of political positions. According to the leaders of the bureau, they were themselves the "lucid and free intellectuals," and their superior theoretical capacity along with their political experience was what enabled them to exercise leadership. The honorable task of the true intellectuals, moreover, was only to divulge the official line of the party or, if unwilling to do so, to opt for silence, as Louis Aragon did after the Soviet invasion of Hungary.[14]

Yet Althusser's strategy, which knew when necessary how to exhibit an orthodoxy more certain of itself than the orthodoxy of his critics, momentarily baffled the party leadership. When they finally decided to condemn his theses during the 1966 Congress of Argenteuil, Althusser had already become a prestigious figure, much more so than any of the theoretical executioners, many of whom, as history would ironically have it, eventually abandoned the party or were expelled from it. For that reason, it did not occur to the party leadership to pursue more drastic sanctions against Althusser; they of course condemned his theses but did not go any further than that.

At this point, I will return to my own adhesion to Althusserianism. Nothing was more gratifying or welcoming than the project to which Althusser summoned us, we young students who were, or believed that we were, aspiring leftist intellectuals and revolutionary militants. On the one hand, the project entailed becoming the bearers of a Marxist knowledge that was both aggressive and new, as well as up to date on all that France was producing at the time in philosophy and the human sciences (the peak of Lévi-Strauss's work, the first Foucault, the publication of Lacan's *Écrits*, the promising beginnings of Jacques Derrida). On the other hand, by virtue of our possession and utilization of said knowledge, the project entailed being authentic revolutionary militants who intervened on the "theoretical front," the front that, so we were told, was the priority of the moment. And finally, by way of Maoism and the defense of China and its Cultural Revolution, the project entailed being to the left of everyone, supporting not only the most advanced theoretical positions, the most lucid theorists, but also the militant philosophers that were situated furthest to the left, to the left of the communists and also the Trotskyists (tangled up in their unconditional defense of the Soviet Union). This was all terribly seductive and gratifying. It was only logical that many of us young university students would adhere almost unconditionally to Althusser's theses.

Althusser's was a philosophy that intended to influence politics, even if at the same time, in strict consistency with the postulation of Marxism's theoretical antihumanism, it vigorously affirmed the ideological character of any notion of the "autonomous subject" (or simply of the "subject"). It was a philosophy of structural laws that seemed to insist on escaping those laws, a philosophy of science that was frankly, positively, and fervently militant. It was an inquisitor of notions, a defender of scientific nomenclature—conceptual chains of a new *Nomenklatura*—that nevertheless welcomed with warm hospitality the contributions of Foucault, Canguilhem, Bachelard, Lacan, and many others. It was a philosophy provocative enough to avoid being considered trivial, prudent enough to avoid becoming suspicious. This was how the philosophy of Althusser appeared in the mid-1960s. It was a philosophy that was theoretically and politically very seductive, although it did not lack lacunas or difficulties. In any case, if many of us agreed with it, it happened not *despite* but *because* of the problems and theoretical and political challenges that it presented.

AS PREVIOUSLY MENTIONED, this was the *declared* project of Althusser and his followers. I have already specified that, construed in this way, the project did not take into consideration a number of "signs" (formulations, concepts, theses) that could not easily fold into its complicated but intelligible logic. These signs also gave rise to the suspicion or to the certainty that another project, or perhaps another philosophy, existed in a larval state underneath the explicit positions. Except for sudden appearances, this dimension remained hidden for a long time. Such hiding was in no way deliberate but rather, on the contrary, the irritating consequence of powerful reasons.

In effect, the other project posed problems of a different magnitude than those that—so it was thought—the declared project should confront. Likewise, due to the complexity of its intrinsic difficulties, the subterranean project, which should have functioned as the foundation and theoretical verification of the declared project, only managed to solidify or deploy itself at an intermittent and slow rhythm. That which did allow itself to be seen in the ephemeral brilliance of a word, a statement, or a thesis furthermore permitted speculation that what was at stake here was something much more difficult, profound, and indefinable than suggested by the word "project."

That said, since delays and the buildup of suspense seem to me to be advisable only in detective novels, I will finally put forward without further ado the two theses that are intimately connected to what is called the "subterranean project," and I will attempt to justify their pertinence here. I will only say as a forewarning that these theses possess both an explicit assertion and an implicit, although easily grasped, polemical twist.

THESIS 1: Levi-Straussian structuralism is the horizon *with* which and *against* which Althusserian thought struggles.[15] Althusserian thought addresses this form of structuralism *in the declared project*, though not without criticizing it with some generally convincing arguments, but also with some low blows. In any case, the principal virtue of this struggle resides in the fact that it opens a path for Althusser's *subterranean* thought. Within the *problematic* of Althusser's subterranean thought, structuralism is an object of radical scrutiny.[16] While leaving some of structuralism's accomplishments standing, this scrutiny irreparably weakens structuralism's theoretical and philosophical foundations. ■

THESIS 2: Althusser's *subterranean* thought takes on the form of a philosophy that sets as its objective and assumes the responsibility of rendering politics thinkable and possible. In the beginning, this subterranean thought, which aimed to philosophically ground the declared project, collides again and again with the very theories of the classic Althusser—in particular, with the theses that affirm the necessity of establishing "historical materialism" as a science in the strong sense of the term. But already from the beginning some of Althusser's formulations tend to undermine, still sporadically and interstitially, the basic axioms of the declared project.[17] With vacillations and incoherencies, but on occasion with courage and theoretical profundity, this thought laboriously and gradually becomes clearer and more coherent, eroding the foundations of the declared project. In Althusser's last writings, finally free of all restraints, the subterranean philosophy achieves its explicit, though not fully developed, expression. The havoc that the new philosophy causes for the declared project and for the totality of Marxism matters very little at this point. Formulated in these terms, Althusser's subterranean thought anticipates and in essence surpasses in profundity the production of his former disciples; it enters onto post-Marxist terrain various years before the term *post-Marxism* would be coined.[18] ∎

THE GRAND MAJORITY of Althusser's interpreters—friends and foes alike—agree with the assertion that Althusser set out to reestablish through his philosophical "interventions" the foundations of historical materialism, which is to say the science, in the strict sense, of the history of social formations. But to accomplish that goal, Marxist philosophy itself, so-called dialectical materialism, had to be profoundly transformed. "Official" Marxist philosophy, in particular, had to relinquish its idealistic and Hegelian commitments, present in the explicitly philosophical production of Marx, to accomplish once and for all its specific task, which consisted in liberating historical materialism from said commitments and opening up the path for its development into a science. To aid in that process, Marxist philosophy had at its disposal what Althusser called philosophy in a "practical state," delicately underlying Marx's authentically scientific production.

This epistemological reading, which does not lack supporting evidence in the various texts of Althusser and his disciples, is usually associated with the thesis that holds that Althusserianism (despite denying it) found, in the structuralist thought that was fashionable at the time, the basic theses and conceptual tools for laying down the foundation of its own scientific project. In *For Marx* and *Reading Capital*, works to which we should often return, that project would achieve its first brilliant expression. From that point forward, however, the inaugural momentum would wane. On the one hand, Althusser and his team would encounter grave theoretical difficulties that would be the source of disagreements between the group's members and even of the first desertion (Rancière). On the other hand, once past the early infatuation, when the initial praise had quieted down, the theses of both books would become the preferred target of innumerable theoretical and political critiques from within the French Communist Party and from without. Having bypassed an initial state of perplexity, it seemed that the next option was to condemn the theses of Althusser's books.

Indeed, defying the generalized enthusiasm, Althusser's exoteric project was destined from the outset to confront problems that would be very difficult to resolve. I would almost say that his project faced these problems because of the very premises of the project's formulation. In a nutshell, the most explicit formulations of that project sought to shed light on and reinvigorate the *science* founded by Marx, historical materialism conceived as a science of history, a "hard" science dealing with the functioning and transformation of social formations. Marx had inaugurated this science as a science of the economic dimension of the capitalist mode of production. It was now the time to complete and develop it with a science of the political and ideological instances and with a theory of the combined effects of these instances.[19]

Althusserianism tended to openly characterize its theoretical objectives in these or similar terms. But such a schematic formulation already obscured the problem. Indeed, if these were its objectives, Althusserianism could not be limited to the assertion that it represented a "mere" strategy of combating, for subsequent political purposes, the weakest link (the theory) of the political line of the French Communist Party. *In reality, it had to be concluded that it was a vast and ambitious theoretical enterprise whose political consequences were dangerously unpredictable.* At the beginning, however, few seemed to notice that there was something excessive in the formulation of these objectives. Its critics limited themselves to pointing out that Althusser's theses falsified or distorted true Marxism. None of them saw anything "beyond" the declared.

Yet Althusserianism effortlessly announced an explicit proposal that consisted in nothing less than reestablishing the entire Marxist theory of history on the solid terrain of Science. It would use for this purpose philosophical tools stemming from a dialectical materialism that was also reinvented and renewed at its very core. All of this was possible by way of recourse to new theoretico-philosophical categories, many of them extracted from non-Marxist disciplines. Critics curiously challenged Althusserianism more for its use of these categories than for the nature and scope of what it aspired to accomplish with them. They also completely ignored the fact that the eventual success of this enterprise should lead to the reconsideration, and in many cases the rejection, of foregone conclusions rooted in the theoretico-political history of the French Communist Party and the communist parties of the West.

Nonetheless, I reiterate that very few critics paid attention to that disturbing dimension of Althusser's exoteric project. None of them noticed, moreover, that a theoretical enterprise as vast as the one that Althusserianism sought to carry out was closer to a utopia of brilliant but inexperienced intellectuals than to a viable proposal. I tend to believe that Althusser eventually became conscious of this, at least by the second half of the 1960s. It is also my opinion that the project of teaching a collective course on philosophy directed toward scientists should be framed within this context. That project was carried out at the École Normale Supérieure, and it was very well attended and made possible the brilliant interventions of Étienne Balibar, François Regnault, Pierre Macherey, and, above all, Althusser himself.

From the start, the "Course on Philosophy for Scientists" introduced an important modification into the principles of the Althusserian framework that had prevailed until that point: philosophy was no longer posited as a science. Philosophy's specific task now consisted in tracing a line of demarcation "between the scientific and the ideological" within scientific practices, with the aim of liberating these practices from the harm produced by the impact of ideologies on scientific work. Other theses would follow that, despite being qualified as politically decisive, tended to convert Althusserian philosophy into a kind of "policing" epistemology obsessed with the detection and elimination of the virus of the ideological within the scientific practices.

However, neither the philosophical brilliance of certain theses, nor the acuity of certain analyses, nor even the presence of self-criticism within these analyses impeded Althusser, his collaborators, and the participants of the "Course on Philosophy for Scientists" from realizing that their chosen path and the results obtained, particularly from the point of view of politics, had carried them down a dead-end street. After Bachelard and the French tradition of the philosophy of science, it was at least possible—if talented—to do quality epistemology. It was not possible, on the other hand, to do politics, not even experimentally. The propositions and theses of the course led more often to problems than to clear formulations from Althusser.

It is strange to perceive today the extent to which the contributions of Althusser and his collaborators, as well as the expectations of those in attendance, were, irrespective of their theoretical quality, surrounded by a quasi-religious aura, appropriate for someone pursuing a transcendental mission. The language of the theses, presented provocatively as "dogmatic," the references to the "fundamental tasks of our time,"[20] the ironic attitude directed toward Lévi-Strauss and Jean-Toussaint Desanti and even Foucault, the slightly inquisitional and proud tone of certain analyses and critiques, together with the sharpness and even profundity of some reflections, brought the "Course on Philosophy for Scientists" close to achieving what many felt while attending Lacan's seminars.[21]

Without a doubt an important difference remained: Lacan did not return to his previous positions, he did not practice self-criticism, while the "Course on Philosophy for Scientists"—which, by the way, was put together on the fly—abounded in rectifications of Althusser's previous positions and of some theses presented at the meetings. The abundant exchange of terminological formulations, bold (yet cautious) assertions, minor debates, and unexpected encounters that accompanied the teaching of the course clearly explains why Althusser and his collaborators attributed such importance to it. Yet very little remains from all of that, with the exception of a few incomplete and considerably altered publications that are among the least read of Althusser's oeuvre.

It is not difficult to see that this was Althusserianism's darkest and most sterile moment. There are few intellectual experiences more disarming than the intention to recuperate for today the theoretical formulations of Althusser and his disciples during that period. More than feeling certain of the arbitrariness of numerous theoretical formulations, and more than appreciating the continued pertinence of others, there is a prevailing sensation of irreducible distance, of irreparable separation. Very little of what Althusserianism judged to be essential in the formulations of that period remains valid today. Interest in those issues has disappeared without a trace as time has passed. The urgent theoretical tasks that, as Althusser declared back then, had to be carried out at that moment, were never completed and sometimes never even begun. The systematic defense of science against an invariably demonized ideology, the construction of a "theory of the process of production of scientific knowledges," considered in the "Course on Philosophy for Scientists" to be one of the "strategic theoretical tasks of our time," and many other formulations momentarily attracted university students and young militants.[22] But today I am not sure what is more surprising: the illusion that made those questions seem to be of fundamental importance or the pathetic transience of that illusion.

In recent years, now aware of Althusser's various unpublished texts from that period, it may be possible to take advantage of certain extenuating circumstances. "Three Notes on the Theory of Discourses" was written toward the end of 1966 but remained unpublished until it was released posthumously in 1993 as a section of the book *Writings on Psychoanalysis*.[23] The text reveals that Althusser struggled in those years; he struggled intelligently and passionately but also with the certainty of not having at his disposal the conceptual tools that he needed, searching for answers to problems that preoccupied him at that time. In his own words, "the theory of discourses [. . . requires] a reflection on the status of unconscious discourse and its articulation with ideological discourse."[24] He sent the three notes to his disciples-collaborators, gathering from them ideas, opinions, and, above all, information.[25] This leads me to believe that, in that period, something had begun to unsettle Althusser's convictions. The "Course on Philosophy for Scientists" wanted to be a new start [*una salida*] and, in a certain sense, it was. But it was a false start [*una salida en falso*].

The essay "Ideology and Ideological State Apparatuses," published in *La Pensée* in June of 1970, almost indiscreetly reveals some of the theoretical and philosophical problems in which Althusser found himself entangled.[26] That text would be at one and the same time the last text of what has been called the "classic" Althusser and the first text of a long series of writings (essays, prefaces to re-editions of his own work and the work of others, seminars) in which Althusser would deploy a wide range of rectifications and self-critiques.

Accordingly, to the condemnation of the inappropriate use of structuralist terminology, which lent itself to confusion, the notion of "theoreticism" was added, as well as "the forgetting of the class struggle," reiterated various times with repeated emphasis.[27] Some of Althusser's disciples followed him, at least for some time, during this laborious effort of reformulation. But classic Althusserianism as a collective project and school of thought had already shown clear signs of exhaustion by the end of the 1960s.

That said, I conclude this chapter by pointing out that such exhaustion did not impede Althusser from continuing to think and produce work, generally in solitude, until shortly before his death in 1990. He did this while facing serious problems and despite the tragedy of 1980.[28] Freedom from party ties and academic obligations, and freedom above all from theoretical and political conventions, would give free rein to a form of thought in which the topics, theses, and ideas of Althusser's "subterranean current" would occupy center stage. This current flowed below, and often against, Althusser's explicit thought. After a laborious journey, however, the much-delayed "encounter" would take place,[29] the encounter of Althusser with himself, which is to say, with the most profound and authentic aspects of his theoretical and political thought.

This does not exempt us, however, from the task of following that prolonged trajectory. I will undertake this task in subsequent chapters.

> *I want to wreak havoc* [foutre le bordel] *in the world of Marxist philosophy.* — LOUIS ALTHUSSER, *Lettres à Franca*

TWO. THE "CLASSIC" ALTHUSSER AND HIS SLIPS

It is commonly assumed that the relative opening that led to the Soviet Union's Twentieth Congress of the Communist Party in 1956 had an impact on Althusser's production since his first theoretical writings. This implies that Althusser would have been perceived from the start as an "open Marxist," permeable to other influences, free to critique other Marxists, including, when appropriate, Marx himself. In reality, though, things were not so simple.

At first, before the rise and rapid apogee of Althusserianism, some readers saw Althusser's texts as diligent revalorizations of familiar orthodox positions, novel principally and solely insofar as these positions were presented in a form of writing that stood out significantly from the poverty-stricken editions of Althusser's party comrades. On occasion, this "orthodoxy" looked like a more refined version of an archaic Marxism: Althusser praised Stalin;[1] whenever he had the chance he reiterated as a fundamental criterion the metaphor of the three instances, a metaphor Marx used in the

1858–59 preface to the *Contribution to the Critique of Political Economy*; he would also mention as a precaution, so as to not break with custom, the ad hoc and widely accepted thesis concerning the superstructure's "relative autonomy." He likewise emphatically sustained the opposition—not to say war—between Science and Ideology,[2] and he returned with astonishing ease to the Stalinist distinction between dialectical materialism and historical materialism, the former designating a Marxist philosophy (which had acquired, after Marx, the status of science) and the latter designating the science of the history of the modes of production and of social formations.[3] With a habitually provocative style, Althusser presented these statements as final. To not accept them was tantamount to renouncing the right to call yourself a Marxist.[4]

When his great works, *For Marx* and the two volumes of *Reading Capital*, came to light, things took on a different tone and dimension, right when the *Cahiers marxistes-léninistes* and especially the *Cahier pour l'analyse* were born and disseminated. To the consternation of those "open" Marxists who had already become aware of Althusser's dismissal, along with his disciples, of the notion of alienation, these works, gaining quickly in popularity and reach, now targeted Marxism's supposed humanism and historicism. Yet the high philosophical and theoretical level of the analyses and of the positions expressed therein, as well as the rigor and depth of Althusser's contributions and the contributions of his collaborators,[5] forced his opponents to recognize that a new Marxism had been born. It was, in fact, the first and only Marxism produced in France deserving of the name. This Marxism reached the height of the greatest contributions hailing from other locales, rich in its proposals, its concepts, and its theoretical and political possibilities. Having said that, as I mentioned in the previous chapter, these foundational works, which ratified Althusserianism as a reading and an interpretation of the legacy of Marx and Engels and as an autonomous ideological and political phenomenon, appeared in the 1960s in France during the heyday of diverse forms of structuralism. The term *structuralism* helped bring together into a single theoretical current, above all and most principally, the works of Claude Lévi-Strauss, Jacques Lacan, Michel Foucault, and Roland Barthes.[6]

Nevertheless, as I also noted earlier, in juxtaposition with the formulations and the developments of this new Marxism were other statements and theses that irrupted here and there without further comment, like the fictitious conclusion to an absent argument. This time, however, Althusser's statements were by no means orthodox; they were unintelligible to some and irritating to those capable of deciphering them. Few became aware of the scope of those unexpected statements, and no one recognized that they often condensed within themselves impasses and theoretical difficulties. While Althusser did not ignore these impasses and difficulties, he could not satisfactorily resolve them.[7] If the overall meaning of the Althusserian enterprise was clear,[8] if its theoretical orientation made it possible to view it as a specific (Marxist) variant of the structuralist turn, what was less clear or, to be precise, more enigmatic, was the fact that other statements emerged here and there, coexisting in singular fashion with his often novel and intelligible theoretical theses, statements that were literally unclassifiable and sometimes practically incomprehensible.[9]

One of my aims is to show that these enigmatic or surprising formulations, these unexpected breaks, represented certain milestones that were tracing, between the lines and at the cost of apparent incoherence and true confusion, the principles for a new conception of philosophy, one that Althusser intuited more than fully understood. These principles were linked in diverse ways to the ones that culminated in what I have called the "classic" Althusser, ranging from convergences to contradictions. When, with some astonishment, vulgar readers discovered these "deviations," they attributed them to the coquetries or fallacies of Althusser's argument. Today we can attempt to offer a response that is not so lazy.

WITH THE PUBLICATION of his book *Montesquieu, la politique et l'histoire*, Althusser found himself in a predicament with certain French intellectuals. Written in clear and elegant prose and light years away from the pitiful lectures of the French Communist Party's "thinkers,"[10] Althusser's writings confront Montesquieu with Montesquieu's own arguments and not with some alleged truth that had been previously revealed. Like Leo Strauss, Althusser places Montesquieu's enterprise in the context of writings marked by *persecution*. For Althusser, Montesquieu's thought was vigilant; it was aware of how to advance as well as how to retreat (not without a conspiratorial wink at the reader); his thought confronted real or potential persecution with a masterly politics of writing. This is how he was able to overcome the constrictions that inquisitional powers of all kinds sought to impose upon him. Montesquieu declared that he was a believer, but his notion of God diverged from the image of an all-powerful being made in our image and likeness. God spoke through "the sweetest of all sounds," which is the sound of nature, and if he spoke through that sound it was because nature and God were "the same thing."[11]

Montesquieu wrote that "[p]articular intelligent beings may have laws of their own making; but they have some likewise which they never made."[12] The first and even the second kind of law can be violated or disobeyed, at least up to a certain point, since, in one of its possible meanings, "'[l]aws are the relations substituting between it (primitive reason, i.e. God [or nature]) and different beings, and the relations of these to one another' (*The Spirit of Laws*, Book I, Chapter I). Add to this the fact that God himself, the instituter of these laws, in creating beings sees his own primordial decree subordinated to a necessity of the same nature, and even God falls inwardly victim to the universal contagion of the law!"[13] Under the protective covering of the invocation of God, Montesquieu outlined the idea of scientific law in the modern sense: the idea of a necessary and invariable relationship between objects. He also tended to endorse this Newtonian notion of law.

According to the early Althusser, this would be one of the principal ruptures produced by Montesquieu's thought. It is no coincidence that Althusser emphasizes this point. The idea of scientific law presupposes a synchronous or continuous relation established on its own and irrespective of the will or beliefs of human beings. This law subordinates man to a necessity that determines and drives him. The "positivist" slant of this thesis is enormously interesting—the reader will already anticipate why—for the budding scientism of Althusser's first book, for *this is the first, indirect sign of Althusser's rejection of the subject, of any kind of subject.*

Something Montesquieu mentioned in passing, through the use of metaphor, inspires a second line of inquiry in Althusser's book. Despite its weak enunciation, it can clearly be heard. Referring to Montesquieu's distinction between different forms of government, particularly between despotism and monarchy, Althusser writes:

> It is very remarkable that the metaphor that haunts despotism is taken from colliding bodies—while the one that haunts monarchy derives from a flowing spring. Water which flows from an elevated spring, passes into channels which moderate its speed and guide its course—and at the bottom reaches the lands which owe it their verdure. The image of colliding balls implies immediacy in time and space, and the "force" entirely transmitted by the impact. That is why in despotism

power is either exercised or handed over. The image of the irrigating spring implies, on the contrary, *space* and *duration*. Its temporality being its course, time is needed for the water to flow. And it never all flows away: a spring does not empty like a basin, it always contains more than it gives away. And contrary to the ball which may be ejected in the opposite direction to the one with which it collided, their instantaneous impact sharply separating them, flowing water never breaks with itself. It is the same uninterrupted stream, from the spring to the most distant lands.[14]

The images of the spring and the colliding balls are presented here as mutually exclusive, alluding on the one hand to an acceptable but also perfectible regime of government and on the other hand to a defective and ultimately unacceptable form of government. The last Althusser will return to these images to refer to the contingent, though not arbitrary, unfolding of the history of social formations.

In these pages from the book on Montesquieu, there also emerges, for the first time, the metaphor of the aleatory, of the accidental: "The infinite plain of despotism is a kind of narrow horizon before the despot, precisely because it contains none of those *accidents* constituted by the inequalities of men: it has been leveled. [. . .] And the *time* of the royal power is merely this space *experienced*. As a man endowed with the supreme power, the king is a prey to haste, everything seeming to be a matter of decree."[15] In despotism, everything is determined; there are no unexpected accidents, but to the prince, on the contrary, it seems that everything is decidable and subject to either his unhurried or urgent freedom. These observations gesture toward the theses that would reappear and would be reformulated by the posthumous Althusser. In other words, after reading Althusser's first published book, I vaguely suspected that the essential could already be found at the beginning.

An essay published shortly thereafter in *La Pensée*, titled "On the Young Marx," provoked renewed commotion and discussion.[16] This is an essay resolutely critical of Marx's early works. It questions the characterization of these works as authentically Marxist and criticizes in particular the thesis—morosely accepted by "orthodox" Marxists after the Soviet Union's Twentieth Congress of the Communist Party—that the kernel and early developments of Marxist philosophy can be found in those early texts, especially the 1844 manuscripts. Althusser deals with these positions by offering an alternative. He holds that starting with *The German Ideology* and the "Theses on Feuerbach," Marx would enact an epistemological break with the "prior philosophical consciousness" of his early writings,[17] founding at the same time the Marxist science of history (historical materialism) and a scientific Marxist philosophy (dialectical materialism).[18] In other words, according to Althusser, Marx only began to "be a proper Marxist," and not without some vacillation, in *The German Ideology* and the "Theses on Feuerbach." With those texts, Marx enacted the change in problematic that broke with inherited bourgeois ideology, the ideology in which Marx's thought had moved up until that point, and arrived at the firm ground of science. That arrival would also constitute a double theoretical foundation: historical materialism as the science of the history of social formations and dialectical materialism as scientific philosophy.[19]

The positions Althusser adopted in this essay, particularly his fierce anti-Hegelianism, fell like a bucket of cold water on his party comrades, as well as on the wide range of French, German, and, to a lesser extent, Italian intellectuals who had reclaimed the influence of Hegelian philosophy and had greeted the publication of Marx's early writings as a felicitous theoretical and political event. On this issue, which was considered fundamental by the aforementioned intellectuals, Althusser seemed to return to positions that had already been surpassed.

As for Althusser's original contribution, very few individuals recognized or praised the proposal of a notion that was clearly novel and undoubtedly of heuristic value. I am referring to the notion of "problematic," which Althusser expounds upon for the first time in the following terms:

> Indeed, to say that an ideology constitutes an (organic) totality is only valid *descriptively*—not *theoretically*, for this description converted into a theory exposes us to the danger of thinking nothing but the empty unity of the described whole, not a *determinate unitary structure*. On the contrary, to think the unity of a determinate ideological unity (which presents itself explicitly as a whole, and which is explicitly or implicitly "lived" as a whole or as an intention of "totalization") by means of the concept of its *problematic* is to allow the *typically systematic structure* unifying all the elements of the thought to be brought to light, and therefore to discover in this unity a *determinate content* which makes it possible both to conceive the *meaning* of the "elements" of the ideology concerned—*and to relate this ideol-*

ogy to the problem left or posed to every thinker by the historical period in which he lives.[20]

Despite the fact that Althusser rarely returned to this category explicitly, its importance should not be underestimated, for it can be found underlying all his future proposals. Although Althusser resorts to the category "problematic" in the passage just cited to explain an aspect of ideology's unity and functioning, the relevance of the category far exceeds the ideological terrain. In fact, its scope spans the structure and functioning of any system of concepts or notions: ideological, scientific, or philosophical. As the reader will have anticipated, it is especially susceptible to self-referential deployment. In that sense, the category "problematic" has functioned permanently as a kind of schematism of Althusserian reason, as a principle that not only granted logical consistency to Althusser's thought but also silently, effectively, made possible the invariable translation of that thought to determinate (historical, political, ideological) referents or cases.

Returning to the essay on the young Marx, beyond some of its "deviations," the unusually argumentative and polemical rigor of its style and tone was an arduous challenge for those accustomed to denouncing all divergent opinions with a simple stroke of the pen or a disdainful paragraph. However, Althusser only truly began to show his teeth—and become an intellectual that worried the French Communist Party leadership—when he published "Contradiction and Overdetermination," a brilliant and incisive text that was met with immediate replies from party supporters like Gilbert Mury and Roger Garaudy. What most strongly unsettled these authors was Althusser's rejection of the thesis according to which Marx had inverted Hegel's idealist dialectical method in a materialist sense. They considered it almost a sign of disrespect toward Marx, who had articulated his theoretical restructuring in these or similar terms, as well as a sign of disrespect toward the party's official doctrine. They likewise felt that by negating the so-called rational kernel of the Hegelian dialectic, Althusser had abandoned the simple and clear light of the self-evident and had entered an obscure, marshy territory with unclear consequences, not to mention unclear intentions. Althusser writes: "So I think that, in its approximation, this metaphorical expression—the 'inversion' of the dialectic—does not pose the problem of *the nature of the objects* to which a *single method* should be applied (the world of the Idea for Hegel—the real world for Marx) but rather the problem of the *nature of the dialectic* considered itself, that is, the problem of *its specific structures*; not the problem of the inversion of the 'sense' of the dialectic, but that of the *transformation of its structures*."[21]

Based on historical information, the protocols of Lenin's experience during the Russian Revolution, and the political works of Marx and Engels, as well as, provocatively, Mao's categories presented in the essay "On Contradiction," Althusser puts forward a complex and plural conception of Marxist contradiction. If, according to Althusser, Marxist contradiction has as its general framework the contradiction between the forces of production and the relations of production, embodied in the struggle between two antagonistic classes,[22] this framework unfolds into an accumulation—multiple and heterogeneous—of specific contradictions. These contradictions, moreover, cannot be considered mere epiphenomena or manifestations of the base contradiction. Rather, they have their own reality and their own specific weight. When these contradictions fuse into a "ruptural unity," they give rise to a revolutionary situation.

Althusser condenses these notions of multiplicity, fusion, and ruptural unity into his concept of *overdetermination*, modestly noting that he is borrowing from "other disciplines."[23] The historical contradiction is always and in principle overdetermined: it can obstruct or open a path to historical change, but it can never be found in a "pure" state as a simple contradiction. The historical process that led to the Russian Revolution—the "weakest link" of the imperialist chain, according to Lenin's slogan—was the product of a prodigious accumulation, articulation, and fusion of contradictions. It was said to be an "exceptional" case. Yet Althusser writes: "[W]e should perhaps ask what is *exceptional* about this 'exceptional *situation*,' and whether, like exceptions, this one does not clarify its rule—is not, unbeknown to the rule, *the rule itself*. For, after all, *are we not always in exceptional situations?* The failure of the 1849 Revolution in Germany was an exception, the failure in Paris in 1871 was an exception, the German Social-Democratic failure at the beginning of the twentieth century pending the chauvinist betrayal of 1914 was an exception . . . exceptions, but *with respect to what?*"[24] This question would lead Althusser to inquire into the raison d'être and the contents of overdetermination. It would also lead him to consider how the Marxist conception of the history of social formations calls for, so to speak, the importation of that category.

Momentarily showing signs of returning to orthodoxy, Althusser explains that the Marxist conception of the history of social formations recognizes the distinction between the infrastructure (the economic base composed of the forces and the relations of production) and the superstructure (the State, law, ideologies) and that they relate to each other through the double rule of the economic base's determination in the "last instance" and the superstructure's relative autonomy. This was meant to reassure worrisome spirits. The good old concepts of the previously mentioned preface to the *Contribution to the Critique of Political Economy* had finally returned.

Yet Althusser places an unexpected card on the table by way of a diversion tactic that presents itself as a tribute to Engels, a tribute consistent with the situation insofar as it designates as a "problem" what was in Engels's writing a simple and straightforward solution. In "Contradiction and Overdetermination," Althusser suggests that Engels poses the problem of last-instance determination and the determinations that proceed from the superstructure. This problem is better understood as "the *accumulation of effective determinations* (deriving from the superstructures and from special national and international circumstances) *on the determination in the last instance by the economic.*"[25] Fortified by the concept of overdetermination, which he has managed to surround with theoretical guarantees and empirical illustrations, Althusser releases his conclusion like a heavy blow: "*From the first moment to the last, the solitary hour of the 'last instance' never comes.*"[26]

Althusser would later pretend to soften the subversive resonances of this declaration, appealing once more to the distinction between "determination in the last instance" and "domination." But he will do so in an almost purposely complicated way:[27]

> Overdetermination designates the following essential quality of contradiction: the reflection in contradiction itself of its conditions of existence, that is, of its situation in the structure in dominance of the complex whole. This is not a univocal "situation." It is not just its situation "*in principle*" (the one it occupies in the hierarchy of instances in relation to the determinant instance: in society, the economy) nor just its situation "*in fact*" (whether, in the phase under consideration, it is dominant or subordinate) but *the relation of this situation in fact to this situation in principle*, that is, the very relation which makes of this situation in fact a *"variation" of the—"invariant"—structure, in dominance, of the totality.*[28]

In my opinion, this passage is of decisive relevance for understanding Althusserian thought as it presented itself in the prolific years of the 1960s. Drawing on a category that is abundantly used in "Contradiction and Overdetermination," I would say that the essay condenses the principal conclusions, but also problems, doubts, and questions, that gave Althusserianism its peculiar theoretical physiognomy and style of reflection. Its style was more complicated, more aware of its insufficiencies, less sure of itself, and more profound than the style that is commonly attributed to Althusserianism by the power and grace of certain textbooks and the sheer will to simplify things. It was a style and, as anticipated, an "esoteric" form of thought that little by little revealed its strength and, above all, its devastatingly critical pertinence. Allow me then to examine the issues of the Althusserian problematic that are "put into play," so to speak, in the passage just cited, dwelling at some length on their analysis. This merits, I believe, a separate section.

Cause of the Structure

If in psychoanalysis the category of overdetermination is open to multiple interpretations, its importation into dialectical materialism does not simplify things but rather makes them more complicated.[29] This is how Jean Laplanche and Jean-Bertrand Pontalis define the category in 1967:

> The fact that formations of the unconscious (symptoms, dreams, etc.) can be attributed to a plurality of determining factors. This can be understood in two different ways:
>
> a   The formation in question is the result of several causes, since one alone is not sufficient to account for it.
> b   The formation is related to a multiplicity of unconscious elements which may be organized in different meaningful sequences, each having its own specific coherence at a particular level of interpretation. This second reading is the most generally accepted one.[30]

Laplanche and Pontalis note that version (b) is the most common understanding of the term but that it is nonetheless possible to find "points of intersection" between the two versions.

In principle, Althusserian overdetermination accommodates both versions, while, at the same time, it not only acknowledges their points of intersection but emphasizes them. Indeed, when considering a determinate historical phenomenon—Althusser's example is the October Revolution—it must be recognized that in order for that phenomenon to have occurred, it was necessary: (a) that 1917 Russia was the site of an immense accumulation of (economic, political, ideological) contradictions, extremely different in terms of their origin, scope, and effects yet nevertheless possessing a common trait—namely, their critical character; (b) that, even if this multiplicity should converge, as indeed it did, into what Althusser called a "ruptural unity," each contradiction would preserve its own consistency and efficacy; that, in the terms of Laplanche and Pontalis, the contradictions were organized "in different meaningful sequences"; (c) that, as previously mentioned, the contradictions in question "fused" into a ruptural unity, bringing together the immense majority of the popular sectors against a regime that was then incapable of defending itself, leading in that way to a revolutionary situation.

These features of overdetermination are not, however, exhaustive with respect to the Althusserian version of the category. The category could not truly be accounted for without confronting a lingering problem: the theoretical status of the determinate contradiction in the last instance (designated as "the economy" in the previously cited passage from "On the Materialist Dialectic") and, more broadly, the theoretical status of the category of determination itself.

The Althusserianism of those climactic years nevertheless hid under its triumphant mask the arduous difficulties this problem posed, along with the often frustrating effort of Althusser and his disciples to offer satisfactory answers to the problem without diverging from the "declared" project. The different theorizations of the category of "structural causality" were both the sign and the result of this effort.

Apart from occasional allusions and some terminological disputes, it was Althusser who offered the first explicit formulation of the problem in the final paragraphs of his essay "The Object of *Capital*":

> *By means of what concept is it possible to think the new type of determination which has just been identified as the determination of the phenomena of a given region by the structure of that region? More generally, by means of what concept, or what set of concepts, is it possible to think the determination of the elements of a structure, and the structural relations between those elements, and all the effects of those relations, by the effectivity of that structure? And a fortiori, by means of what concept or what set of concepts is it possible to think the determination of a subordinate structure by a dominant structure; in other words, how is it possible to define the concept of a structural causality?*[31]

The solution to this problem, first formulated by some of Althusser's disciples, is very well known. The determining structure exercises its "causality" insofar as it establishes the hierarchy of the respective efficacies of the others, with the capacity to "place" in the position of the dominant instance either politics (feudalism), ideology (certain "primitive" societies), or even the economy itself (capitalism). Echoes of a footnote in *Capital* can be heard in this distinction, a footnote that seems to authorize this interpretation and thereby ratify the separation between determination and domination.[32]

Nevertheless, as Alain Badiou indirectly demonstrates, this solution is unsustainable.[33] To put it simply, a function (in this case "determination," conceived of as the application of a set of structures or instances onto a set of hierarchically ordered positions: 1-dom, 2-dom, etc.) cannot be at the same time an element of the "first set" (the "economy" in the list of instances). In reality, this negative demonstration brings to light the main concerns for at least one of the lines of thinking opened up by Althusser's advancement of the concept of structural causality, a line of thinking that counts Badiou as its most significant representative as well as its most lucid genealogist.[34] Regarding precisely this last point, Badiou writes in "The (Re)commencement of Dialectical Materialism":

> The fundamental problem of *all* structuralism is that of the term with the double function, inasmuch as it determines the belonging of all other terms to the structure, while itself being excluded from it by the specific operation through which it figures in the structure only in the guise of its *representative* (its *lieu-tenant*, or place-holder, to use a concept from Lacan). It is the immense merit of Lévi-Strauss, in the still mixed form of the zero-signifier, to have recognized the true importance of this question [. . . in the *Introduction to the Work of Marcel Mauss*]. Pinpoint the place occupied by the term indicating the specific exclusion, the pertinent lack—that is to say, the *determination* or "structurality" of the structure.[35]

The allusion to Lévi-Strauss is of interest for two reasons. The first reason, which I will focus on now, is that it takes the reader back to the exact time and place when the issue was first formulated within the framework of a theoretical perspective not foreign to Althusserianism. *I will accordingly maintain that not only Althusserianism but also poststructuralist Marxism and even Lacanian psychoanalysis struggled, and to this day continue to struggle,* with a nodal point that Lévi-Strauss first clearly articulated in his writings from the 1940s and 1950s.[36]

The previous passage from Badiou's essay refers to Lévi-Strauss's *Introduction to the Work of Marcel Mauss* and, more precisely, to Lévi-Strauss's interpretation of the theses Mauss developed in *The Gift* (1925).[37] The issue revolves around *mana* and analogous notions that certain societies use to designate anything that appears, at least initially, to be unfamiliar, enigmatic, or strange. Lévi-Strauss observes that these notions, whose employment is generally attributed to exotic societies, are, on the contrary, present in many different kinds of societies, whether "archaic" or modern, "primitive" or civilized, including the society of the observer himself. This leads Lévi-Strauss to hypothesize that this type of phenomenon is universal in scope. It would consist of a form of thinking exercised before an object, a situation, or an individual that appears to the observer or the actor as unknown or not immediately decipherable, as lacking a name that would identify or classify it. Consider expressions like *truc* [thingy] or *machine* [thingamajig] in French, or terms like *coso* [whatchamacallit], *invento* [contraption], and also *truco* [trick] in Spanish, with their respective connotations— "machinery [*maquinaria*]," "strange but effective object [*objeto raro y eficaz*]," "stroke of luck [*golpe de suerte*]," etc.—that evoke, at the same time, certain ideas (force, fate, power) that bear witness, even if only marginally in everyday language, to the fact that some phenomenon is foreign to us.[38]

In any event, these notions appear to express a *quantum* of undetermined signification, devoid of meaning in itself, that could, for that reason, acquire any kind of meaning. This is the case when the relationship between signifier and signified becomes unbalanced—due to the meddling influence of that strange "something," without a name or an accepted identity—and the objective is to reestablish the complementarity between signifier and signified. In our societies, these notions are used spontaneously and informally; in exotic societies, they commonly contribute to the construction of elaborate and socially recognized systems of interpretation.

Following the path laid down by Mauss, Lévi-Strauss deploys a dense argumentation that, starting with certain reflections on the origins of language, delves into issues related to what I have been discussing. His exposition begins with the following thesis: "Whatever may have been the moment and the circumstances of its appearance in the ascent of animal life, language can only have arisen all at once. Things cannot have begun to signify gradually. In the wake of a transformation which is not a subject of study for the social sciences, but for biology and psychology, a shift occurred from a stage when nothing had a meaning to another stage when everything had meaning."[39] The exposition continues with the following points:

1. If the entire universe became significant in this way, it does not follow that the world for that reason would be better *known*. The birth of language and therefore of signification was discontinuous in nature, whereas that of knowledge was continuous.
2. Accordingly, the categories of signifier and signified are simultaneously co-constitutive, whereas knowledge, "that is, the intellectual process which enables us to identify certain aspects of the signifier and certain aspects of the signified [. . .] only got started very slowly."[40]
3. In other words, "the universe signified long before people began to know what it signified." But, Lévi-Strauss adds, "from the beginning, the universe signified the totality of what humankind can expect to know about it."[41]

Hence, to sum up, all that we can aspire to do is bring about regroupings, rectifications, and reductions at the center of what Lévi-Strauss calls "a totality which is closed and complementary to itself."[42] That said, there is a difference between nonindustrial societies and ours, a difference that consists in the fact that the birth and development of science in industrial societies, as well as the central role that scientific knowledge plays in these societies, makes it such that the operation of making equivalent [*adecuación*] the signifier and the signified is more rigorous and methodical than in other societies.[43] But this is only a difference of degree. For a long time still, the relationship between symbolism and knowledge will preserve common attributes in both forms of society. In the words of Lévi-Strauss, this is because,

> a fundamental situation perseveres which arises out of the human condition: namely, that man has from the start had at his disposition a signifier-totality which he is at a loss to know how to allocate to a signified, given as such, but no less unknown for being given. There is always a non-equivalence or "inadequation" between the two [. . .]; this generates a signifier-surfeit relative to the signifieds to which it can be fitted. So, in man's effort to understand the world, he always disposes of a surplus

of signification (which he shares out among things in accordance with the laws of the symbolic thinking which it is the task of ethnologists and linguists to study). That distribution of a supplementary ration [. . .] is absolutely necessary to ensure that, in total, the available signifier and the mapped-out signified may remain in the relationship of complementarity which is the very condition of the exercise of symbolic thinking.[44]

4 Notions like *mana*, *orenda* (and many others, including those used in our societies) represent that floating signified, the inevitable destiny of all finite thought, but also, as Lévi-Strauss notes, the opening for poetic invention, be it mythical or artistic. These notions would be, for Lévi-Strauss, the "conscious expression of a *semantic function*, whose role is to enable symbolic thinking to operate despite the contradiction inherent in it."[45]

5 In summary: "In the system of symbols which makes up any cosmology, [the notion of *mana*] would be a zero symbolic value, that is, a sign marking the necessity of a *supplementary* symbolic content over and above that which the signified already contains, which can be any value at all, provided it is still part of the available reserve, and is not already, as the phonologists say, a term in a set."[46]

Badiou's reference to Lévi-Strauss's text alludes exclusively to this point in his argument. But nothing prohibits us from examining other passages from the *Introduction to the Work of Marcel Mauss*. In fact, everything encourages us to do so, to consider passages that seem to preserve, at least in principle, a formal analogy (or should I say "structural analogy") with the preceding analysis and, in that way, considerably extend its domain of validity.

For example, at the beginning of the *Introduction*, while reflecting on the virtues and limits of Mauss's theses concerning the relationship between culture and individual psychical processes, Lévi-Strauss returns to, amends, and deepens his well-known essay published in 1949 with *Les Temps Modernes*, "The Sorcerer and His Magic."[47] In that earlier work, Lévi-Strauss compares, and to a certain extent groups together, the conduct of the neurotic in our societies with the shaman's trance and scenes of possession in exotic societies.

But this approximation encapsulates a difficulty, for psychiatry is revealed to be completely incapable of assimilating cases of possession or of trances documented with video footage into the known forms of neurosis, while anthropologists call attention to the fact that shamans or people who have experienced continual or occasional possession are, except in those moments, normal people who can in no way be considered mentally ill. According to Lévi-Strauss, there are two possible solutions to this problem: "Either the modes of behavior described by the names of 'trance' or 'possession' have no connection with the behavior that we, in our own society, call psycho-pathological, or else they can be considered as being of the same type. In the latter case it is their connection with pathological states that we need to consider as contingent, and as resulting from a condition peculiar to the society in which we live."[48] As anticipated, Lévi-Strauss chooses the second option, from which he proceeds to develop a vast and unexpected generalization. Starting from an idea that he had already outlined in previous writings and that he would develop further in the future, the idea that society can be thought of as a set of symbolic systems (language, kinship structures, economy, religion, etc.), systems that express determinate aspects of physical and social reality as well as the relations between these realities (and the relations between the aforementioned systems), he reexamines the problem Mauss poses concerning the connections between the individual's psychical processes and the social group. For Lévi-Strauss, the symbolic expression of material and social reality can never be fully achieved. This follows, on the one hand, from each system's specific mode of functioning, which makes it incommensurable with the other systems, and, on the other hand, from the fact that historical becoming introduces strange elements into these systems, making one society slide toward another and producing asynchronicities in the rhythm of development of each.

Some remainder always persists that is inexpressible, ineffable, inapprehensible for social symbolism. It follows that

> no society is ever wholly and completely symbolic; [. . . or] it would be more accurate to say that it can never manage to give all its members, to the same degree, the means whereby they could give their services fully to the building of a symbolic structure which is only realizable (in the context of normal thinking) in the dimension of social life. For, strictly speaking, the person whom we call sane is the one who is capable of alienating himself, since he consents to an existence in a world definable only by the self-other relationship. The

saneness of the individual mind implies participation in social life, just as the refusal to enter into it (but most importantly, the refusal to do so in the ways that it imposes) corresponds to the onset of mental disturbance.[49]

Shamans in exotic societies, the mentally ill in industrial societies, and "zero-signifiers" in language would all stand in for, but at the same time display, at the margins of institutions and practices, the impossibility of a total social bond. They would allude to that something "real" that undermines the completeness of the Symbolic.

According to Lévi-Strauss, society could be compared to a universe in which only discrete large masses would be fully structured. It would accordingly be mandatory for all these masses that a certain (and variable) quota of individuals be placed outside of the system or straddling, as it were, irreducible systems. Society expects, and even requires, that these individuals figuratively represent forms of compromise that are inaccessible at the level of the collective, that these individuals simulate fictitious transitions or imaginarily realize incompatible syntheses.[50] In more contemporary terms, society imposes upon them the task of suturing the abyss, the void opened by intersystemic irreducibility, which is to say, to "suture" in the imaginary what the social structure is incapable of apprehending at the symbolic level to which it, so to speak, pertains. Through these apparently abnormal proceedings, the so-called mentally ill, situated at the periphery, become an indispensable element of the system's equilibrium.[51]

From this it follows, according to Lévi-Strauss, that in each society the relationship between normal and abnormal conduct is not one of expression, reflection, or anticipation; it is a relationship of complementarity.[52] In more explicit terms:

> Individual psychical processes do not reflect the group; even less do they pre-form the group. If we acknowledge that they complete the group, that will be a quite adequate legitimation of the value and importance of the studies that are being pursued in that direction today. That *complementarity* of individual psychical structure and social structure is the basis of the fruitful collaboration, called for by Mauss, which has come to pass between ethnology and psychology.[53]

As one can see, in response to a problem that remains to be interrogated, Lévi-Strauss formulates at this point a logical and philosophical theory, analogous to and in many ways convergent with what he expounds, a few pages later, on the notion of *mana, orenda*, and the like. But what is of particular interest, glimpsed by Badiou in the aforementioned essay, is the vast theoretical space that Lévi-Strauss opens with this formulation, anticipating Lacanian speculation years later on the Symbolic and the Real, including Althusser's reflections on these issues. It is a theoretical space rich with misunderstandings, overlaps, allegiances, and multiple intersections; it is a philosophical move with consequences that are still felt in the present, a move that remains unfinished even today.

It is almost impossible to unravel the tangle of intersections and debates that took place in the 1960s in the form of essays and the exchanging of texts, some of which, as in the case of Althusser, would only be published much later. Badiou recovers what could be considered a second moment in the constitution of this theoretical space: Jacques-Alain Miller's essay "Suture," to which I would add another text by the same author titled, "Action of the Structure." Borrowing an expression from Badiou himself, I will show how this new beginning or (re)commencement already entailed some turbulence.

"Suture," Miller's famous intervention in Lacan's seminar, describes the minimal elements of what he and others will call the "logic of the signifier," which, according to the author, governs the field of psychoanalysis as well as that of historical materialism: "Suture names the relation of the subject to the chain of its discourse; we shall see that it figures there as the element which is lacking, in the form of a stand-in [*tenant-lieu*]. For, while there lacking, it is not purely and simply absent. Suture, by extension—the general relation of lack to the structure—of which it is an element, inasmuch as it implies the position of a taking-the-place-of [*tenant-lieu*]."[54] From this point, Miller attempts to characterize Lacan's particular theorization of the figure of the subject while clearing the path for a definition of the concept of structural causality that joins together contributions from Althusserianism and Lacanianism.

To achieve this, Miller turns to Gottlob Frege's analysis of the construction of number, which aims to account for a series of numbers and accordingly for their "successor" function, as well as for the status of zero. According to Miller, the function of the subject anonymously plays a role in the genesis of a numeric series and in the process of its construction. The key is to be found in the double figuration of zero:

> The counting of the 0 as 1 (whereas the concept of the zero subsumes nothing in the real but a blank) is the general support of the series of numbers. [. . .] In the order of number, *there is in addition the 0*, and the 0 counts for 1. The displacement of a number, from the function of reserve to that of term, implies the summation of the 0. Whence the successor. That which in the real is pure and simple absence finds itself through the fact of number (through the instance [*instance*] of truth) noted 0 and counted for 1.[55]

Miller notes that Frege introduces zero into the series through the concept of an impossible object: an object that is not identical with itself. The set that is constituted from this concept is an empty set. "It is this decisive proposition that *the concept of not-identical-with-itself is assigned by the number zero* which sutures logical discourse."[56] Yet this impossible object is in its own way possible: the subject, as support of the unconscious, can be defined as self-contradictory (the principle of contradiction is unknown to the unconscious).

> The impossible object, which the discourse of logic summons as the not-identical with itself and then rejects as the pure negative, which it summons and rejects in order to constitute itself as that which it is, which it summons and rejects *wanting to know nothing of it*, we name this object, insofar as it functions as the excess which operates in the series of numbers, the subject. Its exclusion from the discourse which internally it intimates is suture.[57]

For Miller, as anticipated, suture and especially the logic of the signifier that it presupposes make intelligible the specificity and the novelty of the concept of structural causality: "If structural causality (causality in the structure insofar as the subject is implicated in it) is not an empty expression, it is from the minimal logic which I have developed here that it will find its status."[58]

It is well known that there is no room for the subject in Lévi-Strauss's vision. The concept of the subject is not at all pertinent for him; he does not even make explicit references to it. If the term is occasionally mentioned, its mention does not in any way aspire to have theoretical or philosophical import. As for the status of that which is absent or of absence itself, of the need for a representative, a stand-in that balances the structure, Lévi-Strauss avoids pronouncing a clear position, despite at certain moments appearing to offer pragmatic or functionalist responses of a sociological nature. He does not, however, insist on these responses, nor does he develop them. On this point, his thought prefers to observe studied prudence. What nonetheless remains excluded from his approach, I repeat, is recourse to a Subject, whatever form it might take. As I mentioned earlier, for Lévi-Strauss, the zero-signifier and, on a different level, scenes of possession and the expression of symptoms of mental illness are what completes or "sutures" the structure under the forms of a representative.

Miller curiously and ostensibly elides this aspect of Lévi-Strauss's thought in a transcribed talk produced much later, titled "S'truc dure."[59] He addresses issues pertinent to this discussion, limiting himself to mentioning Lévi-Strauss's "The Sorcerer and His Magic" and to evoking the enthusiasm that that text aroused in the 1950s when a new edition of *Structural Anthropology* was published. For Miller, the analogies Lévi-Strauss revealed between the analyst and the shaman, particularly the thesis that the unconscious is always empty—the critique of a "content-ist [*contenidista*]" idea of the unconscious—prepared the groundwork for and almost foretold the Lacanian distinction between the Imaginary and the Symbolic. But, just as in "Suture," "S'truc dure" completely omits any mention of Lévi-Strauss's *Introduction to the Work of Marcel Mauss*.

Miller's talk includes other references to Lévi-Strauss, in this case critical in nature, but the silence surrounding the latter's *Introduction* persists. This is strange and even suspicious. In reference to what Miller calls the "structural hypothesis," a formulation that he recognizes honestly as belonging to Lévi-Strauss, Miller states the following in "S'truc dure":

> I would go so far as to say that I can deduce from the structuralist hypothesis the distinction between the symbolic, the imaginary, and the real. [. . .] At this point, something must be decided: Is the Freudian unconscious of the order of imaginary inertia or of symbolic law? This is the initial choice of Lacan's teachings. From that moment, the real appears as that which must persist, as a given that is irreducible to symbolic law and representation. It is at first only introduced as an excluded term in Lacan's teachings. [. . .] Let us say that Lacan identifies the real as that element which is structurally flawed [*qui fait structurallement défaut*] within the symbolic order. Regarding this point—it must be remembered—Lacan depends on Lévi-Strauss's guidance, which is why I brought his *Structural Anthropology*.[60]

Of course, as Miller notes more than once in "S'truc dure," Lacan and Miller himself oppose Lévi-Strauss's objectivist negation of the subject with a form of structuralism that makes room for the subject, for a subject that would not be the traditional, conscious subject, the subject that is the master of himself, the only subject for Lévi-Strauss and the subject against which Lévi-Strauss struggles. It would be, on the contrary, a "barred" subject, a subjected subject, absent from the structure (although "represented" in it), but a subject nonetheless, one that speaks, acts, and produces effects.

Miller seeks to go even further: the inclusion of the barred subject in Lacan's theory and writings even entails an improvement over classical structuralism: "To write the subject, $ is added to S1, S2, as a decisive and fundamental structural term. This imposes something that evidently exceeds the structuralist perspective, the perspective that entails that the set of signifiers be complete, that the set accounts for everything and to a certain extent can name everything. From the structuralist perspective, no word is lacking inside a language for the designation of some thing. There are of course distinctions that a language does not make in comparison to another language, but there is no lack in language as such."[61] Nevertheless, toward the end of the talk, with another turn of the screw, he revises the previous statement: "Let us add once more that it is not simply the case that, in this sense, the structure lacks [*la structure manque*], which is to say that it is incomplete. Lacan's correction of the structuralist hypothesis is not the following: within the set of signifiers comprising your hypothesis, one is always missing [*il en manque toujours un*]. No. Because it absolutely does not lack. As Lacan says, one must always write [-1]. This is still a signifier! That is why it is written S(A̶)."[62] Miller nonetheless concludes that even if the symbolic structure were completed in this way, the Subject would remain incomplete and above all affected by a constitutive inconsistency, only accessible via the hypothesis that ultimately refers to what Freud called the "navel of the unconscious," its most intimate nucleus, its secret.

Be that as it may, these reflections are not enough to make us forget Miller's forgetting of the *Introduction to the Work of Marcel Mauss*. These reflections are not enough, among other reasons, because a similar fluctuation, though in theory more stable and with rigorous limits, can be found in Lévi-Strauss. The marginal or peripheral position, be it the shaman, the mentally ill, or the zero-signifier, can be conceived of as what Ernesto Laclau calls a "constitutive outside."[63] Jorge Dotti, regarding precisely this formulation, rightly notes that it almost constitutes an *oxymoron*.[64] I would add as well

The "Classic" Althusser and His Slips 49

that the formulation could be interpreted as a *synecdoche*, depending on the perspective one chooses to adopt. Lévi-Strauss tends to prefer the figure of synecdoche, indicating more than once that the apparently aberrant conduct of the shaman or the psychotic, as well as the distinct variations of the zero-signifier, form "integral parts of the total system."[65] As I have shown, this does not impede Lévi-Strauss from defining the zero-signifier as a "supplementary ration" of signification that makes possible the equivalence [*adecuación*] of the signifier and the signified, as well as the complementarity and therefore relative exteriority of the relationship between society and individual psychic processes.[66] It would not be merely anecdotal to add that Lévi-Strauss alludes to Jacques Lacan's essay "Aggressiveness in Psychoanalysis" precisely in the passages dedicated to what Lévi-Strauss calls the "relationship of complementarity" between society and individual psychic processes.[67] This essay, which stands out for its profundity, gives cause for the conclusions that Lévi-Strauss's *Introduction* develops concerning this topic.[68]

In any case, from this *racconto* at least the following conclusion emerges: the problem "of all of structuralism," the problem Badiou would define as that of the term with a double function that determines the belonging of the other terms to the structure, this problem possesses a history whose beginnings can be traced back to a decade before Lacan "recognizes" the Real and twenty or thirty years before the publication of Althusser's first great works. *In that sense, regarding this point, which for some would constitute a decisive rupture, so-called* poststructuralism *did nothing more than repeat what Lévi-Strauss's structuralism, "plain and simple," had laid out point by point and with absolute clarity a decade prior.*

Returning to the problem of structural causality after this long but necessary digression, I would say that Badiou presents his own take on the problem in "The (Re)commencement of Dialectical Materialism," although not without emphasizing its unresolved difficulties. He also presents the path that, in his opinion, must be taken to solve the problem of structural causality. I will consider here the differences, as well as the commonalities, between his solution and Miller's.

The context in which Badiou situates his discussion is explicitly and—when possible—literally Althusserian. He poses the problem in the same terms as Althusser and punctuates each moment of his argument with passages from *For Marx* and *Reading Capital*. To put it concisely, his proposal consists first in sketching out an "axiomatic" of the "primitive" notions of historical materialism ([i] the labor force; [ii] the means of labor; [iii] the forms of application of force to the means). With these notions, he defines what he calls the most general concept of historical materialism: "practice," understood as a specific combination of the three "undefined" terms, a combination "considered in the structure that is proper to them."[69] It is inferred that in the "social whole" there exist only practices[70] that conform to a "complex unity [. . .] in a determinate society."[71] It evidently becomes necessary to ask at this point what kind of unity would link these practices.

Badiou responds, first, that this unity is an *articulated* unity. He will also stipulate that insofar as a practice is conceived of as articulated with all others, it will be called an "instance" of a social formation: "An instance is entirely defined by the specific relation it maintains with all others: what 'exists' is the articulated structure of instances."[72] At this point, it is a matter of thinking about "their *degree of independence* and their type of 'relative' *autonomy*,"[73] as well as a matter of thinking about their hierarchical position, either dominant or subordinate, within the social formation:[74] "Let us agree to call *conjuncture* the system of instances such as it is thinkable according to the trajectory prescribed by the mobile hierarchy of efficacies. The conjuncture is first of all the determination of the *dominant* instance, whose mapping fixes the *point of departure* of the rational analysis of the whole. The first great thesis of DM [dialectical materialism . . .] posits that the set of instances *always* defines a conjunctural kind of existence."[75] Yet the conjuncture is susceptible to changes; its concept refers to the forms of existence of the social whole, not to the (invariant) principle of the variation of these forms. Be that as it may, given that an analysis of a conjuncture must begin with the localization of its dominant instance, Badiou admits that every "conjunctural type" can be characterized by the instance that plays the "principal role" in it.[76] Logically speaking, multiple types of conjunctures are conceivable: political, ideological, economic, scientific. But the issue is to define the principle that governs these variations, or, as Badiou also states, "the *mechanism for the production of the conjuncture effect*."[77]

This mechanism leads to the introduction of a new concept, that of determination, which is, evidently, equivalent to Althusser's frequently deployed notion of "determination in the last instance," in conformance with the classical nomenclature:[78] "Let us agree to call *determination* the production of this effect. It will be remarked that determination is exhaustively defined by its effect: the change in the conjuncture, which itself can be identified with the displacement of the dominant. This being said, what is the efficacy from which this displacement is the result?"[79] At this point, Badiou confronts the difficult problem of forging a concept of determination capable of functioning as an explanatory tool while at the same time construing it in such a way that, given its position in the conceptual structure of historical materialism, it blocks the path to economism. Economism postulates that the economy is always dominant, that every conjuncture accords to the economy the role of principal instance (as well as, accordingly, the role of principle of intelligibility): "To believe that one *instance* of the whole determines the conjuncture inevitably means to confuse determination (law of displacement of the dominant) with domination (hierarchizing function of the efficacies in a given conjunctural type). Besides, such is the root of all ideological deviations of Marxism—especially the most notorious among them, economism."[80] It is therefore incorrect to search for determination in the *instances*, since they only exist at the level of already constituted conjunctures, which is to say in each moment of the articulated structure in dominance that defines the social whole. Even though the economic instance is present in any conjuncture—a presence that should be interrogated—it can be dominant or it can *not be* dominant.

If the determination cannot be attributed to any *instance*, it could be attributed to a *practice*, defined according to its specific structure, "a structure that is so to speak *dislocated* [décalée] with regard to the one that articulates this practice as an instance of the whole."[81] It could be speculated that the variations of the dominant, and therefore the changes of the conjuncture, are "the effect of the presence, subjacent to one of the instances, of a structure-of-practice in non-coincidence with the instance that *represents* it in the totality."[82] In other words, it is possible that one of the levels of the social formation (a level that in this case is invariant) would be the site of production of *two* functions: that of the instance of the articulated whole and that of the "determinate practice" that "in real history," as Badiou asserts by once again citing Althusser, "is 'exercised precisely in the permutations of the principal role between the economy, politics, theory, etc.'—in short, in the displacement of the dominant and the fixation of the conjuncture."[83]

Nevertheless, this practice, as the site of determination, will always and invariably be the same. On this point, the second great thesis of dialectical materialism holds: "There exists a *determining practice*, and this practice is the 'economic' practice."[84] However, "*qua determining* [. . .] it would remain 'invisible,' not being *presented* in the constellation of instances, but only *represented*."[85] Badiou concludes this point by calling attention to the unprecedented nature of the form of causality bestowed upon this determining practice.

> Indeed, thought of as principle of determination, the economic practice *does not exist*: that which figures in the articulated whole in dominance (which is the only effective existent) is the economic instance which is nothing but the representative of the homonymous practice. Now, this representative is itself *caught* in the determination (according to whether the economic instance is dominant or subordinate, according to the extent, prescribed by the correlation of instances, of its conjunctural efficacy, etc.). The causality of the economic practice is thus the causality of an absence on an already structured whole in which it is represented by an instance.[86]

The parallels with the logical form of Miller's formulations are clear, just as clear as the Lévi-Straussian inspiration to which Badiou refers. Also at issue for Badiou is the problem posed by the localization of the term that delineates the relevant exclusion, the term with the double function that determines the belonging of the other terms to the structure or, to put it differently, the "structurality" of the structure. This, incidentally, makes Miller's silence regarding Lévi-Strauss's *Introduction to the Work of Marcel Mauss* all the more mysterious. The reader will have noticed, in any case, Badiou's careful omission of any reference to the subject. This point marks his divergence from Miller,[87] as well as from Lacan: "Lacan's most recent speculations on the subject of science should not disguise for us that, for Marxism, the subject is a *properly ideological* notion."[88] In this way, Badiou (re)poses the question of the subject. It is now time to reexamine that question as well as analyze, given the force of his intervention, Althusser's contribution to the debate.

The Subject in Question

Althusser was of course not absent from this discussion.[89] In his classic writings,[90] along with being, as previously mentioned, the first to explicitly state the problem, he develops a series of reflections in which:

a he underlines the transcendental importance of this problem not only for dialectical materialism and historical materialism, but also for psychoanalysis, linguistics, biology, and perhaps even physics;[91]

b he links the problem in question to his theory of overdetermination;
c he points at that Marx, despite not having arrived at the solution to the problem in its "theoretical state," nevertheless resolved it in his own way, "practically" (illustrating this point with two passages from *Capital*, one about the rate of profit and the other about ground rent);[92]
d recalling the distinction between *Vorstellung* and *Darstellung*, he discusses the issue of structural causality conceived of as an "absent cause," which Miller and Badiou abundantly mention, and urges that "the other aspect of the phenomenon" not be forgotten—namely, the presence of the cause in its effects, "i.e., *the existence of the structure in its effects*";[93]
e finally, to describe structural causality, he promotes the concept of "metonymic causality," which Miller developed and Jacques Rancière utilized.[94]

Althusser's interventions, moreover, demonstrate that he was perfectly aware of the difficulties—as well as the theoretical possibilities—of the concept being discussed. His allusions to *Darstellung* in particular contribute to highlighting this kind of double status of cause, both absent and present, exterior and interior to the structure. He even suggests that to speak of the absence or the presence of a cause in its effects depends on "*the level at which one is placed.*"[95]

But in my opinion, what stands out sharply from this series of considerations, and what appears to be in continuity with the theses developed in *Reading Capital*, is Althusser's determined opposition to granting the (ideological) notion of the subject a theoretical status, his exclusion of *any kind* of subject. Permit me to include below a well-known and decisive passage on this point:

> [T]he structure of the relations of production determines the *places* and *functions* occupied and adopted by the agents of production, who are never anything more than the occupants of these places, insofar as they are the "supporters" (*Träger*) of these functions. The true "subjects" (in the sense of constitutive subjects of the process) are therefore not these occupants or functionaries, are not, despite all appearances, the "obviousness" of the "given" of naïve anthropology, "concrete individuals," "real men"—but *the definition and distribution*

of these places and functions. The true "subjects" are these definers and distributors: the relations of production. [. . .] But since these are "relations," they cannot be thought within the category subject.[96]

In 1993, Stock/IMEC released an unprecedented collection of Althusser's unpublished texts, titling the volume *Writings on Psychoanalysis*. I would like to focus on one of those texts, "Three Notes on the Theory of Discourses," which was written in 1966 yet was never printed during Althusser's life.[97] The principal motivation for reviewing this text is that it allows us to return to the insistent—and still open—question of the subject from the strategic (although also problematic) point at which the theory of ideology and the theory of the unconscious intersect.

Althusser's "Three Notes on the Theory of Discourse" constitutes a valiant yet inconclusive attempt at epistemological realignment. In these notes, Althusser pursues a laborious inquiry into the relationship between the unconscious and ideology, an inquiry not exempt from setbacks and questions without answers. Through preliminary speculation, to both clear the path for the independent treatment of each issue and to organize his own thought, he elaborates a kind of "cartography" in which he attempts to define the status and the relevance of those disciplines and theories that he judges to be pertinent for the clarification of the aforementioned relationship.

To begin, he proposes a distinction between what he calls "general" and "regional" theories. Psychoanalysis would be a regional theory, dependent on a general theory (the Theory of the Signifier) still in the making, and its object would be the unconscious.[98] Although it will soon be discarded,[99] Althusser postulates four "subjects" that correspond to the four kinds of discourses he discerns during his reflections, which include the ideological discourse, the unconscious discourse, the aesthetic discourse, and the scientific discourse. Nevertheless, these distinctions, which were postulated before they were fully demonstrated, create more confusion than clarity for Althusser's reflections, so much so that, with nervous urgency, he calls on his collaborators to weigh in with their responses and opinions regarding the issue.

In the second and third notes, Althusser advances a series of conclusions that he labels "provisional," an awfully frequent precautionary qualification in Althusser's writings. First of all, by engaging in a self-criticism of the first note, Althusser rids himself of the search for the subjects that would correspond to the aesthetic discourse, the scientific discourse, and the unconscious discourse. The only "subject" would be *in* (and *of*) the ideological discourse. The scientific discourse would not have a subject, and the subject of the unconscious would be none other than the subject of the ideological discourse.[100]

Although "provisional," these propositions, particularly the last ones, are announced with an apodictic tone, the tone of someone clearing up a problem and arriving at a conclusion. Althusser's rejection of the "subject of the unconscious" is of interest in this sense, for it reveals a clear divergence from Lacan's position on the matter, a divergence that Althusser mentions to Lacan himself in the form of a confused questioning of the Lévi-Straussian conception of structure.[101]

There is no "subject of the unconscious," not even a "divided" subject. According to Althusser, one cannot speak of the *Ich-Spaltung* in terms of a subject separating itself from the ideological subject (*der Ich*) and opening before it the abyss, the "gap of the unconscious."

> [I]t seems to me unwarranted to talk about the "subject of the unconscious" in connection with the *Ich-Spaltung*. There is no *divided* or *split* subject, but something else entirely; alongside the *Ich*, there is a *Spaltung*, that is, literally, an *abyss*, a precipice, an absence, a lack, a gap.[102] This abyss is not a subject, but that which opens up *alongside a subject*, alongside the *Ich*, which is well and truly a subject (and falls within the province of the *ideological*; Freud, it seems to me, gives us the necessary grounds for thinking this on a number of different occasions). This *Spaltung* is the type of specific differential relation or articulation that binds (in the form of an abyss, a lack) unconscious discourse to the element or, rather, structural category of ideological discourse called the *Ich*. In a word, Lacan would appear to *establish the abyss* or *lack as a subject*, by way of the concept of the division of the subject. There is no "subject of the unconscious," although the unconscious can exist only thanks to this abyssal relation with an *Ich* (the subject of the ideological). This lack of the subject cannot be called a subject, although the (ideological) subject is implied or reflected in Freud's second topography, in an original way, *through* this lack, which is not a subject, but something *altogether different*.[103]

That said, it is probable, although impossible to verify, that Badiou's essay, with which Althusser must have been familiar, played a role in this now reinforced continuity of the rejection of the idea of the subject. Perhaps a subsequent exchange between the two likewise played a role. But Althusser also developed ideas of his own that did not figure in Badiou's work.

AT THIS POINT, I would like to take a step back to examine the route traveled so far. First, one might ask if the problems that Althusser and Badiou aim to resolve are left effectively resolved by the proposals discussed so far. There are basically two fundamental issues at play—namely, that of elaborating a theorization of the conjuncture that would be free of economism and that of "deciding" the status of the subject in said theorization.

Regarding the first issue, my opinion is that Badiou's elaborate argument, despite its acumen and the brilliance of its unfolding, is not able to fully absolve Marxism from the allegation of economism. Badiou is able to show without a doubt that what he calls dominant at the conjunctural level is not always, perforce, the economy; it can also be politics, ideology, science, etc. In this way a space of "indetermination" seems to open up. But that space reveals itself to be clearly determined at a deeper level. It is determined by the practice that is axiomatically qualified as determinant, an invariable practice that is *none other than the economy*. Since it is impossible that the variations at the conjunctural level are merely a "whim" of economic practice, and it is evident that these variations are thorough and necessary effects of that which is determinant, economism, thrown out the front door, reenters through the back. It is an issue of "second-order" economism, which makes the analysis of concrete situations more flexible, freeing it of certain restrictions. In that sense, it constitutes what Badiou himself, when addressing other issues, tends to call an "intra-ideological progression,"[104] but it does not constitute a true overcoming of economism. In any case, these inquires have contributed, many years later, to breaking free from the theoretical tethers (notions like the instance, relative autonomy, "social whole in dominance," etc.) that placed insurmountable obstacles in the way of truly putting an end to the economistic vision.

Regarding the problem of the "subject," things get more complicated. Without a doubt, on this specific point, the positions of Althusser and Badiou completely coincide. It would not be incorrect to maintain that this concordance was a substantial and long-lasting one, since it has managed to live on to this day. During a talk in Vienna given not that long ago, Badiou polemically reaffirmed his agreement with Althusser: "[I]t seems to me that two ideas dominate research into his theoretical work. [. . .] The first is to place Althusser in relation to Marxism. The second is to try to find in his work a theory of the subject."[105] I will return later on to Badiou's position regarding the first idea and will instead focus my attention for now on the second. Badiou continues: "On the second point, my verdict is stark: there is no theory of the subject in Althusser, nor could there ever be one. For Althusser, all theory proceeds by way of concepts. But 'subject' is not a concept. This theme is developed with the utmost clarity in 'Marx's Relation to Hegel.' For example: 'the concept "process" is scientific, the notion "subject" is ideological.' 'Subject' is not the name of a concept, but that of a notion, that is, the mark of an inexistence. There is no subject, since there are only processes."[106] He then immediately highlights, just as Althusser, what in his judgment cannot be articulated by the Lacanian theory of the subject (and of the *objet petit a*):

> The very frequent attempt to supplement Althusser with Lacan on this question, which seeks support in some of Althusser's passages on psychoanalysis, is in my view unworkable. In Lacan there is a theoretical concept of the subject, which even has an ontological status. For the being of the subject in Lacan is the coupling of the void and the "objet petit a." There is no such thing in Althusser, for whom the object exists even less than the subject. Althusser writes: "object = mirror reflection of *subject*." The object is therefore the image of an inexistence. The process without a subject functions just as effectively as the process without an object.[107]

In my view, Badiou's conclusions are pertinent despite the fact that they constitute an ex post commentary (although concurrent with what Badiou has always maintained). The tragedy of 1980 and its aftershocks left Althusser unaware of the extended meetings, prolonged debates, and infinite speculation that proliferated at the time concerning the register of the Real, which Lacan converted into a central issue during the 1970s. It is already too late to mourn that missed encounter. Those who have read the stories that chronicle, with a modicum of objectivity, Lacan's role in putting an end to the Freudian School of Paris in March of 1980 will recall that Althusser's last "intervention" regarding Lacan—an untimely intervention that no doubt was more representative of the philosopher's illness than of the annoyance of psychoanalysis[108]—all in all came from someone who could not exactly be considered Lacanian, despite having come to appreciate Lacan's work like almost no one else.[109] Althusser had been free from the Subject—including the split or divided Subject—since 1966. Leaving for another time a discussion of the controversy surrounding the status of the Subject within the framework of structural psychoanalysis or Lacanian psychoanalysis, both ultimately the same thing, it is my opinion that this freedom from the Subject represented an important advancement down the path toward making explicit the physiognomy proper to the profound thought of Althusser.

The Structuralist Controversy

The previous discussion of Lévi-Strauss prompts me to rethink an issue that many other individuals have already discussed and taken as definitively resolved: Can Althusser's "classic" stage of theorization be characterized as structuralist? This question can only be answered in the affirmative. Structuralism is vibrantly present throughout the development discussed in this chapter, in Althusser's contributions to *Reading Capital* as well as in those of his disciples, Étienne Balibar, Jacques Rancière, Pierre Macherey, and Roger Establet. Althusser quickly and repeatedly attempted to refute this presence, to reduce it to terminological resemblances or, at the very least, to engage in self-criticism of partial aspects of his work; however, its gravitational pull was apparently too strong for such gestures to nullify it.

These gestures were even less capable of enabling Althusserianism to escape the summary but not erroneous characterization that it was the Marxist iteration of structuralism. This interpretation of Althusserianism is confirmed from the very beginning of *Reading Capital* when Althusser states the following in a laborious passage with Derridean accents: "[T]he text of history is not a text in which a voice (the Logos) speaks, but the inaudible and illegible notation of the effects of a structure of structures."[110] There were, of course, already implicit convergences with structuralism, like the critique of the humanist reading of Marx carried out in the essays of *For Marx*, which evoke Lévi-Strauss's theses from the final chapter of *The Savage Mind* (1962), where the latter enters into a polemic with the Jean-Paul Sartre of the *Critique of Dialectical Reason*.[111] But Althusserianism's convergence with Lévi-Straussian ideas becomes explicit, although always embarrassingly, in the two volumes of *Reading Capital*.

Althusser is not only the one who most forcefully renounces this convergence; he is also the one who is most invested in distancing himself from

Lévi-Strauss. His best efforts to achieve this are nevertheless condemned to fail from the start. This is so "from the start" because even if the terminology had been different (as in Lacan, Foucault, Barthes), even if the not unavoidable notion of "combinatory" discussed by Balibar had been dispensed with,[112] even if Lévi-Strauss—unlike Marx—had lacked, as Althusser once said, a theory of social complexity (an unjust accusation, by the way),[113] the *problematic* in which Althusser's declared project is inscribed would have been no less enveloped by the global axiomatic of Lévi-Straussian structuralism, an "epochal" ideology whose origins can be traced back to the late 1940s and early 1950s.[114]

Althusser's declared project inherited or borrowed from structuralism not only its concepts but also its problems. As I attempted to demonstrate earlier, the issue of "structural causality" in particular, which Althusser held to be decisive, is a notorious inheritance from structuralism. Among his disciples (those who, as Marx would say, tend to extract the most absurd consequences from the master's theories), Balibar takes the cake in *Reading Capital*,[115] arguing that the concept of the "mode of production" can be defined as the "combination"—governed by two fundamental connections or relations, "property" and "real accumulation"—of "a small number of elements which are always the same"— namely, the "means of production, direct producers, even 'non-laborers.'"[116] This definition gives rise to the following thesis: "By varying the combination of these elements according to the two connections which are part of the structure of every mode of production, we can therefore reconstitute the various modes of production."[117]

These theses are in perfect harmony with one of Althusser's, which uses the same terms and coincides, as in many of his texts, with the (more diplomatic) anti-historicism of Lévi-Strauss: "[I]t is clear that the theoretical nature of this concept of 'combination' may provide a foundation for the thesis [. . .] that Marxism *is not a historicism*: since the Marxist concept of history depends on the principle of the variation of the forms of this 'combination.'"[118] Nevertheless, Althusser, Balibar, and the other coauthors of *Reading Capital* insist systematically on establishing critical distance from Lévi-Strauss, be it indirectly, through the critique of the validity of Lévi-Strauss's frequently used concept of "model" (which Balibar nevertheless uses in *Reading Capital*),[119] or directly, through scornful references to Lévi-Straussian formulations that cautiously avoid touching on the central aspects of structural anthropology.[120]

One passage from "The Object of *Capital*" could perhaps be considered a (no-doubt very partial) exception to this rule. In effect, Althusser states the following:

> There is hardly any need to show how diachrony admits its destitution in those thinkers who assign to it the role of history. Diachrony is reduced to the sequence of events (*à l'événementiel*), and to the effects of this sequence of events on the structure of the synchronic: the historical then becomes the unexpected, the accidental, the factually unique, arising or falling in the empty continuum of time for purely contingent reasons.[121] In this context, therefore, the project of a "structural history" poses serious problems, and a laborious reflection of this can be found in the passages devoted to it by Lévi-Strauss in *Structural Anthropology*.[122]

Yet Althusser does not develop or justify his assertions. Political reasons are without a doubt at work here. Lacan can be praised, no matter what position is taken on the political terrain, because his terrain is psychoanalysis. The same does not apply to Lévi-Strauss, since his object of investigation pertains to the field of historical materialism, and despite his complicit nods toward Marxism, Lévi-Strauss was not a Marxist, let alone a Marxist-Leninist.

In my opinion, however, these political reasons are not the only reasons at play, nor are they the principal ones. After Althusser's death, those in charge of publishing his writings included a critical note on Lévi-Strauss from 1966. That text was addressed as a letter to Emmanuel Terray. According to the editors, Althusser not only gave permission for this text to be published but also suggested that it appear as an appendix to Terray's book titled, *Marxism and "Primitive" Societies* (1969). This did not happen. The editors also maintain that Althusser sent the note along with his suggestion of where to publish it to Badiou, but it is unclear if Althusser ever received a response.

The fact is that this text remained unpublished.[123] It seems that Althusser did not insist that it be published. It is my opinion that this can be explained by the fact that his own colleagues and disciples found the text to be, at bare minimum, excessive. Althusser recognized this himself in the note's final lines. In truth, it is a weak text: there is an inconsistency, even a contradiction, between what it says that it is going to do and what it effectively does. The critiques of Lévi-Strauss are never backed up with arguments derived from a serious reading of his work. After declaring and reiterating that he will not judge Lévi-Strauss for his adequate or inadequate understanding of

Marx's work, Althusser proceeds to attack Lévi-Strauss on the sole basis of having ignored, according to Althusser, the elementary concepts of historical materialism, the concepts of the science founded by Marx, the concepts that, to be more precise, were none other than those of Althusser himself. I believe this is not an insignificant deficiency; it is a symptomatic forgetting that deserves to be interrogated.[124]

As I have suggested, this kind of involuntary forgetting no less symptomatically marks Miller's text, "S'truc dure." The absence of any mention of the *Introduction to the Work of Marcel Mauss* can only be interpreted as a (no doubt unintentional) concealing of an approach that forms the basis not so much of Miller's exposition as of the problematic of structural causality in all its iterations.

It is impossible to justify these omissions, but it is possible to attempt to understand them. To put it briefly and therefore schematically, an inquiry like that of Lévi-Strauss's, which wholly pored over structures (of kinship, myth, etc.) and, in his own words, had to bow before "the power and the inanity of the event," an inquiry that exiled history and politics from its horizon of investigation—that kind of inquiry had to be viewed by Althusserianism as opposed to its own project.[125] But this could not be the case without difficulties. I repeat that this is not merely a question of terminology. The structuralist turn of Althusserianism, viewed as a project that aimed to be scientific (just as Lévi-Strauss wanted to be scientific), was no doubt one of the key elements of the problems that needed to be faced, not by the declared project but rather by what I have called Althusser's esoteric thought.

The obsession with establishing distance, with avoiding confusion between Althusser's Marxism and structuralism, also stems from the fact that what aspired to give true meaning to the Althusserian enterprise was not just any kind of politics but rather a politics that called for the revolutionary transformation of society. In this way, Althusser and his collaborators remained faithful to the ideals and projects that marked the 1960s. The supposed philosophers of structuralism placed structuralism very far away from those same ideals and projects, almost to the point of being at odds with them. Without taking communion with Sartre, Althusser felt closer to the author of the *Critique of Dialectical Reason* than to Lévi-Strauss.

That said, and leaving aside for now the exoteric project, it should be recognized that Althusser's initial rejection of structuralism, more surface-level than substantial, was none other than the other side of the intermittent occurrence of his still-larval esoteric thought. The latter is in fact profoundly incompatible with structuralism. Giving ontological priority to chance, to historical conditions, to the event, and especially to *contingency*, this form of thought questions one by one the fundamental premises of any instantiation of structuralism (not only the structuralism of its founder but also of authors like Lacan). In that sense, Althusser's esoteric thought exchanges the first blow that injures structuralism at its very core. It is the first sign that foretells structuralism's imminent death.

The most fundamental of aporias, the one which in fact governs the whole fate of Marxism (as Althusser had perfectly understood and shown), is the aporia of the concept of ideology. — ÉTIENNE BALIBAR, "The Infinite Contradiction"

THREE. **THE TRAPS OF IDEOLOGY**

In the previous chapter, I had the opportunity to consider in detail the notion of the subject insofar as it is directly implicated in one version of the theory of structural causality. There is nevertheless another angle to consider that was also previously mentioned, which invokes and interrogates the notion of the subject regarding its relation to the concept of ideology.

The relation subject-ideology puts into relief an issue to which Althusser always—including in his final writings—accorded special attention, an issue that has kept Althusserianism and its inheritors on both sides of the Atlantic occupied for the past forty years. It is well known, and was mentioned in chapter 1, that the majority of Althusser's exegetes place him among the toughest and most consequential critics of the notion of the subject. There is, of course, no absence of texts that sustain this thesis. Since the book on Montesquieu, and especially since the essay on the young Marx, Althusser submits the category of the subject to permanent questioning and unceremoniously relegates it to the realm of ideology. The critique of so-called theoretical humanism points in reality to what Althusser considers to be the hegemonic form—both inside and outside of Marxism—of the ideology of the subject. Althusser will modify and fine-tune his opinions on these matters with time, but he never compromises on his rejection of any theory centered on the subject.

In Althusser's first writings, the question of the subject even seems to refer to a secondary dispute, already decided in advance and lacking in interest: that which is called "subject" is none other than the figure with which individual actors—in reality mere supports (*Träger*) of social relations—imaginarily, which is to say falsely, represent their relation to their conditions of existence. The ideology of the subject would enjoy the privilege of being the most complete form of expression of the illusion that the actor himself has instituted this relation by his own will. In sum, the actor forges the fantasy that he is himself the lord and master of his destiny, and he believes in this fantasy.

But this privilege comes with a price. While effective as an ideological operator, the category of the subject lacks all theoretical pertinence. There is no "subject" other than the illusory phantom of individuals. In reality, individuals are submitted to the joint and irrevocable determination of the social relations of production, the political relations of domination, and ideology itself.

Althusser forcibly outlines these theses in his classic works, attempting to bolster them with varying references to psychoanalysis and particularly to the Lacanian reading of Freud.[1] This is the case, for example, when Althusser names as "doubly specular" the structure of recognition that characterizes the ideological effect.[2] This expression, inspired by Lacan, refers to the thesis of the mirror stage and more specifically to that "irreducible line of fiction" in which, for Lacan, the individual ego, before any social determination, would remain imprisoned forever.[3]

This is, of course, also the case when Althusser refers to the registers of the imaginary and the symbolic as structuring the aforementioned fiction. Althusser addresses this last point in "Freud and Lacan," an essay that was published—not without some difficulties—in *La Nouvelle Critique* (1964).[4] In that text, everything seems to rely on what I will cautiously call a "cognitive [*cognoscitivo*] plane," even though the text's consequences far exceed the realm of knowledge. The subject—or better yet the little wannabe subject [*el pequeño aspirante a sujeto*]—constitutes its identity in such a way that this identity rests, from the start and permanently, on a structure of misrecognition. This misrecognition at the same time misrecognizes itself in the comfy positivity of an ideological formation, such that the subject, constituted in this way, lives its relation with itself and with the world in the form of an unconscious, soothing, and constant self-deception. To inevitably conceive of oneself as a subject is to ignore, no less inevitably, one's condition as "support." Of course, to fill this misrecognition with meaning and reinforce it,[5] the individual will later have at his disposal the almost always discreet services of a rich array of ideologies.

I mentioned the terms *ideology* and *ideological formation* previously. Jacques-Alain Miller, one of Althusser's disciples at the time, advances some propositions in a Lacanian idiom that open a path to the incorporation of these concepts. Miller writes:

> In the structural system in which production is articulated in a specific mode, the zone of displacement of the subject—insofar as it is held up at the level of the actual, which is to say insofar as the structure concedes it the perception of its state (of its apparent motion) while stealing from it the perception of its system—is defined as *illusion*. Illusion perpetuates itself in the form of ideology when the subject reflects it, signifies it, or in a word, redoubles it. Illusion and ideology, if they are thought in the continuity from a "seeing" to a "saying," form the element natural to a subject rigorously qualified by its insertion into the structure of a social formation.[6]

The "action of the structure" should be retained from this passage; it only allows subjects to perceive the apparent motion (that of the structure and that of themselves as supports of the structure), and it robs from them the real motion (its system).[7]

From this it must be inferred that illusion is inherent to all perception—physical and intellectual—and to the discourse that prolongs and rationalizes the illusion without questioning it, which is to say the ideological discourse. Without explicitly stating it, this proposition presupposes the radical opacity of the social for "spontaneous" individual perception, and it can find support in some of Marx's well-known maxims.[8] The proposition also presupposes Miller's (and Lacan's) conception of the subject, as discussed in chapter 2. Likewise, as a vague corollary, the proposition gives strong theoretical backing to the Kautskyian thesis on the necessity of importing socialist consciousness into the working class, incapable as they are of overcoming spontaneity and reformism on their own. The strategic importance of this thesis for the Althusserian *dispositif* was explained in chapter 1.

For a few years, Althusserianism accepted these positions, including with some oscillation between the Millerian and Badiouian options concerning the notion of the subject, though clearly predisposed to the latter. Linguists and philosophers close to Althusserianism's positions added some theoretical elements and above all strove to translate Althusserianism's theses into methodological criteria for analysis. The main representative of this school was Michel Pêcheux, who was accompanied by, among others, Régine Robin, Françoise Gadet, Pierre Henry, Jacques Guilhaumou, Denise Maldidier, Claudine Haroche, and Bernard Conein.

Althusser would once again take up his theses on ideology and the subject in his most well-known essay on the topic: "Ideology and Ideological State Apparatuses" (1969–70), which was published for the first time in *La Pensée* (1970) and reproduced in various anthologies.[9] This essay's point of departure is the same as in Althusser's prior writings [such as in the following passage from *For Marx*]:

> In ideology men do indeed express, not the relation between them and their conditions of existence, but *the way* they live the relation between them and their conditions of existence: this presupposes both a real relation and an "*imaginary*," "*lived*" relation. Ideology, then, is the expression of the relation between men and their "world," that is, the (overdetermined) unity of the real relation and the imaginary relation between them and their real conditions of existence. In ideology the real relation is inevitably invested in the imaginary relation, a relation that *expresses a will* (conservative, conformist, reformist or revolutionary), a hope or a nostalgia, rather than describing a reality.[10]

This passage raises the issue of explaining why the individual's representation of his relation to the real conditions of existence, which is to say to the "objective" relations that govern his existence, must necessarily be "imaginary" (or distorted regarding the reality of these relations). This issue presupposes another one, that of clarifying the nature and the functioning of said imaginary. The essay on Ideological State Apparatuses attempts to elaborate a response to these questions.[11]

Regarding the first issue, Althusser affirms in this essay that the mode of functioning proper to ideology is the "interpellation" of individuals as "subjects." Beyond his new formulation, this affirmation does not add much to what has already been discussed before—namely, that the invariable mechanism of ideology (called "interpellation" here) produces, as its specific effect, individuals that live their relation to their conditions of existence in such a way that they imaginarily, which is to say illusorily, constitute themselves as the *autonomous principle* of determination of this relation. Accordingly, through ideology, every individual who occupies a determinate position in (and through) social relations qua individual perceives himself as that upon which said position depends. In this way, the functioning of ideology produces an illusory inversion of determinations, making the determined appear determining "in the eyes" of the determined. This happens through the elementary mechanism of interpellation: "[I]deology 'acts' or 'functions' in such a way that it 'recruits' subjects among the individuals (it recruits them all),[12] or 'transforms' the individuals into subjects (it transforms them all) by that very precise operation which I have called *interpellation* or hailing, and which can be imagined along the lines of the most commonplace everyday police (or other) hailing: 'Hey, you there!'"[13] This implies that the trivial and commonplace act that we direct toward "someone"— hailing them by their own name or nickname—is none other than the putting in motion of the ideological operation that is at once *universal* (because all ideology functions in this way) and *specific* (because this mode of functioning distinguishes ideological practice from all other social practices). In every quotidian interpellation, we repeat mindlessly the operation that ideology has always accomplished.

At this point, Althusser does introduce some new elements, for the illusion of the "subject's" autonomy is only one aspect of ideology's functioning. This aspect is subordinated to another complementary and no less essential aspect: at bottom this illusion of autonomy conceals the real submission that affects subjects. More precisely, it hides this submission behind the appearance of a consensual self-subjection.

Indeed, according to Althusser, the interpellation of individuals as subjects has as one of its conditions the existence of another Subject, with a capital "S," in whose name ideology conducts its specific operation. It is naturally to the Subject par excellence that obedience and subjection are due. Althusser states:

> We observe that the structure of all ideology, interpellating individuals as subjects in the name of a Unique and Absolute Subject is *spec-

ulary, i.e. a mirror-structure, and *doubly* speculary: this mirror duplication is constitutive of ideology and ensures its functioning. Which means that all ideology is *centered*, that the Absolute Subject occupies the unique place of the Center, and interpellates around it the infinity of individuals into subjects in a double mirror-connection such that it *subjects* the subjects to the Subject, while giving them in the Subject in which each subject can contemplate its own image (present and future) the *guarantee* that this really concerns them and Him, and that since everything takes place in the Family [. . .] "God will *recognize* his own in it," i.e. those who have recognized God, and have recognized themselves in Him, will be saved.[14]

From the previous passage it can be inferred that ideology in general:

a interpellates individuals as subjects;
b guarantees the subjection of these subjects to the Single, Absolute, Central Subject;
c ensures the mutual recognition between subjects and the Subject, between the subject and itself, and between the various subjects;
d furnishes the absolute guarantee that everything is fine and that, if the subjects recognize who they are and act accordingly, everything will work out marvelously.

What is the ultimate result of this four-part operation? Naturally, that the subjects fulfill their duties, that they do what is required of them, in short, that they assume, freely and without recourse to external coercion, that which is prescribed to them by virtue of the position they hold in the fabric of social relations into which they are inserted.

We thus arrive at a new thesis, which maintains that the global effect of ideology's mechanism within a social formation is "to ensure the cohesion of the social whole by regulating the relations of individuals to their tasks."[15] This thesis, advanced in a less developed form in a prior work,[16] acquires its precise and complete meaning in the essay on Ideological State Apparatuses. To ensure social cohesion in general means to ensure the reproduction of existing relations of production and of the relations that follow from them. This would ultimately be the specific effect of ideology.

With this thesis it seems that the theory of ideology proposed by the classic Althusser comes—belatedly—full circle. Nevertheless, in a postscript from 1970, a year after drafting the essay, Althusser returns to the arguments developed therein and reformulates or corrects some of its theses. These rectifications are generally the result of Althusser introducing an element that up until this point had been practically absent from his reflections (at least his reflections on the subject and on ideology)—namely, *class struggle*. For Althusser, self-criticism becomes a normal turn of events. Rather than modify the theses put into question by the insertion of a new element, he prefers to label them "abstract" without refuting them or limiting their scope. Accordingly, there is ideology "in general" and concrete ideologies, the invariable and "eternal" mechanisms of the former and the historically variable mechanisms of the latter. What's more, the *factum* of class struggle would be unthinkable without the existence of antagonistic classes. And "[w]hoever says class struggle of the ruling class says resistance, revolt, and class struggle of the ruled class."[17] It accordingly follows that,

> this point of view of the class struggle in the ISAs is still an abstract one. In fact, the class struggle in the ISAs is indeed an aspect of the class struggle, sometimes an important and symptomatic one: e.g. the anti-religious struggle in the eighteenth century, or the "crisis" of the educational ISA in every capitalist country today. But the class struggles in the ISAs is only one aspect of a class struggle which goes beyond the ISAs. The ideology that a class in power makes the ruling ideology in its ISAs is indeed "realized" in those ISAs, but it goes beyond them, for it comes from elsewhere. [. . . It comes] from their conditions of existence, their practices, their experience of the struggle, etc.[18]

Althusser limits himself to these observations without developing them and notably without extracting conclusions from them that would affect his theory of ideology. The dense and suggestive work on Ideological State Apparatuses concludes enigmatically, without any explanation regarding the notorious imbalance between the body of the text and the postscript, like a story abruptly interrupted right in the middle of its telling. As I will demonstrate, many years will pass before this same interruption is interrupted.

In any event, the central theses of the essay on Ideological State Apparatuses reopen the discussion regarding the status of the notion of the subject. I have shown that in the published and unpublished work, after examining alternative positions, the "subject" remained reduced to merely an ideological *notion*, from which it was necessary to be liberated, at least in the realm of theory. Nonetheless, it is important to note here that the issue is open to interpretation, at the very least because the term *subject* seems to be indispensable for describing the effects of ideology's functioning. The "general" theory of ideology as it is developed in the aforementioned text must necessarily include the concept of the subject in its terminology. The thesis according to which "ideology interpellates-constitutes individuals as subjects" presents itself, in fact, as a scientific statement.

In my view, this is not merely a terminological issue. What is truly at stake here is the choice between, on the one hand, a conception of ideology as a "specter to dispel," a conception that Althusser calls into question while often remaining attached to it, and, on the other hand, a conception of ideology as an irremovable element, active and operational in all social formations.

In an attempt to shed some light on this and other points, it would be useful to draw once more from the *Writings on Psychoanalysis* (unpublished until 1993), since the texts of that volume, which were not available to the public during Althusser's lifetime, go into the most obscure aspects of the Althusserian theorization of ideology and the subject. In the previously cited "Three Notes on the Theory of Discourses,"[19] Althusser in fact engages with the problem discussed above:

> In every social formation, the base requires the support-[*Träger*] function as a function to be assumed, as a place to be occupied in the technical and social division of labor. This requirement remains abstract: the base defines the *Träger*-functions (the economic base, and the political and ideological superstructure *as well*), but the question of *who* must assume and carry out this function, and how the assumption of it might come about, is a matter of *perfect indifference* to the structure, [. . .] it "doesn't want to know anything about it." [. . .] It is ideology which performs the function of *designating* the subject (in general) that is to occupy this function: to that end, it must *interpellate it* as subject, providing it with the reasons-of-a-subject for assuming the function. [. . .] These reasons-of-a-subject appear explicitly in its ideological discourse, which is therefore necessarily a discourse that relates to the subject to which it is addressed, and therefore necessarily includes the subject as a signifier of this discourse; that is why the subject must appear in person among the signifiers of ideological discourse. In order for the individual to be constituted as an inter-

pellated subject, it must recognize itself as a subject in ideological discourse, must figure in it: whence a first speculary relation, thanks to which the interpellated subject can see itself in the discourse of interpellation.[20]

Summarizing these points again later on, Althusser writes, "Ideology is articulated with the economic and political structures in that it enables the '*Träger*'-function to function by transforming it into a *subject*-function."[21] In other words, the support-function "functions" as a void to fill, from which it could be inferred that ideology interpellates-constitutes this structurally determined "void" as subject. This constitution is not "imaginary," but it unfolds, so to speak, and furnishes effects in the register of the imaginary. In fact, the function of the *Träger* designates, to use a Lacanian term that Althusser failed to take into account, the "real" of the supposed "subject." "Support" (*Träger*) would be, then, the concept that designates that which attains self-recognition/misrecognition via the subject-function. But this is not an entirely satisfactory solution to the problem.

Indeed, the essays on the young Marx and on Ideological State Apparatuses, as well as the unpublished notes on the theory of discourse, introduce a third term along the way between the support and the subject—namely, the "individual." Ideology interpellates "individuals" as subjects. But what then would be the theoretical status of the term *individual*? This question is never even formulated, which is why it remains without an answer. Without the slightest hesitation, Althusser distractedly sneaks in the term *individual* as if it were self-evident and then continues right along.[22]

This is, however, not the only enigma that remains unresolved. As is evident, two different focuses coexist in the essay on Ideological State Apparatuses, and Althusser perceives their incongruence insofar as he tries, although with debatable success, to neutralize it. This incongruence is expressed in various ways: (a) ideology (in general) is eternal, which is to say that, just like the unconscious, it has no history; (b) ideology (in general) encompasses all of history, which, according to Althusser, *is the same as saying "the history of class societies."*[23]

As is well known, (a) does not get along with (b), which leads Althusser to introduce the ad hoc statement that (b) imposes a merely *provisional* limit on (a). Yet the formulation "ideology in general" serves another purpose, as can be noticed when Althusser states the following in the postscript: "The 'mechanism' of ideology *in general* is one thing. We have seen that it can be reduced to a few principles expressed in a few words (as 'poor' as those which, according to Marx, define production *in general*, or in Freud, define *the* unconscious *in general*). If there is any truth to it, this mechanism must be *abstract* with respect to every real ideological formation."[24] This is a strange way of referring to "the general" and of utilizing the category of "abstraction." With these precautionary qualifications, Althusser feels confident addressing concrete ideological formations as if the effective modalities of their functioning were not necessarily subsumable under the characteristics inherent to all ideology. By incorporating class struggle only at this "concrete" level and referring to the ideology of the dominant class, on the one hand, and to the ideology of the dominated class, on the other, Althusser hints that some determinations of ideology "in general" do not apply urbi et orbi. For example, it cannot be held that the ideological forms of expression of the exploited classes must necessarily contribute to the reproduction of the relations of production, since certain openings exist that enable the dominated classes to struggle against exploitation *through ideology itself*, turning against the exploiting classes one of their principal weapons of nonviolent subjection. This nevertheless requires that the theory of ideology *in general* be rethought and revised, which, as anticipated, Althusser will eventually do, even if only partially. I will return to this point later.

Before that, however, permit me to consider a problem that is logically prior and of interest insofar as it makes visible a kind of unexpected—but also productive—incoherence in Althusser's work. As is well known, one of the theses that Althusser most fervently proposes in his major writings is the thesis that affirms the scientific character of historical materialism. The concepts Marx introduces in *Capital* (constant capital, variable capital, surplus value, labor power, labor process, process of production, *Träger*) are for Althusser classic scientific concepts in the strict sense, with rules of use that are deemed to be rigorous and controlled. The laws that Marx set forth with the help of these concepts and others derived from them are laws in the strong sense.[25] They are scientific laws, independent from the will of individuals. They are by no means, as in the case of juridical or moral laws, *instituted* (by a society or a social class).[26] As it was customary for Althusser and his collaborators to say in those years: "This is a crucial point."[27] Any confusion or vacillation regarding this point would incurably compromise, in its entirety, the project that Althusserianism put together and endorsed.

However, in a very significant late text from 1975, Althusser attempts to retrospectively attend to and justify the essential elements of his theoretical propositions, sketching out an unexpected interpretation, to say the least, of some of the theses examined thus far. Returning to the question of the individual as a mere support (*Träger*) of social relations, he writes:

> It is very important to understand why Marx considers men in this case only as "supports" of a relation, or "bearers" of a function in the production process, determined by the production relation. It is not at all because he reduces men in their concrete life to simple bearers of functions [. . .]. In effect, the man of production, considered as an agent of production, *is only that* for the capitalist mode of production [. . .]. But to treat individuals as simple bearers of economic functions has consequences for the individual. It is not Marx the theoretician who treats them as such, but the capitalist production relation! To treat individuals as bearers of interchangeable functions is, within capitalist exploitation, which is the fundamental capitalist class struggle, *to mark them* irreparably in their flesh and blood, to reduce them to nothing but appendices of the machine, to cast their wives and children into the hell of the factory, to extend their working day to the maximum, to give them just enough to reproduce themselves, and to create that gigantic reserve army from which other anonymous bearers can be drawn in order to put pressure on those who are in employment, who are lucky enough to have work.[28]

In this and other passages from the text, which Althusser offers to his peers for judgment, with the idea of obtaining a doctorate, a line of interpretation is insinuated that, if brought to its logical conclusion, would shake loose some of the fundamental building blocks of "exoteric" Althusserianism's theoretical and philosophical edifice. Indeed, the *Träger*-function and the Subject-function—two key pieces of the edifice—are presented here as effects of the capitalist relations of production and thus of the historical domination exercised by the capitalist class on the open (and therefore susceptible to change) terrain of class struggle. Laws are no longer conceived of as invariable but rather as the potentially variable result of historical processes. This implies that laws can change [*pueden cambiar*] or more precisely *that they are contingent and can be changed* [*pueden ser cambiadas*].

Without a doubt, these interruptions that sneak into the letter of Althusser's discourse converge toward the introduction of a coefficient of contingency and indeterminacy in historical becoming, thereby breaking the linearity of a discourse that always claimed to situate itself within the domain of scientific necessity. We thus encounter, at this point, another irruption of the esoteric discourse and consequently a new rupture that affects the logic of the discourse in which Althusser's declared project presents itself.

Be that as it may, this last development illustrates, in continuity with what was mentioned before about ideology, the fact that the insertion of the concept of class struggle produces turbulence and contradictions in Althusser's theoretical *dispositif*. In an attempt to refine our gaze, I will risk going a bit further and will make an incursion into the expository strategy that serves Althusser when he has to contend with theoretical imbalances of this kind. It will become clear that in many cases, although of course not in all of them, Althusser, when pressured by two logics that cannot come to terms with each other, simply ignores or displaces this pressure. He proceeds on occasion as if no problem existed at all. Before the unrest of his readers and the joy of his critics, he leaves unresolved many of these difficulties—that without a doubt did not escape him—and leaves standing all the elements of the problem. The aforementioned essay on Ideological State Apparatuses, including the postscript, is in this sense a paradigmatic example.

In my opinion, behind this strategy lies the conviction that being limited to reordering the theoretical *dispositif* by opting for one of the terms and throwing away the others is equivalent to misrecognizing that which the very emergence of the problem allows us to glimpse—namely, the existence of a richer and more complicated register in which theses that seem at first glance to be incompatible can not only coexist but also mutually illuminate each other,[29] no matter how incapable one might be of defining with precision their respective realms of pertinence. To illustrate this point and to advance my argument, I will return to the examination of the Althusserian theory of ideology at the difficult point where we left it: the imbalance provoked by the insertion of class struggle into some of the theory's basic axioms.

I will draw from a very late text of Althusser's, the interviews conducted by the Mexican philosopher Fernanda Navarro between 1984 and 1987, which is to say around fifteen years after the publication of the essay on Ideological State Apparatuses. In these interviews, Althusser reiterates, in almost the same terms, the major topics of that essay and develops an argument that aims to resolve—and sometimes dissolve—the difficulties it set forth. Allow me to reproduce in extenso some of the questions and answers of the interview:

FERNANDA NAVARRO: Could you please say something more about this relationship between philosophy and ideology?

ALTHUSSER: [... W]e ought first to explain what we mean by "ideology." [... On this point,] I would like to add two clarifications. First, man is so constituted that no human action is possible without language and thought. Consequently, there can be no human practice without a system of ideas (I would prefer to say a system of *notions* inscribed in words; this system thus constitutes the ideology of the corresponding practice). Second, I insist on the fact that an ideology is a *system of notions* only to the extent that it refers to a system of *social relations*. It is not a question of an idea produced by an individual imagination, but of a system of notions that can be projected socially, a projection that can constitute a corpus of socially established notions. Ideology begins only at this point. Beyond it lies the realm of the imaginary or of purely individual experience. One must, then, always refer to a social reality which is singular, unique and factual.

FERNANDA NAVARRO: But could you explain how the "consciousness" of a concrete individual can be "dominated" by an ideological notion or a system of ideological notions?

ALTHUSSER: I could begin by responding that this mechanism operates whenever a consciousness "recognizes" these ideological notions to be "true." But how does this recognition come about? We already know that it is not the mere presence of the true which causes it to be perceived as true. There is a paradox here. It is as if, when I believe in a notion (or a system of notions), I were not the one who recognizes it and, confronted by it, could say: "That's it, there it is, and it's true." On the contrary, it is "as if,"—the roles having been reversed—it were the idea that interpellated me, in person, and obliged me to recognize its truth. This is how the ideas that make up an ideology impose themselves violently, abruptly, on the "free consciousness" of men: *by interpellating* individuals in such a way that they find themselves compelled "freely" to recognize that these ideas are *true—compelled* to constitute themselves as "free" "subjects" who are capable of recognizing the true wherever it is present, and of *saying* so, inwardly and outwardly, in the very form and content of the ideas constitutive of the ideology in question.

[. . .]

FERNANDA NAVARRO: It follows from what you have just said that man is by nature an ideological being.

ALTHUSSER: Absolutely, an ideological animal. I think that ideology has a trans-historical character, that it has always existed and always will exist. Its "content" may change, but *its function never will*. If we go back to the beginning of time, we can see that man has always lived under the sway of ideological social relations.

FERNANDA NAVARRO: So much for ideology "in general," then. As early as 1970, however, you drew a distinction here, affirming that particular ideologies plainly do have a history, even if it is determined, in the last instance, by class struggle.

ALTHUSSER: Granted; but I continued to maintain that ideology in general has no history.

[. . .]

FERNANDA NAVARRO: You have spoken of the "ideological subject." What, precisely, do you mean?

ALTHUSSER: I mean the subject considered as an effect of structures that precede and found its existence—considered, that is, as an individual subject or determined by ideological social relations. [. . .] In other words, he is a subject structurally subjected to the dominant—or non-dominant—ideology; that is to say, to a society's hegemonic or subaltern norms and values.

[. . .]

FERNANDA NAVARRO: Using the whole set of your theoretical instruments, can we think the transformation of subjects not only at the level of self-consciousness, but also at that of the consciousness of reality and the need to transform it?

ALTHUSSER: Yes. Otherwise there would be no change, and people would never take positions that challenge and oppose that which is established, that which is dominant. There would be no "revolutionary subjects." But a subject is always an ideological subject. His ideology may change, shifting from the dominant ideology to a revolu-

The Traps of Ideology 77

tionary ideology, but there will always be ideology, because ideology is the condition for the existence of individuals.[30]

In the preceding passages there are at least three sets of statements and some silences:

a On the one hand, there is a first set of statements in which Althusser limits himself to reiterating positions already developed, either in prior writings or in the essay on Ideological State Apparatuses. He insists, in particular, on the transhistorical character of ideologies.

b On the other hand, there is a second set of statements in which Althusser reinforces, and to a certain extent develops, the theses that he includes in the postscript of the aforementioned essay. I have underlined these statements, and all of them mention the existence (or the possibility of the existence) of nondominant or nonhegemonic ideologies, of stances that oppose domination, in sum, of revolutionary ideologies, and, although taking the precaution of using inverted commas, even of revolutionary subjects.

c There is a third set of statements that is not clearly developed in which Althusser gives the impression that the previous two sets and therefore the two types of ideologies to which they allude, while opposed in terms of their content and effects, accomplish the same inalterable function, that of interpellating-constituting individuals as subjects in such a way that they recognize themselves in determinate values or stated objects of belief and that they "freely" recognize these values and beliefs to be true. Evidently, this identity of function allows both types of ideologies to be subsumed under the same general concept.

d There is also a set of absences or, better, raturas, particularly regarding the operations that characterize the so-called mechanism of subjection that Althusser holds as proper to ideological interpellation. On the one hand, certain aspects of the theory are recuperated and even fine-tuned, such as the reflection on the modalities assumed by the process of the "ideological subject's" constitution as social being and his relation to ideological interpellation.[31] On the other hand, corrections of certain prior statements are incorporated, almost always implicitly, and certain theses that played an important role in prior moments are uniformly and plainly omitted.

e Indeed, the efficacy of said mechanism, at the level of theory in general, is ultimately restricted in a decisive way because of these recalibrations. No longer is there talk of a general and inevitable subjection that, starting from the imaginary representation of individuals regarding their relation to their real conditions of existence, would lead to the "voluntary" and "free" contribution of said individuals to the reproduction of the relations of production. If there is subjection, it operates on individuals strictly in terms of their recognition within a determinate ideology.

f That said, subjection to an ideology, the belief in its "truth," may be the necessary counterpart to the emancipatory initiatives of individuals. From this it is inferred, to put it simply, that not all ideology contributes necessarily to the reproduction of the relations of production. There can be and are ideologies that oppose and combat these relations of production. Of course, Althusser does not explicitly formulate all these conclusions, but the elements that he offers are more than sufficient, such that it is not only possible but almost mandatory that these conclusions be drawn.

g In this way, the period of interruption to which I referred earlier comes to a close. In a first moment, Althusser unquestioningly maintains incongruent theses on ideology (e.g., ideology is "transhistorical" but has a history; ideology functions as a dispositif of subjection of individuals and classes but also can contribute to their emancipation; ideology contributes to the reproduction of the existing relations of production but, when taking on the form of a revolutionary ideology, it can denounce and combat these same relations). In a second moment, Althusser rearranges the pieces of his dispositif: (i) He retains the thesis that ideology is "eternal" but clarifies that it is eternal with regard to its function, whereas, on the contrary, its contents historically change; (ii) he retains the theses relative to the mechanism of interpellation-constitution of individuals as subjects and the "effect of subjection" that it brings about in individuals, but he clarifies that this mechanism can contribute to strengthening the status quo and to domination as much as it can open a path to the emancipation of the exploited; (iii) he excludes from the general theory the thesis that holds that all ideology contributes to the reproduction of the existing relations of production. The "reproductionist" thesis would only be valid when applied to the ideologies of the dominant classes. Althusser, as mentioned before, never explicitly states this conclusion, but it is necessarily inferred from (i) and (ii).

h Of course, for the purposes of the interview, Althusser strives to express his thought with plain clarity and to avoid technical terms and specialist discussions.[32] In any case, in the interview and other texts (especially letters) included in the book, once repudiated terms, such as social movements, imagination, and even—advanced and called into question in the same paragraph—freedom, often make an appearance.[33] The obsolescence of other terms, particularly contradiction (replaced by antagonism), is also recorded.[34] Without venturing too deeply into muddy waters, and even appealing to the habitual terminology of his writings from the 1960s, Althusser risks advancing some novel theses. The most interesting among them refer to the definition of philosophy and to the relationship between philosophy and Marxism.

Regarding the first point, the definition of philosophy, Althusser returns in part to ideas already developed in previous works ("philosophy as such [. . .] was constituted with the constitution of the first science, mathematics";[35] "philosophy is, 'in the last instance,' class struggle in theory";[36] philosophy advances theses, which is to say it "takes up a position";[37] and these theses cannot be qualified as true or false but rather as correct [*justas*] or incorrect [*no justas*], etc.).[38] But he also introduces and elaborates other ideas, previously mentioned at conferences or in short texts. In particular, he affirms that history shows the properly philosophical struggle to be a conflict between materialism and idealism, with idealism dominating (even when it defines itself as "materialism").[39] Second, he holds that all philosophy is inhabited by its antagonist, by "the spectre of its opposite."[40] Finally, clarifying the political role of philosophy, he contends that "the task which philosophy is assigned and delegated by the class struggle is that of helping to unify the ideologies in a dominant ideology, guardian of the Truth."[41] Althusser likewise shares his conception of aleatory materialism in the interview and in other texts included in the book, but this is an issue that will be considered later on.

Regarding the second point, the relationship between philosophy and Marxism, Althusser affirms that it is necessary to elaborate not a Marxist philosophy but rather a philosophy for Marxism. The construction of a

Marxist philosophy is a task that does not make any sense. Philosophy is a discipline that has its history and effects; Marxism, as historical materialism, is a science. What was called "dialectical materialism" was a theoretically aberrant enterprise, even though it was effective and functional for Stalinism, which promoted both the name and the thing. Althusser's project, in his own words, would be to spend many years demonstrating above all else that Hegelianism—the philosophy to which Marx had recourse to inaugurate and develop the science of history—was never "functional" for Marxism nor for the scientific work of Marx. But Althusser's own efforts were unable to give theoretical status to a philosophy that would indeed be functional. According to Althusser, these efforts drowned in "a philosophy dominated by 'the spirit of the times'; it was a philosophy of Bachelardian and structuralist inspiration, which, even if it accounts for various aspects of Marx's thought, cannot, in my opinion, be called Marxist philosophy."[42] Accordingly, "the task before us today is to work out, not a Marxist philosophy, but a philosophy for Marxism. My most recent thinking moves in this direction. I am looking, in the history of philosophy, for the elements that will enable us to account for what Marx thought and the form in which he thought it."[43]

These final passages foreshadow the philosophical path that Althusser would take in those later years, more resolute with every step. It is clear that they exceed the framework of his standard theory of ideology and of the modest variants of that theory. In the next chapter, I will have the opportunity to return to these passages and explore in detail the new path that Althusser's thinking had begun to traverse.

> *One must think* in extremes. — LOUIS ALTHUSSER,
> "Is It Simple to Be a Marxist in Philosophy?"

FOUR. **THE SOLITARY HOUR**

The previous chapters pointed to some anticipatory traces of what I have termed Althusser's "esoteric" philosophy. These traces slipped in almost imperceptibly behind the dense reasoning and strained writing of Althusser's most well-known works. Among other examples, I noted that some glimpses of the "subterranean current" flowing beneath the exoteric project had already appeared in Althusser's first published book, *Montesquieu, la politique et l'histoire*. Their emergence was untimely and, in a sense, ill-timed, appearing out of the blue in the form of short and unexplained statements, still lacking the direction and force with which they would appear, openly and with a clear foundation, many years later. I also suggested that after reading Althusser's first book I began to suspect that the essential idea was already there from the beginning.

Althusser's *Reading Capital*, to take up again what I have termed precursor traces, went back to some ideas from the *Montesquieu* book concerning the emergence of a new historical reality and emphasized the importance of accounting for what he called, in reference to that emergence, "the necessity of its contingency." Almost haphazardly, this short phrase provocatively broke with the laws of Marxist orthodoxy as well as with the logical syntax of the classical philosophical tradition,[1] laterally incorporating the idea of contingency into a problematic that would supposedly liberate us from contingency forever. The metaphor of *prise*, of that which takes form [*toma consistencia*] or "takes [*prende*]," in the sense of a vaccine or of mayonnaise, was likewise formulated more than once, addressing different topics and appearing at different moments in his work.[2]

Permanent recommencement was the specifically Althusserian mode of philosophizing. For that reason, a necessary incompleteness marked his philosophy, with each point of arrival immediately converting into a new point of departure, into a new beginning. This was a costly effort that led Althusser to stretch his intuitions and the intuitions of others to the limit, scrutinizing all the many "interstices" left open by the culture and the epoch in which he happened to find himself, exploring the most minor nuances of a word or phrase.[3] Many well-known figures inspired his enterprise. As previously noted, in addition to Marx, the main ones were always Engels, Machiavelli, Spinoza,[4] Rousseau, Derrida, and to a lesser extent Lacan. They were interrogated over and over again, with critical insight but also with an anxious minuteness, with a kind of reserved impatience.

In chapter 2, I attempted to demonstrate that a constitutive imbalance inhabited this enterprise, as it had been explicitly taken on, from the beginning: it clearly seemed incoherent to attempt to think politics from within the framework of a philosophy fenced in by the "regulation" of an obstinate scientism and the demanding logic of a theoretical language that did not want to speak its name (structuralism) but was everyone's idiom at the time, since everyone understood each other with it and nothing could be heard without it. For that reason, drawing on Ernesto Laclau's formulation, it could be said that Althusser's structuralism was from the beginning a "dislocated" structuralism. It was a historical materialism that, based on categories with a structuralist bent, proposed nothing less than the forging of concepts capable of accounting for the conjuncture, the so-called current moment [*momento actual*]. It sought to confront, in other words, a challenge that from its very inception appeared to be not only arduous but also strange, both theoretically and practically.

For a structuralist, the conjuncture could only be an object of analysis when it was limited to actualizing a structure;[5] conjunctural analysis, pursued from this perspective, would most certainly be reduced to tedious calculation. For that reason, structuralism washed its hands of such analysis and happily entrusted it to historical investigation, though not without guarding itself—"astronomizing" its objects—from the never dismissible and always uncomfortable interference of historians. It is thanks to Lévi-Strauss that we have the formula that "anthropology is the astronomy of the human sciences."[6]

In contrast, for the kind of Marxist Althusser aspired to be, the conjuncture was the site in which a structure, while presenting itself in its inescapable contingency, exhibited not only its strength but also its fragility, its cracks, its weaknesses, where rupture was possible. Accordingly, and despite his epistemological outbursts, Althusser knew very well that "historical laws," in the strong sense, do not exist. The laws that Marxism believed it had discovered were only tendential: the last Althusser repeatedly paid homage to the expression "tendential law," which he attributed to Marx. As Althusser also noted, if these laws aspired to be more than tendential, they only survived at the expense of an overwhelming list of exceptions.

To make some progress and especially to silence his enemies, Althusser discreetly used the varied and forbidding vocabulary of an intransigent and uncompromising epistemology. He felt comfortable in this realm; the reservations or objections of his adversaries, within or outside of the party, were summarily dismissed, always by appealing to a kind of terrorism of the concept or of "scientific rigor." Without a doubt, this tactic was somewhat malicious, but behind the feint were some real convictions that generated long-lasting effects. To quickly mention one example, these convictions gave birth to the previously discussed project of teaching a course on philosophy for scientists at the École Normale Supérieure.

In any case, if, on the one hand, the new role of class struggle in Althusser's theory introduced serious disturbances into the logic of his thought, it led him, on the other hand, to delve into new terrain that had not yet been explored. The irruption of defiant formulations proliferated from within this budding problematic, formulations that were extremely challenging and even "revolutionary," as we candidly used to say back then.

Taking on the form of a kind of global assessment, the text "Marx in His Limits" (1978) details what, in my opinion, are the main shortcomings of Marxist theory, shortcomings already present in Marx and never recognized by his inheritors. "Marx in His Limits" was published posthumously in 1994.[7] It represents a notable development from Althusser's previous writings. In this text, Althusser relentlessly enumerates the fallacies from which, in his judgment, "Marxism-Leninism" suffers, and he recognizes that these fallacies were not innocent in terms of what would occur a few decades later and, in particular, in terms of Stalinism.[8]

In a profound and illuminating work, the philosopher Miguel Vatter brings to light the innovative aspects of this text from 1978. He points in particular to some of the important milestones that punctuate Althusser's reasoning: "'For Marx, critique is the real criticizing itself,' says Althusser, citing from *The German Ideology* where communism is famously identified with 'the real movement that abolishes the present state of things.' Althusser understands the 'real' to refer to 'the primacy of the struggle between classes with respect to the classes themselves.'"[9] Vatter gives priority to the distinction Althusser establishes between class struggle and classes, and he calls attention to the fact that the notion of class depends on what Vatter calls a "socioeconomic grammar of production" (in the classical Marxist idiom, the forces and the means of production, the division of labor, etc.), while the notion of a conflict between classes, to the extent that this notion logically precedes the others, is independent of the aforementioned grammar and points to what the author calls a "grammar of relations of production." Vatter perceives in Althusser the primacy of a *political* conception of these relations of production, a conception inscribed in the antagonism between domination and resistance, the antagonism that leads to the constitution of classes.

Vatter argues that classical Marxism, for Althusser, has revealed itself to be incapable of thinking social antagonism. Althusser rebels against this kind of Marxism and openly risks a new and provocative thesis: no "superior synthesis" can resolve social antagonism; it is a permanent antagonism that cannot be overcome. As Vatter also states, there is no "end of history."[10] History, I would say, paraphrasing another text of Althusser's, is a process without a subject and without a goal.[11]

In this same work from 1978, Althusser presents a radically "instrumentalist" theory of the State, converting it into a machine whose product is none other than the reproduction of the relations of production. He makes abundantly clear his resolute rejection of the position of Euro-communism, which was in full bloom at the time. Euro-communism, more than trying to present a democratic image of communism, advocated for a noninstrumentalist theory of the State, a conception of the state apparatus as full of contradictions and conflicting power relations. As is well known, the Euro-communist proposal did not survive the profound changes carried over by the winds of the East. In any event, Althusser's reflections regarding the functioning of the machine of the State and his critiques of Marx on this point are of unquestionable interest and are supported by substantial and in many ways convincing reasoning.[12] Some of the political opinions that are expressed, on the other hand, seem to be, at least today, untenable.[13]

Responding to some questions posed to him by the Italian Marxists gathered around the newspaper *Il Manifesto*, Althusser wrote an essay in 1978 entitled, "Il marxismo come teoria 'finita' [Marxism as a 'Finite' Theory]." In this work, Althusser reiterates well-known positions, but he also introduces new ones from which alternatives emerge that are more radical than the options that seem to prevail in the text. Consider the following example: "[T]he idea that Marxist theory is 'finite' totally excludes the idea that it is a *closed* theory. It is the philosophy of history that is closed, for it confines in advance the entire course of history within its thought. Only a 'finite' theory can be truly *open* to the contradictory tendencies that it discovers within capitalist society and open to their aleatory becoming, to the unpredictable 'surprises' that have never ceased to mark the history of the workers' movement, open and therefore alert, capable of taking seriously and accounting for *in time* the incorrigible imagination of history."[14] The (ex?-)"scientific" Marxist's obsession with rendering politics thinkable and possible is in tension with this entire passage: finitude and the opening of theory, the aleatory nature of events, the necessity of accounting for the capricious paths by which history advances (or regresses). The published and unpublished texts that have been discussed so far, written between 1976 and 1978, demonstrate Althusser's will to distance himself from what could very well be described as his "prior philosophical consciousness," even at the cost of putting into question certain deep-rooted convictions. But these texts also demonstrate that this will of Althusser's still lacked a positive alternative. Although conscious of the path he had chosen, Althusser still ignored where it would take him. He only knew, as Oscar Terán wrote, citing Montaigne, "from where he was fleeing."[15] In any event, within the passage that I transcribed previously, a still thin beam of light begins to illuminate the scene.

New "words," moreover, are incorporated into the Althusserian lexicon, corroding a theoretical edifice that, up until then, even with cracks and nicks, conserved a definite physiognomy. Politics is converted simultaneously into the first and last instance.[16] It is worth highlighting as well that Althusser gradually gives up being the spokesperson of an "imaginary" Marx, one of Althusser's inventions according to Raymond Aron.[17] At this point, Althusser seems to speak more and more for himself and at his own risk. And despite the fact that the same faithful references will quickly reappear along with Marx, who is not abandoned, and other new references, Althusser will no longer simply aim to "see clearly" with them but rather to demonstrate that these references bear witness to the presence of a subterranean current that struggles to reach the light.

Two series of writings, very different in nature, will trace the dominant lines of Althusser's thinking at this moment. In these writings, Althusser outlines the principles of his new philosophy, a philosophy that decidedly announces its inscription in this same subterranean current, which he furthermore hopes to enrich with original propositions. He will not give a detailed account of the contents or corollaries of this philosophy but only of its principles: its beginnings. But this is enough to bear witness to a profound shift, a shift that Althusser judges to be just as potentially significant as the shift that led to the formation of classic Althusserianism in the 1960s.

I am referring to texts that make up two heterogeneous groups. The first brings together the famous texts on Machiavelli: the monograph *Machiavelli and Us*, the presentation "Machiavelli's Solitude," the handwritten text "Machiavelli, Philosopher," and the group of short texts and notes (some taken by former members of his seminar) dated from 1955 to 1972 and collected in the 2006 volume titled *Politique et Histoire, de Machiavel à Marx*.[18] The date of the monograph, written as an initial draft, is unknown, but it was probably drawn up between 1971 and 1972. This draft endured a large number of revisions, cuts, and additions between those dates and 1986. No final version of *Machiavelli and Us* exists; those who published it made a selection of the revisions, privileging the most recent ones while trying to integrate the earlier ones into the body of the text. As for "Machiavelli's Solitude," it was a presentation given at the Fondation Nationale des Sciences Politiques in 1977. In 1988, a slightly modified version was published in English.[19] In 1990, a new version came to light in the journal *Futur antérieur* that included some minor additional modifications.[20]

Various texts written between 1982 and 1988 make up the second group of writings. Of these texts, the manuscript titled "The Underground Current of the Materialism of the Encounter" stands out.[21] The other texts included in this group are generally variations of this manuscript,[22] with the exception of the already partially cited book edited by the Mexican philosopher Fernanda Navarro, which includes letters and a series of interviews Althusser completed with Navarro between 1984 and 1987.

Before moving on to the next section, I want to address another important reference for Althusser and Althusserianism: Spinoza. Although mentioned and praised at various moments, to my knowledge Althusser never made Spinoza the subject of a single text dedicated specifically to his work.[23] Spinoza's *Ethics* explicitly inspired Althusser's theory of ideology, and Althusser repeatedly cited Spinoza's formulation that "truth is the standard both of itself and of the false."[24] It is likewise known that between 1967 and 1969 Althusser organized a political and philosophical discussion group that called itself "Spinoza," and he presumably also held in high esteem Spinoza's attempt to regard human beings "not as they should be" but rather "just as they are," which is to say prisoners of prejudices and passions that impede them from acting rationally. Yet, unlike what occurred with Marx and Machiavelli, Spinoza did not have that intellectual and affective component that leads one to identify with a given author. Althusser's relationship with Spinoza was always cordial, but they never became intimate friends. As I have just suggested, this was not the case with Niccolò Machiavelli. But treatment of this issue deserves a separate section.

The Machiavelli Factor

According to Althusser, Machiavelli's theoretical novelty resides in the fact that his theoretical intervention expands or proliferates [*se vectoriza*] from the text—that is to say, from the site of theory's enunciation—to its very exterior, or more precisely to the site where theory is tested by facts, where it is "realized."[25] This exterior is none other than actual politics [*política efectiva*], political praxis operating on the conjuncture, on its referent in the here and now. Writing thus assumes the form of a manifesto, a performative political discourse that is directly activating. Between the text-manifesto's paradigmatic theory and its syntagmatic form there is only the void of a conquered distance [*el vacío de una distancia conquistada*].[26] Yet Althusser maintains that this performative character of Machiavellian writing operates by means of inconclusive leaps, roundabouts, unresolved antinomies, and digressions.[27] What is the purpose of this strange and perhaps unwelcome rhetoric?

On various occasions, particularly during the presentation of "Machiavelli's Solitude,"[28] Althusser characterizes Machiavelli's thought as "strange." It is strange, first, because of its amazing *actuality*, and second, perhaps as a consequence of this unthinkable vivacity, because of the weird sensation of familiarity (*Unheimlichkeit*) that it prompts the reader to feel: "Without our understanding why, we find these old texts addressing us as if they were of our own day, gripping us as if, in some sense, they had been written for us, and to tell us something which concerns us directly, without our exactly knowing why. De Sanctis noted this strange feeling in the nineteenth century when he said of Machiavelli that '*he takes us by surprise, and leaves us pensive.*'"[29] According to Althusser, the simultaneous bewilderment and seduction experienced while reading *The Prince* stems not only from the "weird familiarity" of a text that continues to besiege and move us from within our own thought. It also stems from the fact that this strange effect occurs insofar as the text, taking us by surprise, inserts itself in what we had been thinking or believed that we had been thinking and meddles with it. It acts as a thought that feels close to us, as if it were our own, despite our not having recognized it as such, as if it were something that had always inhabited our thinking but had never been noticed before. This is where its strange and captivating quality comes from. It is also where the interest in Machiavelli's work lies, felt by great classical thinkers like Spinoza, Rousseau, Hegel, and, to a lesser extent, Marx, as well as more recent philosophers and militants like Antonio Gramsci, or even contemporaries like Maurice Merleau-Ponty and Claude Lefort, whose book *Machiavelli in the Making* was praised sincerely and enthusiastically by Althusser.

As previously mentioned, Althusser devotes a 1977 presentation, as well as one of his most developed posthumous writings, *Machiavelli and Us*, to the Florentine thinker. In both works, Althusser intends to elaborate and substantiate a clearly innovative reading of Machiavelli in general and of *The Prince* in particular, a reading of those eighty brilliant pages that—as Althusser was fond of saying—revolutionized political philosophy and politics itself.

For Althusser, in agreement with De Sanctis and Gramsci on this point, Machiavelli aimed to put on the table the political question of the necessary and sufficient conditions for the constitution of a national State in Italy, which is to say in a country prey to frailty and fatal pitfalls, the propitiatory victim of internal divisions and external invasions. In what follows, I will schematically present the essential aspects of the theses that Althusser brings to light through his reading of *The Prince*:

1. Endorsing from the start a radical politics, Machiavelli declares that only a "new prince in a new principality" would be able to satisfactorily accomplish this difficult enterprise. It goes without saying that Machiavelli was confident that the haste to complete this task, Italy's almost congenital political poverty, and the nature of the Italian people would be enough for such a prince to win immediate popular support. The feat of César Borgia, which was quickly thwarted but could have been successful, served as evidence of this. Due to the simple fact that he was in the beginning a nobody, for he was not a prince of any State, Borgia was therefore in no way dependent on the old political formations and obstacles of the feudal State. Had he been accompanied by fortune and had he been the bearer of a greater portion of virtue, he could have triumphed. But this was already a thing of the past, and Machiavelli was interested in the present, with eyes on the future. He was interested in what he called *la verità effectuale de la cosa* [the effective truth of the thing]. For this reason, he speaks in general and anonymous terms of a "new prince in a new principality" without naming names. This anonymity was an expression of his distrust in all existing princes and a summoning of a kind of nobody, an unknown person, who could constitute the new State.
2. Machiavelli refers to the indispensable combination of luck and courage, fortune and *virtù*, that are necessary for the enterprise of constituting the new State to have a chance at succeeding. But it is not only a matter of founding a new State but of founding a State capable of enduring, of growing and uniting Italy.
3. For this to happen, Machiavelli states and Althusser reiterates, it is necessary to "be alone." One must be alone to institute and render effective the armed forces necessary for a political task of this magnitude, alone to issue the first laws and consolidate the foundation of the new State. The inaugural moment of the State requires a solitary hour and the presence of one man alone, a prince, be he monarch or even dictator.
4. But this requirement is not sufficient. If, as already described, it is an issue of the new State, once instituted, being in a position to endure, the Prince—who must be alone in order to bring the State's foundation to fruition—should, according to Machiavelli, become many and institute a system of laws that would protect the people

from the abuse of the nobles. He should do so while establishing a "composite" government in which nobles and peasants, kings and subjects, are represented.

5   Althusser contends that this constitutes the second moment, the moment of the rooting of power in the people, of the class struggle between the people and the nobles. Against the dominant view, Machiavelli proposes the thesis that class conflict is indispensable for the consolidation and growth of the State.

6   This is perhaps an expression of what has been called Machiavelli's "republican moment." But in any event what Machiavelli points to is national unity, to the creation of a State capable of realizing this unity. This constitution requires first of all an individuality—a king, it could be said—capable of founding the new State, of rendering it long-lasting and apt for growth through combined government and through laws. This government would open the path to conflict and would permit the game of struggle between popular classes, a government in which the king and the people would be on the same side of the barricades so as to reinforce the State and give it the necessary resilience to carry through its national mission.

According to Althusser, this constitutes Machiavelli's profound originality. In "Machiavelli's Solitude," Althusser notes, "I should rather say that he is a *theoretician of the political preconditions of the constitution of a national state*, the theoretician of the foundation of a new state under a new prince, the theoretician of the durability of this state; the theoretician of the strengthening and expansion of this state. This is a quite original position, since he does not think the *accomplished fact of absolute monarchies* or their mechanisms, but rather thinks *the fact to be accomplished*, what Gramsci called the 'having to be' of a national state to be founded."[30] The strange character of Machiavelli's thought resides here as well, for the phrase that he holds so dear, "it is necessary to be alone to found a state," oddly reverberates in his work.[31] Why should the Prince be alone? This solitude is in fact isolation. It is necessary to be alone, which means that it is necessary to relinquish ties, roots, and dependencies and to find oneself, due to fortune and *virtù*, absolutely rootless, free from the impositions of Italy's existing political formations, from which nothing can be expected.

Machiavelli himself was alone while writing *The Prince* and the *Dis-*

courses. He was alone, which is to say withdrawn and for that reason free from ties to the old world, unaffected by the ideology that dominated that decadent old world. Machiavelli cut all ties with those ideas. That rupture is not declared, but it is no less profound and forceful.

In "Machiavelli's Solitude," Althusser does not only pose and substantiate these theses but also calls on Marx to testify. Everyone is familiar with the eighth section of *Capital*, where Marx analyzes "so-called primitive accumulation."[32] It is upon this primitive accumulation that the ideologues of capitalism narrate the inspirational story of capital. There once was an independent worker who knew how to save. When some poor soul crossed his path, he did the guy a favor by offering to feed him in exchange for work, which then allowed him to obtain funds to enlist other poor souls and feed them, while at the same time contributing to economic and industrial progress. But Marx, Althusser notes, tells a very different story, a story of forced labor, of plunder, of theft, of the violent dispossession of peasants from their lands, of impositions, whipping, arrogance, mire, and blood.

> I would argue that, *mutatis mutandis*, Machiavelli responds rather in the same way to the edifying discourse maintained by the philosophers of natural law about the history of the state. I would go so far as to suggest that Machiavelli is perhaps one of the few witnesses to what I shall call *primitive political accumulation*, one of the few theoreticians of the beginnings of the national state. Instead of saying that the state is born of law and nature, he tells us how a state has to be born if it is to last and to be strong enough to become the state of a nation. He does not speak the language of law, he speaks the language of the armed force indispensable to the constitution of any state, he speaks the language of the necessary cruelty of the beginnings of the state, he speaks the language of a politics without religion that has to make use of religion at all costs, of a politics that has to reject hatred but inspire fear, he speaks the language of the struggle between classes, and as for rights, laws and morality, he puts them in their proper, subordinate place.[33]

The reader will have already anticipated that, to conclude this section of the argument, I want to note that the last Althusser, the Althusser who gives free reign to his esoteric thought, speaks a language that occasionally situates itself at the opposite pole of the language of the classic Althusser. It opposes the structure's constriction with the fortune and virtue of individuality. It responds to the discourse on the unavoidable necessity of processes, which science guarantees will be successful, with a discourse that makes radical contingency an inherent principle of each moment, of each conjuncture, and of the entire course of history.

THOUGHT HAS THE rewarding possibility of inquiring into those who have previously inquired and encountering traces or fragments among them. Take the Greek philosopher Epicurus, from whom we have inherited only that: fragments, a few pages. But we know much more about him, thanks to the care of the Latin philosopher Lucretius and, later, with the passing of years and centuries, thanks to Machiavelli, Spinoza, Marx,[34] Engels, and finally, thanks to our contemporaries, Lacan, Foucault, and Derrida.

"Sometimes," wrote Lucretius, "at uncertain times and places, the eternal, universal fall of atoms is disturbed by a very slight deviation—the 'clinamen.' The resulting vortex gives rise to the world, to all natural things."[35] The clinamen, that unpredictable and minimal swerve, tends to be considered the main fallacy of Epicurean and Lucretian physics and philosophy. But in reality, the novelty and strength of both fields reside in this thesis.

In contemporary physics, the clinamen allows theoreticians to account for how a laminar flow becomes unstable and spontaneously veers toward turbulent flow. Today's specialists in fluid dynamics test the stability of fluid flow by introducing a disturbance that expresses the effect of molecular disorder added to the regular flow. Epicurus and Lucretius inspired these specialists, perhaps without the latter knowing it. They also inspired the last Althusser, who borrowed his concepts from them. As I have attempted to demonstrate, these concepts had already been present from the beginning, from that radical void that is the raw material of philosophy.

SUBJUGATED BY A diversely enigmatic present, nurtured by a history rich with events and readings, perplexed by dizzying changes, both expected and unexpected, changes that delight and upset at the very same time, Althusser's inquiry persists at the risk of going astray or, even worse, of not seeing anything at all. It is an inquiry without an object that at least at the beginning does not know what it is inquiring about nor how to orient itself. It fears giving in to self-deception or frustration, but it continues its march almost blindly.

In sum, it is an inquiry that can only *encounter*. And if fortune is favorable toward it, if it "encounters" something, it knows that it cannot for that reason consider the task completed. The inquiry by definition is open, always recommencing or beginning again. When the gaze glimpses something new, generally a blade of grass, a pebble, a minor variation in the landscape, it knows that this discovery is only the threshold of a path not yet taken that must be traveled so that the inquiry can continue. Apart from this, it could be discovered that the blade of grass forms part of an old and well-known herb, that the pebble is a common rock without value, or that the variation in the landscape is simply a mirage. In other words, it could be found that there is no path or that the path is merely a dead end. This does not matter. The gaze expands and multiplies; it gives over to itself. It is no longer only a gaze but also imagination, affect, reasoning, invention. It is thought in the fullest sense.

Epicurus, Althusser notes, explained that before the formation of the world an infinite number of atoms were falling parallel to each other in the void. *They are falling and will continue to fall until the end of time.* This implies, first of all, that there was nothing before the world and, at the same time, that all the elements of the world existed for all eternity before the existence of any such world. The clinamen intervenes in this "before," what we could call the "originary operation." The clinamen is precisely an infinitesimal swerve, and, as Althusser explains, "no one knows where, or when, or how" it occurs.[36] It causes an atom to "swerve" from its fall into the void and, ever so slightly breaking with parallelism, provokes an *encounter* with the neighboring atom and then from encounter to encounter "multiple collisions [*carambolaje*]" and the birth of a world, which is to say, as previously expressed, the becoming-world of the set of atoms, provoked by the chain reaction of the first swerve and the first collision.

I maintain that it is not enough to say that the swerve is first. It is important to go further. For the swerve to result in an encounter, from which a world can emerge, it must persist; it cannot be a fleeting encounter but rather one that endures, that then becomes the basis of the new world, of the new situation. But it is possible that the encounter does not endure and that a world will therefore not emerge. Or, somehow, the encounter can give off the appearance of "enduring," despite the fact that in reality it has become rigid and denaturalized, protecting itself with the mask of a skillfully distortionary discourse and the paraphernalia of ceremonies and liturgies that "re-create" the inaugural moment.

All of this can be said in another way. Paraphrasing Althusser from "The Underground Current of the Materialism of the Encounter," any world can be thought of as a fait accompli, which, *once accomplished as such*, affirms itself as a new world (in this case, a profound sociohistorical transformation). But the accomplishment of such a thing is merely a question of contingency insofar as it depends on the chance encounter of atoms, the product of the swerve. However, it is not only the case that this encounter happens but rather also that on occasions it takes form [*toma consistencia*]; it "takes [*prende*]" (like a vaccine takes), which means that the encounter does not break apart once it happens but rather resists and persists, resulting in stable and enduring relations. Yet what interests Althusser is not so much these relations as their aleatory character of "having taken [*haber prendido*]" from the encounter that gives way to the new phenomenon.[37]

Finally, how does one explain the advent of the clinamen, of the swerve? It cannot be explained; it occurs.[38] "It is the case," Althusser says to Navarro, delighted by that old formula of symbolic logic that he had recently discovered in the works of Ludwig Wittgenstein and Bertrand Russell.[39] In other words, following Althusser, it could have been the case that the elements had failed to take form and that the encounter had been thwarted. It is possible to go even further and conjecture that many encounters have occurred in history but that nothing new emerged from them because an element was lacking or because the elements lacked a favorable arrangement.[40] There was *virtù* but not fortune, or sometimes, in a fortunate context, what was lacking was that "element" of *virtù*. Finally, this constitutive contingency obviously softens and gives plasticity to historical time, since everything could have been different. *Everything*, including Althusser's stormy, extremely difficult, and persistent inquiry and the unjust and disgraceful destiny that for years was reserved for his philosophy.[41]

Subjectivity and Politics in Althusser

In chapter 2, the analysis of the problem of structural causality led to the conclusion that, unlike Lacan (and, of course, many other renowned thinkers), Althusser denied any theoretical pertinence to the category of the "subject." The idea of the subject referred to an *ideological notion* in the sense that Althusser habitually construed the concept of ideology. From the perspective of cognition, ideology was an effect of misrecognition, an illusory fiction, a pseudo-science. From the perspective of its function, moreover, ideology played a role in social cohesion and was an indispensable weapon of political struggle, *though never an instrument suitable for the production of knowledge.*

However, the theses on aleatory materialism, on the coefficient of contingency inherent to any historical process, on the irreplaceable allotment of will, of *virtù* (and fortune) that is required of any politics worthy of the name (all issues developed by the last Althusser) would seem to place serious obstacles in the way of the decisive conceptual disqualification of the subject. To whom should the qualities of good—or bad—politics be attributed? What or who "does" politics?

A preliminary response, perhaps necessary but also insufficient, would consist in remembering that the negation of the subject is inscribed in the heart of a general theoretical and polemical orientation regarding the question of the "subject of history." In *History and Class Consciousness* (1923), the book of his youth, Georg Lukács develops a philosophical theorization that leads to the thesis that the subject of history exists and that its current name is the *proletariat*.[42] At another point, it was the bourgeoisie. Challenging the category of the subject, affirming the impertinence of the notion, primarily represents a response to this kind of thesis. Yet it was none other than Marx who wrote at the beginning of the *Eighteenth Brumaire* the often-cited line "Men make their own history." And if he immediately explains that "they do not make it under circumstances chosen by themselves, but under circumstances directly encountered, given and transmitted from the past," it still remains the case, as Sartre noted more than fifty years ago, that it is *men who make history and not circumstances* (which can be obstacles but also bridges).[43]

It is nevertheless the case that this kind of "headlong rush forward" is incompatible with Althusser's often affirmed and never refuted theoretical antihumanism. And it is in the realm of theoretical antihumanism that figures like Lévi-Strauss, Foucault, and Althusser converge without the slightest disagreement. That said, crossing (and, above all, mutually restricting) Lukács's references to the proletariat and the bourgeoisie with the passage from the *Eighteenth Brumaire*, a position begins to take shape that Althusser himself affirms and reiterates, particularly during his various self-criticisms of the 1970s onward: *class struggle is the motor (not the subject) of history.*[44] But, unhappy with just that, Althusser resumes the controversy with the inconceivable John Lewis. Against the latter's position, that "man makes history," Althusser replies that, for Marxism-Leninism, "*it is the masses*" who make history.[45] Nevertheless, as though he noticed a problem, Althusser formulates at this point (for himself) a question: *Should we accordingly say that "the masses" are the subject of history rather than man?*

Althusser does not at first seem to give a univocal answer, writing, in effect, the following:

> Yes and no. When we started to sketch out a definition of the masses, when we talked about this idea of the masses, we saw the whole thing was rather complicated. The masses are actually *several* social classes, social strata and social categories, grouped *together* in a way which is both complex and *changing* (the positions of the different classes and strata, and of the fractions of classes within classes, *change* in the course of the revolutionary process itself). And we are dealing with huge numbers: in France or Britain, for example, with tens of millions of people, in China with hundreds of millions! Let us do no more here than ask the simple question: can we still talk about a "subject," identifiable by the *unity* of its "personality"?[46]

Althusser later proceeds to put at the center of the theoretical scene the class *struggle* as the "motor" of history. From his perspective, this is the principal thesis of Marxism-Leninism. What happens then to the other thesis about the masses, earlier defended against John Lewis's man? It is still valid, but it is subordinated to the principal thesis: "[T]he revolutionary power of the masses comes precisely from the *class struggle*."[47] The masses cannot be thought under the category of the "subject," no matter what kind of theoretical acrobatics are attempted. Instead, the masses should be thought in terms of the class struggle and, more precisely, in terms of the materiality of this struggle, its rootedness in the material (or *economic*) conditions of its existence and its activity. If these principles are strongly upheld, the problem of the subject evaporates. Althusser writes, "[h]istory is an immense *natural-human* system in movement, and the motor of history is class struggle. History is a process, and a *process without a subject*."[48]

Following this classic line of reasoning, Althusser clarifies that denouncing the ideology of the "subject" absolutely does not forget about real people, political action, or the party. It is simply limited to situating them and subordinating them to the operative forms of exploitation and forms of resistance to exploitation, to the general and particular conditions of the class struggle in each epoch and at each location, to their organization, to the ideologies and slogans that emerge from this struggle—in sum, to the existing state of things. This "putting into relation," rigorously understood and oriented, could give way to a mass line that would open a path to revolution.

From this set of statements, it seems that the "Reply to John Lewis" provides very little in terms of clarifying the problem that it poses. The solution that it puts forward does not even come close to offering a valid alternative to the issue in question. It simply oscillates like a pendulum between the two opposed poles of antihumanism and "the point of view of the proletariat."

There is nevertheless one argument in that text that is worth retaining—namely, the impossibility of subsuming collectives (in this case classes, fractions of classes, and social strata) composed of tens or even hundreds of millions of people, as occurs in Europe or in Asia, under the traditional category of the "subject." The complex and changing reality of the division of classes and of the divisions, subdivisions, and alliances between classes and fractions of classes, of the transformations of a class into another, the frequent "absorptions" of a class by another, and even the partial or total fusion of different classes all refer to phenomena that Marx anticipated and analyzed on many occasions in *Capital* and other works. It is not possible to think these ample, heterogeneous, and mobile collectives under the notion of the subject and the suppositions that this notion carries with it, particularly what Althusser called the "unity of its personality." To continue making use of that notion, it would have to be so thoroughly reworked that it would end up losing its defining features. It is difficult to find something positive in such a chore, and it is very easy to notice the difficulties and confusions that it would cause.

If what has been discussed up to this point is accepted as valid, it would be possible to conclude that the contributions of the "Three Notes on the Theory of Discourse," which I analyzed in detail in chapter 2, would recover their cogency. They would represent the most stable point of arrival of all the proposals that Althusser had formulated up to that moment. However, the conclusions developed in the "Three Notes," precisely regarding the theoretical disqualification of the notion of the subject, become debatable—to say the least—in light of the theses on the "materialism of the encounter." This is the case particularly in light of the corollaries of these theses: the contingency inherent to the sociohistorical, the promotion of the event, the aleatory nature of the primary and the secondary, swerves, encounters that "take form [*toman consistencia*]" and persist. This is, as Alain Badiou states, "the real stuff of partisanship, the militant's opportunity, the moment of choice."[49]

In 1996, Badiou also presented some considerations of unquestionable interest regarding the problem that I am attempting to clarify here.[50] For this "late" Badiou, Althusser's proposal would consist in "[attempting] to think the characteristics of politics after Stalin under the aegis of a philosophical rupture."[51] This passage adequately summarizes the thesis that I have attempted to put forward in this book. For Badiou, Althusser's principal theses on philosophy move toward that conclusion:

> Philosophy is not a theory, but a separating activity, a thinking of the distinctions in thought. Therefore it can by no means theorize politics. But it can draw new lines of partition, think new directions, which verify the "shifting" of the political condition.
>
> Philosophy has no object. In particular, the "political" object does not exist for it. Philosophy is an act whose effects are strictly immanent. It is the discovery of new possibles *in actu* which bends philosophy towards its political condition.
>
> Philosophy is guarded from the danger of confusing history and politics (therefore science and politics) on account of itself lacking history. Philosophy authorizes a non-historicist perception of political events.[52]

On this basis, which Badiou shares with Althusser, the latter's enterprise cannot avoid interrogation regarding the "singular space" of a politics construed as lacking a subject.[53] According to Badiou, Althusser would respond to this interrogation in an "incomplete" way. He would do so particularly through the deployment of terms like partisanship, choice, decision, or revolutionary militant, emblematic terms that allude to the fact that what is at stake at the level of politics possesses an undoubtedly *subjective* character. He continues: "Let us say that the point to which Althusser leads us, without being able to say that he realized it himself, is the following: is it possible to think *subjectivity without a subject*? What's more, is it possible to think subjectivity without a subject whose figure is no longer the (scientific) object? It is towards this enigma of subjectivity without a subject as the intra-philosophical mark of politics that the whole of what might be termed Althusser's *topographical* framework [*l'appareillage topique*] is directed."[54] Badiou reiterates that Althusser did not reflect on this enigmatic—but also decisive—site of politics that is condensed in the formula "subjectivity without a subject," a site that would be protected from the objectivity of scientific necessity and the ideological effect of the "subject," a site that would be open to "the possible," that, without guarantee, may open the way to a real trajectory. Nevertheless, Althusser's work, which amplified and deepened the vision of Marx and Engels, cleared a path that made this thought possible. Badiou then concludes that Althusser deserves "our most rigorous respect" for this undeniably decisive achievement.[55]

I am in total agreement with Badiou on this point. But I would like to take things in a direction that I fear Badiou would not be willing to go: over the embankments surrounding a region that has been ostensibly and systematically left out by—for once in agreement—both classical Marxism and Althusserianism. I have in mind the field of sociology and more precisely the most recent contributions to the sociological theorization of collective action.[56] In what follows, I will attempt to succinctly demonstrate how these contributions can aid in thinking and resolving the problem analyzed in this section of the book.

Daniel Cefaï affirms in an important recent work that "[t]he dramaturgy and rhetoric of collective identities poses the problem of the ontological status of the existence of the collective and the problem of representation, in both the theatrical and political sense of the term."[57] For Badiou, Althusser likewise proposes, among other things, to clarify "the problem of the ontological status of the existence of the collective" and the multiple forms that the collective—and politics in particular as a collective intervention—can assume.

In another work, by way of the passage cited previously, I have referred to the mechanisms, *dispositifs*, and initiatives that constitute an action and one or many subjects as "collectives."[58] To do this, I took up Francisco Naishtat's promising theses. From a pragmatic (not utilitarian) perspective that is greatly inspired by an original and productive reading of the theory of speech acts and an acute reflection on the nature of the *decision*, Naishtat puts forward some extremely suggestive ideas. Allow me to cite a passage that condenses what is essential in his proposal: "What is hidden behind the usual way we talk about collective action? In my view, that which is hidden is the double performativity of the decision. The 'We,' in effect, is simultaneously the speaker who enunciates the act and the illocutionary result of that enunciation: in the *collective decision* or in the *common declaration of intention*."[59] Naishtat emphasizes that the employment of a "we," which syntactically is figured by the first-person-plural pronoun as well as by the verb's conjugation, is pragmatically irreducible, since the affirmation "We, the people gathered together here, declare that we are on strike" cannot be substituted, without semantic variation, for "*I decide* to declare that I am on strike along with Pedro, Juan, Maria, and Sylvia."

The declaration of collective decision enacts the emergence of a newly arising figure as the immediate result of the enunciation, just as in J. L. Austin the individual promise appears as an effect of its enunciation. Such a statement then gives visibility to the pact and the decision that, due to the same movement, becomes a collective decision. Accordingly, from the pact emerges an unprecedented effect, what I will call, following Badiou on this point, "subjectivity without a subject."

Nourished by a creative analysis of the late Wittgenstein, this focus addresses the issues of the decision and of the constitution of collectives. In my opinion, its novelty resides as much in the fact that it delivers a strong blow to the more celebrated theses of "methodological individualism" as, above all, in its own theoretical relevance. Consider, for example, Jean-Paul Sartre's concern for shining light on different kinds of collectives in *Critique of Dialectical Reason*, on what he calls "seriality," and in particular his reflections on the modes of constitution of the "group in fusion," the "pledged group," and finally the "statutory group."[60] That arduous exploration that would quickly suffer attacks from a steadily rising structuralism, that laboriously advancing thought that delved into *impasses* from which it did not always escape unscathed, lacking the instruments necessary to account for the performative and illocutionary aspects of language, can now be reactualized, its rights restored.[61]

Naishtat's contributions illuminate for us the illocutionary and practical forms in which the collective is born and at the same time opens itself to political intervention. But, in my opinion, these contributions also allow us to extend his thinking, asking ourselves how this nascent collective persists and endures.[62] Sartre wondered about the logic that presides over the emergence of different "practical ensembles" and about the obstacles that should be confronted due to what he called the "anti-dialectic" of the practico-inert. Naishtat wonders about how a collective political intervention is constituted. And each new political intervention is a new birth,[63] a new process of forming identities, a new ideological idiom that is affirmed. Sartre's reflections, like Naishtat's, are marked by the unsolved mysteries of their political present, Stalinist bureaucratization for the one and the new forms of sociopolitical protest for the other. In both, the figure of the encounter is at stake, which congeals and affirms itself as a collective subjectivity capable of intervening politically in any situation that summons it.

At the end of this journey, I have thus arrived at an encounter that will hopefully take form, that of a renewed *sociology*, redefined as a theory of action and of collective intervention, with *Marxism* (or better yet aleatory materialism) as its philosophy of politics. If this encounter yields results, it will recognize at that time the essential debt that ties it to the thought of Althusser.

> [Althusser's] generous multiplicity [...] makes it incumbent upon us not to totalize or simplify, not to immobilize him or fix a trajectory, not to seek some advantage, not to cancel things out or try to get even, and especially not to calculate, not to appropriate or re-appropriate (even if it be through that paradoxical form of manipulating or calculating re-appropriation called rejection), not to take hold of what was inappropriable and must remain so. — JACQUES DERRIDA, "Text Read at Louis Althusser's Funeral," October 1990

CONCLUSION. ALTHUSSER'S LAST LESSON

The objective of the preceding chapters was to explore, against the backdrop of what I have called the "classic" version of Althusser's philosophy, certain fugitive points that intermittently invaded his discourse, altering the expositional logic while insinuating, with progressively increasing coherence, the exertion—vague at first, then firm, and ultimately tumultuous—of a form of thought that was different from, though not necessarily opposed to, what the classic discourse had been expounding. This investigation aimed not to be an erratic endeavor; it was guided by the hypothesis that those anomalous signs, already present in Althusser's very first writings, should be read as symptomatic traces of that other thought that, despite Althusser himself,[1] cleared its way, gradually, laboriously, until it achieved in his last writings its first explicit, albeit not fully developed, formulation. This inquiry traveled many paths that did not yield positive results. However, while on other paths, at times lost in the thick jungle of phrases, of brief analytical sketches or long enigmatic reflections, and after patient and often provisional reconstructive work, it was possible to weave together fragments, to articulate and prioritize concepts, in order to gradually unravel the thick tangle that had been unexpectedly encountered. The reader already knows the results at which I arrived or believe to have arrived, so here, a final synthesis.

Expressed at the beginning in brief, fleeting formulations, what I have called Althusser's "esoteric thought" gradually took shape and disordered his exoteric thought. Having weathered all manner of harsh difficulties, advances, setbacks, contradictions, self-criticisms, and theoretical snags, Althusser's esoteric thought finally culminated in the rough outline he termed *materialism of the encounter*. As previously stated, this arduous journey was the subject matter of the preceding chapters. There is, however, a remainder that I have reserved for this conclusion.

In these final pages, I will take a detour in the exposition to introduce themes that freely reveal certain traces which allude directly or indirectly to my personal history (in the form of opinions, preferences, choices, value judgments, and even affections). I managed to keep these issues out of the theoretical argument, but, having concluded that section, they may now contribute to a greater understanding not of the reasoning behind the thesis of this book but rather of the motivation behind writing it. These references also emphasize the inevitably individual character of the opinions that have been expressed herein.

At the beginning of this volume, I referred to the bitter rejection directed toward all versions of Marxism since the early 1980s. This rejection was not entirely unforeseeable, as it stemmed from the false hopes that Marxism had breathed into us, which a series of injurious defeats implacably and catastrophically destroyed. A set of events diverse in character and scope made it so that this repudiation, at least for Latin American Marxism,[2] had a first and last name: Louis Althusser. The dense and elegant style of his prose in the 1960s that would later smack of arrogance; the dispersed character of his inquiries and the wavering of his theoretical and political positions in the mid- to late 1970s; his philosophical impasses; and, of course, his heartrending personal tragedy; all of this managed to convert Althusser into a perfect scapegoat in an age far too eager to unload its rage (and also its responsibilities) on others. For once, we political scientists, philosophers, and intellectuals of the Latin American Left clearly knew where to direct our hatred. The name of Althusser and the significance of his writings were excluded from the intellectual and philosophical scene for far too many years, almost as if he had never existed, as if he had been an illusion from which we had finally broken free.

Yet, for two decades and to a much greater extent than anyone else, Althusser had been the Marxist thinker that mobilized and animated philosophical debate in France, Italy, Spain, the United States, England, Latin America, and many other places. His work sparked impassioned polemics, not only between Marxists but also among non-Marxist intellectuals who found themselves obligated to recognize the relevance and the productivity of a form of thought that they had believed to be completely exhausted. Without the sharpness and the profundity of Althusser's work, Marxism might have been summarily dismissed as a relic of the past, just another milestone that had come and gone in the history of ideas. Instead, thanks to his writings, it had to be approached as a philosophical proposal of the highest caliber. Its achievements and conceptual richness enabled it to play a major role on the stage of contemporary philosophy for many years.

I have noted that Althusser, at his peak, was perfectly aware of the problems that the development and extension of Marxism's philosophical options entailed. Althusserianism Triumphant lived itself as Althusserianism Militant and Althusserianism Suffering, engaged in an enterprise the difficulties of which it knew far better than its adversaries.[3] Perhaps for that reason the first serious critiques directed at Althusserianism emerged from its own progeny, signed by Althusser's former disciple, Jacques Rancière.[4] Not long afterward, Althusser's prolonged silences,[5] combined with the rapid succession of revelations concerning the Gulag, the diligent media-based intervention of the so-called New Philosophers, and the already visible process of decline and ultimate collapse of Eastern European regimes, represented heavy blows for Marxism and its principal representative at the time.

Overnight the theoretical figure of classic Althusserianism became blurred and faded, nearly to the point of caricature. Many Latin American intellectuals were quick to reduce Althusser's thought to the coarse and catechistic version of it found in Marta Harnecker's manual.[6] Shortly thereafter, the important role Althusser played in cultural, theoretical, and political realms during the 1960s and early 1970s was consistently and plainly repressed. With remarkable speed, it was forgotten that it had been thanks to Althusser that Marxist thought, particularly in those decades, was something more than a mere repetition of dogmatic slogans taken from Marx, Engels, Lenin, or Mao. It was also forgotten that at the very heart of Marxist thought it had been possible to forge conceptual instruments and original theoretical formulations for grasping the new circumstances that history had brought to the social and political scene.[7]

In the view of his detractors, Althusser had the good sense to die in 1990. Already by the mid-1980s it was no longer necessary to despise him or to refer to his work with scorn. Forgetting him sufficed. And for several years he was buried in the deepest oblivion. This was a voluntary and active forgetting that exiled Althusser from publishing houses and libraries, from critical commentaries and bibliographies. The youngest students today ignore his very existence.[8] Yet that forgetting forgot that Althusser still had much to say. As I pointed out in the prologue, the posthumous appearance of his autobiography and the still ongoing release of his previously unpublished works has breathed new life into a form of thought that continues to live on and to make itself heard, despite the fact that Althusser is no longer with us.

The act of reading Althusser's unpublished writings in an abbey in Normandy, with the havoc of the 1944 bombings still in plain view, reanimated and revived in me an idea that I had sketched out some time earlier in a confused and clumsy way.[9] My experience reading some of Althusser's texts prompted me to offhandedly conjecture that, beneath the outermost layer of the text, something new was pushing through to the surface. That intuition, however, did not take me very far; I felt that it was impossible to untangle this "new" dimension that I thought I had observed. Though not without some unease, I ended up concluding that this impossibility was due to the fact that those glimmers, if they existed, had never gone beyond the status of isolated formulations with no overall connection. Reading those texts, still unpublished at the time, illuminated and gave meaning (a far richer and more complex meaning than I had imagined) to my initial speculation.[10]

ALTHUSSER FORTUNATELY HAD disciples that did not forget about him. It is only fair that they be briefly mentioned here. Althusser's "legacy" is extensive and heterogeneous. Apart from the significant influence that his work has had in areas such as psychoanalysis, political theory, and sociology, Althusser's thought quietly but indelibly continued to mark the work of those who had been his disciples. This happened even though his thought was declared theoretically obsolete for many years for the reasons mentioned previously, drowned out later by the overwhelming influence of other emerging intellectual trends. This happened, moreover, despite Althusser's own long absence from the visible philosophical scene. He had loyal disciples like Étienne Balibar, Pierre Macherey, and, in his own way, Alain Badiou, the author of a vast and gifted oeuvre, in addition to other more critical disciples, such as the previously mentioned Rancière. Likewise, in England, the United States, and in both Hispanophone and Lusophone Latin America,[11] Althusser's thought provoked and still provokes debates and controversies. It was and remains, above all, unshakably seductive. Convergences, frequently profound ones, will surely be found among these readers of Althusser, along with divergences and distinct lines of attack and points of interest. But these tensions—aside from one or two exceptions—only serve to confirm the richness of the Althusserian legacy.[12]

Althusser's work furthermore produced a curious effect, that of the "usurped legacy." The clearest example of this is without a doubt to be found in the writings of Jacques Bidet.[13] In any case, Althusser inaugurated a movement of thought that has survived him and, in my opinion at least, continues to be valid today. Althusser embarked on a difficult path. He only managed to advance down this path by virtue of provisional responses, ambiguities, self-critiques, and partial solutions to the problems that he repeatedly had to confront. In 1985, and perhaps beforehand, it was already debatable whether he should be categorized as a Marxist, unless one was willing to offer a long series of caveats and qualifications. It may not even have been adequate to consider him "Althusserian," at least in what I have termed the *classic* sense.

I BELIEVE IT was during the final months of 1965. There were about ten of us, all young, half from South America. Despite the absence of all flashiness, in a school that looked the same as any other, some secret strategy of our unconscious drove us to walk through the corridors and approach the classroom, walking with a reverential trepidation that was vague and (we believed) indispensable. Althusser, the eternally present cigarette in his mouth, dressed in a sweater and no tie, elbows propped on his desk, received us cordially yet informally. We had seen him at one point or another, at least in photographs, and yet we all felt that indefinable seduction in that still youthful visage, not yet damaged by depression, illness, and tragedy, the amiable and transparent gravitation of that serene, cordial, and subtly profound gaze. We had calculated that Althusser would concede to us—which was already a lot—some forty-five minutes of questions and answers. He spent about two hours with us. Two hours that could have been three or four; Althusser did not keep time. He was interested above all in clearly and exhaustively responding to each question; he was more interested in posing further problems than in subduing us with ready-made formulas. He did not hesitate to disclose his difficulties, nor did he hesitate to scrutinize ours. He respected our way of speaking, which was not always correct and was less often refined. At that time, he used to say that his principal concern resided in not having managed to define the theoretical status of the concept of social class. Without false modesty, I would almost say that he was asking us for help.

In those years, we attended his courses at the École thanks to his authorization. They were, as we expected, brilliant. But my memory seeks above all else to retain, as a rare privilege, the vivid recollection of that first encounter.

ON CERTAIN OCCASIONS, such as this one, it is difficult to come up with the right words and compose the adequate phrases to bring a text to its conclusion. Arguments, convictions, memories, joys, and hardships crowd together at the end and struggle for the right to have the last word, that inevitable act of writing that will close and crown the whole.

I am part of the generation upon which it fell the task of bearing witness to Althusser's enterprise and becoming its interlocutor. Perhaps some hidden inclination leaves me unable to find the right tone and the adequate terms to draw this conclusion to an end. I signaled earlier that Althusser's close friend Jacques Derrida, when informed just ten hours before returning to Paris that Louis had passed away, put some words together that he read at the funeral. Beyond his sorrow, his weariness, and the haste with which he had to scrawl his oration, he managed to sum up in one hurried and moving passage all that I myself would have liked to say, as I too had been a part of that time that Derrida mentioned. It is accordingly for that reason that I grant him the right to conclude this book, transcribing those final words:

> Our belonging to this time, and I believe I can speak for all of us here today, was indelibly marked by him, by what he sought, experimented with, and risked at the highest of costs; it was marked by all the movements of his passion, whether determined or suspended, at once authoritarian and hesitant, contradictory, consequential or convulsive, all the movements of that extraordinary passion he had and that left him no respite, since it spared him nothing, with its

theatrical rhythms, its great voids, its long stretches of silence, its vertiginous retreats; those impressive interruptions themselves interrupted by demonstrations, forceful offensives, and powerful eruptions of which each of his books preserves the burning trace, having first transformed the landscape around the volcano.[14]

NOTES

FOREWORD

1. The book first appeared in Argentina with the publishing house Siglo XXI, which has made a major contribution to the intellectual life of the Hispanophone world over the past half century.

2. *Translator's note:* This foreword originally appeared as the preface to the French translation of de Ípola's *Althusser, el infinito adiós*; see Emilio de Ípola, *Althusser, l'adieu infini*, trans. Marie Bardet (Paris: Presses Universitaires de France, 2012), vii–xxi. In his preface to that edition, Balibar adds, "I am pleased, therefore, that the Presses Universitaires de France has decided to take on the publication of this text in France, in a collection that I had the honor of directing for many years with Dominique Lecourt."

3. *Translator's note:* The IMEC (Institut Mémoires de l'édition contemporaine) archive in France houses Althusser's papers.

4. *Translator's note:* See Régis Debray, *Revolution in the Revolution? Armed Struggle and Political Struggle in Latin America*, trans. Bobbye Ortiz (New York: Grove Press, 1967).

5. De Ípola will, very rightly, accord a fundamental significance to the title and content of an essay published by Alain Badiou in 1967 when he "rallied" to Althusser's project, exhibited in *For Marx*: "The (Re)commencement of Dialectical Materialism," granting this idea not simple punctual sense, but that of an infinite process; see Badiou, "Le (Re)commencement du matérialisme dialectique," *Critique* 240 (1967): 438–67; trans. Bruno Bosteels as "The (Re)commencement of Dialectical Materialism," in *The Adventure of French Philosophy* (London: Verso, 2012), 133–70.

6. Jean-François Lyotard published an essay in *Les Temps Modernes* in 1969 with the title, "Dérive à partir de Marx et Freud [Drifting away from Marx and Freud]," later published as a book in 1973; see Lyotard, *Dérive à partir de Marx et Freud* (Paris:

Editions Galilée, 1994); translated as *Driftworks*, ed. Roger McKeon (New York: Semiotext(e), 1984).

7. In his book, de Ípola attributes the development of the most dogmatic forms of Althusserianism in Latin America to Marta Harnecker's book *Los conceptos elementales del materialismo histórico* (Buenos Aires: Siglo XXI, 1971), in particular, which sold over a million copies (the French translation was published in Brussels in 1974). It also bears mentioning that Althusser himself wrote a preface for the second edition of this book, which can also be found in the collection of essays by Althusser titled *Positions* (Paris: Éditions sociales, 1976). Marta Harnecker was Althusser's student in Paris. After returning to Chile she directed the newspaper *Chile Hoy* during the Popular Unity period; she managed to escape arrest during the Pinochet coup d'état and ultimately found refuge in Cuba. She recently served as an advisor to the late President Hugo Chávez in Venezuela.

8. It would be more accurate to say that the group chose Althusser as its guide and asked him to organize its collective research. See the interviews with Yves Duroux and myself with the English editors of the site dedicated to the *Cahiers pour l'Analyse*: http://cahiers.kingston.ac.uk/interviews/balibar-duroux.html. [*Translator's note:* These interviews have been published in English in *Concept and Form*, ed. Peter Hallward and Knox Peden, vol. 2, *Interviews and Essays on the "Cahiers pour l'Analyse"* (London: Verso, 2012).]

9. See the letter from Althusser to Emmanuel Terray on Lévi-Strauss, which de Ípola quotes and comments on in chapter 2.

10. See the collective volume edited by Patrice Maniglier, *Le Moment philosophique des années 1960 en France* (Paris: Presses Universitaires de France, 2011), in which the references to Althusser come from all directions and play a very important role.

11. See Jean-Claude Milner, *Le périple structural* (Lagrasse: Verdier, 2008).

12. To describe the insistent presence of an esoteric thought below the exoteric, de Ípola draws on the metaphor of the underground current that Althusser used to characterize materialism itself. Given that this Straussian hermeneutic is linked to the hypothesis of a writing that takes place under conditions of persecution (Leo Strauss, *Persecution and the Art of Writing* [Chicago: University of Chicago Press, 1988]), it is impossible not to wonder what persecution he has in mind when it comes to Althusser. It cannot really be the university, which provided Althusser with a relatively protected space. It could be the party, though one should not conflate different periods and places, nor should one forget that Althusser also aimed to persecute the persecutors (see Althusser's memoir, *The Future Lasts Forever: A Memoir*, trans. Richard Veasey [New York: New Press, 1993]). More fundamentally, it is Althusser himself—or his internal double—that points our investigation toward the figure of a philosopher *in permanent conflict with himself*, even more so than other philosophers who might come to mind (Pascal or Nietzsche).

13. Karl Kautsky (1854–1938), orthodox theorist of the German Social Democratic Party, hailed by Lenin in *What Is to Be Done* in 1902, and by Althusser in the preface to *For Marx*, for his theory regarding the "importation of Marxist theory into the labor movement" as the condition for passing from "spontaneous" political struggle to

"organized" struggle, considered perhaps to be the inventor of what I am here calling "pedagogism within Marxism."

14. Spinoza: "Curavi, humanas actiones non ridere, non lugere, neque detestari, sed intelligere" (*Tractatus politicus* I, §4). [*Translator's note:* "I have taken great care not to deride, bewail, or execrate human actions, but to understand them"; Spinoza, *Political Treatise*, trans. Samuel Shirley (Indianapolis: Hackett, 2000), 35.]

15. A baton powerfully taken up by Judith Butler in *The Psychic Life of Power: Theories in Subjection* (Stanford, CA: Stanford University Press, 1997).

16. He also juxtaposed these theories, without really articulating them, in the montage of excerpts that resulted in the essay from 1970. In an essay since published in French, as the preface to the new edition of the posthumous work *Sur la reproduction* (Althusser, *Sur la reproduction* [Paris: Presses Universitaires de France, 2011]), I called attention to the opening effect produced by the caesura of the *ellipses* that originally figured in Althusser's essay "Ideology and Ideological State Apparatuses," which recent editors have unfortunately persisted in removing.

17. This calls to mind Marx's theory from the 1857 "Introduction," in *A Contribution to the Critique of Political Economy*: capitalism brings about abstract labor, which is virtually present in every mode of production, and which is in fact a *form of organization* of concrete labor itself. [*Translator's note:* See "Introduction: Production, Consumption, Distribution, Exchange (Circulation)," in *Karl Marx and Frederick Engels Collected Works*, vol. 28, *Marx: 1857–1861* (New York: International Publishers, 1986), 17–48.]

18. In his 1978 conversation with the Italian Communists of *Il Manifesto*, Althusser argued that the Communist Party (as he understood it) is a "party outside the State [*parti hors État*]"—a theory I then considered indefensible with respect to "ideological state apparatuses" in general. In the same vein, it should of course be asked whether communism can be "outside of ideology" from his own viewpoint. Together, these two questions lead us to ask whether the State, in an inevitable and uniform way, is what comes in the *place* of the imaginary, the place from which individuals receive their (auto)interpellation—in other words, whether there exist "ideological apparatuses" other than those of the State.

19. *Translator's note:* On the "labyrinth of freedom," see G. W. Leibniz, *Theodicy: Essays on the Goodness of God, the Freedom on Man and the Origin of Evil*, trans. E. M. Huggard (La Salle, IL: Open Court, 1985), 53.

20. Following my former student Kazuya Onaka (in "Pratique et temps: Louis Althusser et les 'courants souterrains du matérialisme,'" his 2003 PhD dissertation at the University of Paris X, Nanterre), I have called attention to the disconcerting proximity between Althusser's adoption of the phrase "aleatory materialism of the encounter" and Derrida's invention in 1979 of the phrase "contingent [*aléatoire*] experience of the encounter"; see Jacques Derrida, "The Law of Genre," trans. Avital Ronell, in *Acts of Literature*, ed. Derek Attridge (London: Routledge, 1992), 244). [*Translator's note:* On this proximity, see also Balibar, "Eschatology versus Teleology: The Suspended Dialogue between Derrida and Althusser," in *Derrida and the Time of the Political*, ed. Pheng Cheah and Suzanne Guerlac (Durham, NC: Duke University Press, 2009), 57–73.] Guillaume Sibertin-Blanc also rightly brought to my attention the fact that, as

early as 1972, Deleuze and Guattari used the phrase "history is the history of contingencies and encounters"; Gilles Deleuze and Félix Guattari, *Anti-Oedipus: Capitalism and Schizophrenia*, trans. Robert Hurley, Mark Seem, and Helen R. Lane (Minneapolis: University of Minnesota Press, 1983), 195. The reception of Deleuze is a black hole for the Althusserians and a terra incognita for the interpretation of Althusser.

21. The material referent for Francisco Naishtat's analyses to which de Ípola refers is the *piqueteros* movement in Argentina in the 1990s, which resisted the International Monetary Fund's orders to reduce public debt. [*Translator's note:* For Badiou's "subjectivity without a subject," see Alain Badiou, *Metapolitics*, trans. Jason Barker (London: Verso, 2006), 58–67.]

22. *Translator's note:* See G. W. F. Hegel, *Phenomenology of Spirit*, trans. A. V. Miller (Oxford: Oxford University Press, 1977), 110. On the phrase cited from this work, see Étienne Balibar, *Citizen Subject: Foundations for Philosophical Anthropology*, trans. Steven Miller (New York: Fordham University Press, 2017).

23. See my introduction [titled "Une rencontre en Romagne"] to the pocket edition of Louis Althusser, *Machiavelli et nous* (Paris: Tallendier, 2009).

24. A surprising encounter took place between Althusser and his rival E. P. Thompson around the oxymoronic phrase "class struggle without class"; see Thompson, "Eighteenth-Century English Society: Class Struggle without Class?," *Social History* 3, no. 2 (1978): 133–65.

PROLOGUE

Epigraph: Louis Althusser, *Lettres à Franca (1961–1973)*, ed. François Matheron and Yann Moulier Boutang (Paris: Stock/IMEC, 1998), 685.

1. After Althusser's death, the foundation that bears his name took charge, with the permission of Althusser's inheritor, of the classification, organization, and posthumous publication of a large quantity of unpublished manuscripts. This rich material (which spans a period of forty years, approximately 1946–86) includes various essays and studies of great significance.

2. By "classic," I mean the works of Althusser and his disciples that were published during the mid-1960s (essentially *For Marx* and *Reading Capital*). These works made their authors famous and gave rise to "Althusserianism" as a theoretical figure and ideologico-political wager.

3. To all this, we would have to add the deft rhetorical tricks that Althusserian prose frequently adopted—unbeatable at this art—to mitigate the excessively heterodox (or orthodox) nature of this or that statement. Of course, those cunning schemes contributed even further to thwarting my attempts to restrict the scope of my object of analysis.

4. Recall that Rancière later definitively distanced himself both theoretically and politically from Althusserianism. I believe nonetheless that in all of his anti-Althusserian essays the indelible mark of his mentor remains. Rancière had to try to forget about Althusser so as to erase the latter's imprint on him. But his effort failed.

5. Alain Badiou recognizes this kind of parallel and convergent thinking in an interview with Bruno Bosteels: Badiou and Bosteels, "Posmaoísmo: Un diálogo con Alain Badiou," *Acontecimiento: Revista para pensar la política* 24–25 (2003): 63. [*Translator's note:* The English version of this text, with the title "Can Change Be Thought," is included as an appendix in Bosteels, *Badiou and Politics* (Durham, NC: Duke University Press, 2011), 289–317.]

6. In any case, this study will remain focused on Althusser's work. I will of course refer, particularly in the conclusion, to the production of "post-Althusserianism," but I will not offer a detailed or systematic analysis of that ongoing project.

7. A respected Catalan sociologist, Salvador Giner, thus asks himself in the mid-1980s with undisguised contempt, "Who reads Althusser these days?" In reality, Giner did nothing more than say out loud what many, myself included, were thinking at that time; see Giner, "Intenciones humanas, estructuras sociales: Para una lógica situacional," in *Acción humana*, ed. Manuel Cruz (Barcelona: Ariel, 1997), 93n86.

8. The most spectacular example of the anti-Marxist vision that flourished in the mid-1970s can be found among the so-called New Philosophers.

9. *Translator's note:* Althusser, *The Future Lasts Forever: A Memoir*, trans. Richard Veasey (New York: New Press, 1993). Published originally as Althusser, *L'avenir dure longtemps, suivi de Les Faits. Autobiographies*, ed. Olivier Corpet and Yann Moulier Boutang (Paris: Stock/IMEC, 1992).

10. Lavish but also forgettable. See my discussion of Gérard Pommier's book below.

11. See Giner, "Intenciones humanas, estructuras sociales."

12. Oscar Terán, *De utopias, catástrofes y esperanzas: Un camino intelectual* (Buenos Aires: Siglo XXI, 2006), 22. Althusser was both the victim and the victimizer of this moment of hatred toward Marx as well as toward himself *qua* Marxist. See, for example, Althusser, "On Marxist Thought," trans. Asad Haider and Salar Mohandesi, *Viewpoint Magazine*, September 12, 2012, https://viewpointmag.com/2012/09/12/on-marxist-thought/. See also the repeated mea culpas deployed in Althusser, *The Future Lasts Forever: A Memoir*, trans. Richard Veasey (New York: New Press, 1993).

13. Likewise, in the conclusion, I allow myself to refer a few times to my personal experience after completing the theoretical analysis.

14. *Translator's note:* See Althusser, *Positions* (Paris: Éditions sociales, 1976).

15. See Pommier, *Louis du néant: La mélancolie d'Althusser* (Paris: Aubier, 1998). This argument does not apply to León Rozitchner's moving essay entitled "La tragedia del althusserianismo teórico." Rozitchner offers an honest and valiant reading of *The Future Lasts Forever* and masterfully reconstructs with compassion the tragedy of Althusser, whose explicit philosophy Rozitchner rejects point by point for reasons that he explains at the outset. Rozitchner undoubtedly discovers a link between philosophy and tragedy in what I would hastily refer to as "the question of the subject." But that question does not function as an explanatory factor for either philosophy or for tragedy; it is, rather, the conflictual nucleus that both disavow, a conflictual nucleus that, according to Rozitchner, is terribly effective; see Rozitchner, "La tragedia del althusserianismo teórico," *El Ojo Mocho* 17 (2003): 43–50.

16. I am of course referring to the victim of these analyses.

17. If I must take Althusser's autobiography into account, it is because it contains philosophical reflections. This text in particular presents aspects of Althusser's early philosophy and thought with more clarity than other previously unpublished works and deserves our attention.

18. This is true except for in very few cases when it was necessary to refer to Althusser's personal history to clarify some chronological information in relation to this or that aspect of his work.

19. This preoccupation dates back to the first writings of his youth and can even be detected in an almost Stalinist letter he wrote to Jean Lacroix, a letter whose contents would be unimaginable for anyone only familiar with the mature Althusser; see Althusser, "Letter to Jean Lacroix (1949–1950)," in *The Spectre of Hegel: Early Writings*, trans. G. M. Goshgarian (London: Verso, 2014), 207–44.

20. Jean Laplanche and Serge Leclaire, "The Unconscious: A Psychoanalytic Study," trans. Patrick Coleman, *Yale French Studies* 48 (1972): 118–75. Althusser cited the work of Laplanche and Leclaire rather often (above all in his courses and his unpublished texts); see Althusser, *Écrits sur la psychanalyse*, ed. Olivier Corpet and François Matheron (Paris: Stock/IMEC, 1993). [*Translator's note*: Most of the texts collected in this volume are available in English translation in Althusser, *Writings on Psychoanalysis: Freud and Lacan*, trans. Jeffrey Mehlman (New York: Columbia University Press, 1996).]

21. In other words, one must consider not only the semantic level but also the grammatical, phonological, and morphological levels, as well as the logic of the argument and the extra-discursive situations in which that argument is transmitted. It is, accordingly, important to consider not only what is stated but also the conditions of the statement.

22. The clearest example of this is the analysis of the "oversights" of classical political economy that Marx revealed at the beginning of *Capital*. Classical political economy is incapable of seeing that it has produced an adequate answer to a question that has never been formulated; see, for example, Althusser, "From *Capital* to Marx's Philosophy," in *Reading Capital*, by Louis Althusser and Étienne Balibar, trans. Ben Brewster (London: Verso, 2009), 19.

23. See in particular the already mentioned essay "On Marxist Thought" (1982), which remained unpublished until it appeared in 1993. [*Translator's note*: See Althusser, "Sur la pensée marxiste," *Futur antérieur, Sur Althusser: Passages* (1993): 11–29.]

24. *Translator's note*: See Althusser, *Montesquieu, la politique et l'histoire* (Paris: Presses Universitaires de France, 1959).

ONE. **THE PAST, THAT STRANGE LAND**

Epigraph: L. P. Hartley, *The Go-Between* (New York: New York Review of Books, 2002), 17.

Epigraph: Louis Althusser, "From *Capital* to Marx's Philosophy," in *Reading Capital*, by Louis Althusser and Étienne Balibar, trans. Ben Brewster (London: Verso, 2009), 33.

1. *Translator's note:* The English translation of Althusser's book on Montesquieu includes other works on Rousseau and Marx and a modified title; see Althusser, *Politics and History: Montesquieu, Rousseau, Marx*, trans. Ben Brewster (London: Verso, 2007). For the original French version, see Althusser, *Montesquieu, la politique et l'histoire* (Paris: Presses Universitaires de France, 1959).

2. Althusser, *Écrits philosophiques et politiques*, ed. François Matheron (Paris: Stock/IMEC, 1995), 2:8.

3. Althusser, *Machiavelli and Us*, trans. Gregory Elliott, ed. François Matheron (Verso: London, 1999), 67, 68. [*Translator's note:* I have slightly altered the translation, rendering *le vide* as "the void" rather than "emptiness" to preserve how this passage resonates with Althusser's theorization of the materialism of the encounter. For the original French version, see Althusser, "Machiavel et nous (1972–1986)," in *Écrits philosophiques et politiques*, 2:119.]

4. I would mention, among many others, the works of Epicurus and Lucretius, Aristotle, Machiavelli, Hobbes, Spinoza, Montesquieu, Helvetius, Rousseau, Feuerbach, Gramsci, and, among Althusser's contemporaries, the works of Jean Cavaillès, Gaston Bachelard, Georges Canguilhem, Michel Foucault, Jacques Lacan, and—fundamental for the last Althusser—Jacques Derrida.

5. However, the peak of Althusserianism would not last for long. Some consider May 1968 as the date that marked the beginning of the end of the Althusserian enterprise. Be that as it may, this enterprise remained at the forefront for a long enough time to have an impact on, at the very least, an entire generation.

6. Althusser refers occasionally to these meetings in his autobiography. In the *Lettres à Franca*, he also alludes to the interest that his work provoked in the Latin American group; see Althusser, *Lettres à Franca (1961–1973)*, ed. François Matheron and Yann Moulier Boutang (Paris: Stock/IMEC, 1998), 677.

7. I will say more about this rather abrupt conversion later.

8. Yann Moulier Boutang, the author of an excellent biography on Althusser, expresses amazement and incomprehension when confronted with the fact that Althusser despised Garaudy. He insists on the inconsistency of this attitude, since Garaudy and Althusser shared a common Catholic upbringing that would have left its mark on the work of both thinkers. Nevertheless, the fact that Althusser was a first-rate philosopher and theoretician, while Garaudy was never more than an inept and wild ideologue, is not an insignificant detail; see Boutang, *Louis Althusser: Une biographie* (Paris: Grasset, 1992).

9. This reference to Rancière, a philosopher who has my complete admiration and respect, allows me to denounce and deny the validity of certain laughable assertions that an irresponsible publication attributed to me. These assertions stemmed from a distorted transcription of an interview conducted at a noisy locale in Buenos Aires that was not submitted to me for review; see Bruno Fornillo and Alejandro Lezama, *Releer Althusser* (Buenos Aires: Parusia, 2003). I also refer the reader to where I pre-

sent my thoughts on Rancière's writings: Emilio de Ípola, *Ideología y discurso populista* (Buenos Aires: Folios, 1982).

10. Althusser declared more than once that he had to take a "detour" through philosophy to obtain the means to arrive at politics. This is undoubtedly a valid assertion so long as it is added that this detour was each time a (re)commencement. Such a new beginning—as I suggested earlier—was the specific, Althusserian modality of philosophizing. Accordingly, Althusser's philosophy was constitutively affected by a kind of necessary inconclusivity; each point of arrival suddenly became a new point of departure, a new commencement or beginning. This was a costly effort that led Althusser to stretch his intuitions—his own or the intuitions of others—to the limit, scrutinizing all the "interstices" that were left open by the culture and the period that he happened to inhabit, exploring the minute nuances of a phrase or a word.

11. *Translator's note:* See Althusser, "Contradiction and Overdetermination," in *For Marx*, trans. Ben Brewster (New York: Verso, 2005), 87–128.

12. Althusser responds in this text to the criticisms that his essay "Contradiction and Overdetermination" inspired. [*Translator's note:* see Althusser, "On the Materialist Dialectic," in *For Marx*, 161–218.]

13. Claude Lévi-Strauss, *Mythologiques*, vol. 2, *Du miel aux cendres* (Paris: Plon, 2009), 408.

14. The same did not occur, however, when the Soviet Union invaded Czechoslovakia. That time Aragon said "enough," just as José Saramago did in 2002 when faced with the murder and arbitrary imprisonment of dissidents in Cuba.

15. Lacan also inscribed himself in this debate and coincided with Althusser during the early stages of his inquiry. Without losing sight of their shared perspective, they disagreed on one point that was essential for both of them: the question of the subject. This topic is analyzed in detail in chapter 2 of this book.

16. The term *problematic* is utilized here in the sense that Althusser gave to it in his study on the young Marx. [*Translator's note:* See Althusser, "On the Young Marx," in *For Marx*, 49–86.]

17. Though this is not the case for all of them, particularly the formulation that "history is a process without a subject or a goal," which, as Althusser declares to put an end to a long debate, encapsulates the main idea that Marx would inherit from Hegel. This formulation is sustained and deepened in Althusser's esoteric thought.

18. Freely following Leo Strauss, I will reaffirm the term that appeared in the previous footnote and say that in Althusser there exists an "exoteric" thought and an "esoteric" thought. On Strauss, see Claudia Hilb, *Leo Strauss: El arte de leer; Una lectura de la interpretación straussiana de Maquiavelo, Hobbes, Locke y Spinoza* (Buenos Aires: Fondo de Cultura Económica, 2005).

19. On the basis of the economic instance's invariable determination.

20. "The Theories mentioned in Thesis 41 [Epistemology or the Theory of the processes of production of scientific knowledges, the Theory of the history of sciences, the Theory of Philosophy, the Theory of the history of philosophies] do not exist as Theories. Only some of their chapters or sections exist at the theoretical state. These theories do not essentially exist but in the 'practical state.' The constitution of these

Theories is one of the strategic theoretical tasks of our time"; Althusser, "Du côté de la philosophie (cinquième Cours de philosophie pour scientifiques) (1967)," in *Écrits philosophiques et politiques*, 2:295.

21. Among them Althusser himself, who at one point attended the seminar taught by Lacan at the Institute of Sainte-Anne. In his autobiography, Althusser humorously mentions that Lacan had spoken of cybernetics and psychoanalysis at this seminar and that, for his part, he had not understood any of it "because of [Lacan's] tortuous, baroque way of speaking, a phony imitation of Breton's splendid language. He clearly did it so that his listeners would be awestruck"; Althusser, *The Future Lasts Forever: A Memoir*, trans. Richard Veasey (New York: New Press, 1993), 332.

22. Althusser, "Du côté de la philosophie," 2:295.

23. *Translator's note:* For the English translation of this text, which is not included in the English edition of *Writings on Psychoanalysis*, see Althusser, "Three Notes on the Theory of Discourses," in *The Humanist Controversy and Other Writings*, trans. G. M. Goshgarian (London: Verso, 2003), 33–84. For the original French version, see Althusser, "Trois notes sur la théorie des discours, 1966," in *Écrits sur la psychanalyse*, ed. Olivier Corpet and François Matheron (Paris: Stock/IMEC, 1993), 111–70.

24. Althusser, "Three Notes on the Theory of Discourses," 37.

25. The "Three Notes" openly exhibits the theoretical difficulties that troubled Althusser's thought at the time. The notes include urgent requests directed at their readers. For example: "Information, please." Althusser, "Three Notes on the Theory of Discourses," 80.

26. On this point, see chapter 3.

27. The principal references regarding this point include Althusser's 1969 preface to the first volume of Marx's *Capital*, the essay "Comment lire *Le Capital*," which appeared in *L'Humanité* in March 1969, and the text that served as the preface to the second edition of Marta Harnecker's *Los conceptos elementales del materialismo histórico*, titled "Marxisme et lutte de classe." [*Translator's note:* See Althusser, "Avertissement aux lecteurs du Livre I du 'Capital,'" in *Le Capital: Livre 1*, by Karl Marx (Paris: Garnier-Flammarion, 1969), 5–30, translated as "Preface to *Capital* Volume 1," in *Lenin and Philosophy and Other Essays*, trans. Ben Brewster (New York: Monthly Review Press, 2001), 45–70; Althusser, "Comment lire 'Le Capital?,'" *L'Humanité* (March 21, 1969), translated as Althusser, "How to Read Marx's 'Capital,'" *Marxism Today* (1969): 302–5; Althusser, preface to *Los conceptos elementales del materialismo histórico*, by Marta Harnecker, 2nd ed. (Buenos Aires: Siglo XXI, 1971), xi–xvi. This preface was reprinted as "Marxisme et lutte de classe," in *Positions* (Paris: Éditions sociales, 1976), 71–78; translated by Patrick Lyons as "Marxism-Leninism and the Class Struggle," *Theoretical Review* 3 (1978): 17–20.]

28. The topic of solitude, apropos thinkers such as Machiavelli and Gramsci or political leaders like César Borgia and Lenin, returns constantly in the writings of this period. Althusser alludes to his own solitude through these references.

29. A *prise* [take], as Althusser would say.

TWO. THE "CLASSIC" ALTHUSSER AND HIS SLIPS

Epigraph: Louis Althusser, *Lettres à Franca (1961—1973)*, ed. François Matheron and Yann Moulier Boutang (Paris: Stock/IMEC, 1998), 646.

1. See Althusser, "From *Capital* to Marx's Philosophy," in *Reading Capital*, trans. Ben Brewster (London: Verso, 2009), 42n17; Althusser, "Contradiction and Overdetermination," in *For Marx*, trans. Ben Brewster (London: Verso, 2005), 97n16; Althusser, "On the Materialist Dialectic," in *For Marx*, 200n41.

2. Althusser, not without irony, reminded his critics: "For we are all agreed that [. . .] a really existing science has to be defended against an encroaching ideology"; Althusser, "On the Materialist Dialectic," 172.

3. See Althusser, "On the Young Marx," in *For Marx*, 49–86.

4. Jacques Rancière has noted the forceful tone with which Althusser tended to introduce some of his formulations; see Rancière, "La scène du texte," in *Politique et philosophie dans l'oeuvre de Louis Althusser*, ed. Sylvain Lazarus (Paris: Presses Universitaires de France, 1993).

5. Rancière, Étienne Balibar, Roger Establet, and Pierre Macherey all contributed essays to the two volumes of *Reading Capital*.

6. Certain free spirits who also participated in this current were Jean-Pierre Vernant, Maurice Godelier, and Martial Guéroult.

7. See chapter 1.

8. Even if also deemed by many Marxist and non-Marxist theorists alike to be unacceptable.

9. Throughout almost all his works, Althusser would repeatedly turn to argumentative sequences that would begin with the defense of an orthodox thesis, including one that the party had already abandoned, and would then offer an unexpected reinterpretation of the thesis in question, a reinterpretation that at the same time would be in contradiction with some isolated and generally enigmatic formulation. The last version of this roundabout can be found in the critique of the French Communist Party's abandonment in 1978 of the thesis on the "dictatorship of the proletariat"; see Althusser, "Marx in His Limits," in *Philosophy of the Encounter: Later Writings, 1978–1987*, trans. G. M. Goshgarian (London: Verso, 2006), 7–162.

10. Roger Garaudy, Gilbert Mury, Lucien Sève, and Georges Cogniot, among others.

11. Montesquieu as cited by Althusser, in *Politics and History: Montesquieu, Rousseau, Marx*, trans. Ben Brewster (London: Verso, 2007), 39.

12. Althusser, *Politics and History*, 38, 39.

13. Althusser, *Politics and History*, 33 [de Ípola's note in brackets].

14. Althusser, *Politics and History*, 68 [original emphasis].

15. Althusser, *Politics and History*, 69 [original emphasis].

16. This essay, published in 1961, would later be included in *For Marx* (1965). [Translator's note: For the original publication, see Althusser, "Sur le jeune Marx (Questions de théorie)," *La Pensée: Revue du rationalisme moderne* 96 (1961): 3–26.]

17. This is Gaston Bachelard's formulation, which Althusser's writings incorporated and often reinterpreted.

18. Latin America first became aware of Althusser's writings through the publication of Pierre Verstraeten's essay in *Les Temps Modernes* titled "Lévi-Strauss ou la tentation du néant," which cites the text on the young Marx that had appeared in *La Pensée*. It could not but grab our attention that something readable and positively citable could appear in a journal as theoretically bankrupt as *Les Temps Modernes*, associated as it was with the French Communist Party (although without dressing up as an official publication); see Verstraeten, "Lévi-Strauss ou la tentation du néant," *Les Temps Modernes* 206 (1963): 66–109.

19. The latter was present only "in a practical state," which is to say neither reflected upon nor, for that reason, expressed as such.

20. Althusser, "On the Young Marx," 67 [original emphasis].

21. Althusser, "Contradiction and Overdetermination," 93 [original emphasis].

22. Althusser, "Contradiction and Overdetermination," 99. Jean Pouillon highlights and critiques this questionable comparison between contradictions; see Pouillon, "Del lado de Marx," in *Lectura de Althusser*, ed. Saúl Karsz (Buenos Aires: Editorial Galerna, 1970), 231–46.

23. Althusser, "Contradiction and Overdetermination," 101.

24. Althusser, "Contradiction and Overdetermination," 104.

25. Althusser, "Contradiction and Overdetermination," 113 [original emphasis].

26. Althusser, "Contradiction and Overdetermination" [de Ípola's emphasis, translation modified], 113. Étienne Balibar, among others, emphasizes the decisive theoretical range of this formulation; see Balibar, "Althusser's Object," trans. Margaret Cohen and Bruce Robbins, *Social Text* 39 (1994): 157–88. [*Translator's note*: In the cited passage, I modified the existing English translation of the phrase *l'heure solitaire* so that it reads "the solitary hour" rather than "the lonely hour" to preserve more clearly the resonance with later works by Althusser that theorize the solitary and solitude. This resonance is discussed further in chapter 4 of this book, appropriately titled "The Solitary Hour." For the original French passage, see Althusser, *Pour Marx* (Paris: La Découverte, 2005), 113.]

27. "Complicated" for his inept colleagues of the French Communist Party. In reality, for those who know how to read it, the passage holds no mystery.

28. Althusser, "On the Materialist Dialectic," 209 [original emphasis].

29. *Translator's note:* The original Spanish for the heading of this section reads *Causa de la estructura*. This ambiguous phrase, although potentially referring literally to the cause of the structure or to what brings about the structure, seems also, or more likely, to be referring to the kind of cause proper to structure, which is to say to structural causality. I have decided to translate word for word in this instance in part to preserve this ambiguity and in part to preserve what seems to be an oblique reference to an essay by Jacques-Alain Miller cited in this section titled "Action de la structure." For the English translation of this text, see Miller, "Action of the Structure," in *Concept and Form*, vol. 1, *Key Texts from the "Cahiers pour l'Analyse,"* ed. Peter Hallward and Knox Peden (London: Verso, 2012), 69–83.

30. Jean Laplanche and Jean-Bertrand Pontalis, *The Language of Psychoanalysis*, trans. Donald Nicholson-Smith (New York: W. W. Norton, 1974), 292.

31. Althusser, "The Object of *Capital*," in *Reading Capital*, 205, 206 [original emphasis].

32. "One thing is clear: the Middle Ages could not live on Catholicism, nor could the ancient world on politics. On the contrary, it is the manner in which they gained their livelihood that explains why in one case politics, in the other case Catholicism, played the chief part"; Karl Marx, *Capital: A Critique of Political Economy*, trans. Ben Fowkes (New York: Penguin, 1990), 1:176n35.

33. Badiou does so "indirectly" because his reflections on the concept of structural causality presuppose the falsity of this solution.

34. In those years, Althusser would eventually adhere to this line of thinking.

35. Alain Badiou, "The (Re)commencement of Dialectical Materialism," in *The Adventure of French Philosophy*, trans. Bruno Bosteels (London: Verso, 2012), 157n45.

36. As for the second reason, which has to do with the complex and conflictive relationship between Althusser and Lévi-Strauss, I will have to postpone its discussion until the next section of this chapter.

37. And, subsidiarily, to the first draft of these theses delineated in Mauss's much earlier work from 1902; see Marcel Mauss, *A General Theory of Magic* (New York: Routledge, 1972). [*Translator's note*: See also Mauss, *The Gift: The Form and Reason for Exchange in Archaic Societies*, trans. W. D. Halls (New York: W. W. Norton, 1990), and Claude Lévi-Strauss, *Introduction to the Work of Marcel Mauss*, trans. Felicity Baker (London: Routledge and Kegan Paul, 1987).]

38. Lévi-Strauss provides another example that refers to the same signified, though this time the example is not an object but rather—in a sense closer to its use in exotic societies—a property of someone: "X has 'something'" (in Spanish, more frequently: *x tiene algo especial* [there's something special about x] or *x tiene un no sé qué* [x has that certain *je ne sais quoi*]); Lévi-Strauss, *Introduction to the Work of Marcel Mauss*, 55.

39. Lévi-Strauss, *Introduction to the Work of Marcel Mauss*, 59, 60.

40. Lévi-Strauss, *Introduction to the Work of Marcel Mauss*, 60.

41. Lévi-Strauss, *Introduction to the Work of Marcel Mauss*, 61.

42. Lévi-Strauss, *Introduction to the Work of Marcel Mauss*, 61.

43. *Translator's note*: Although de Ípola translates Lévi-Strauss's French term *adéquation* literally, rendering it in Spanish as *adecuación*, the English translation of Lévi-Strauss's "Introduction à l'oeuvre de Marcel Mauss" uses variations of the more common but different notion of "equivalence." Here and further on, I will follow the English translation while including the Spanish word in brackets to preserve de Ípola's allusion to the French original. For more on this notion and its translation into English, see Felicity Baker's note in Lévi-Strauss, *Introduction to the Work of Marcel Mauss*, 71n16. See also the original French here: Lévi-Strauss, "Introduction à l'oeuvre de Marcel Mauss," in *Sociologie et anthropologie*, by Marcel Mauss (Paris: Presses Universitaires de France, 1950), ix–lii.

44. Lévi-Strauss, *Introduction to the Work of Marcel Mauss*, 62, 63.

45. Lévi-Strauss, *Introduction to the Work of Marcel Mauss*, 63 [original emphasis].

46. Lévi-Strauss, *Introduction to the Work of Marcel Mauss*, 64 [de Ípola's emphasis and note in brackets].

47. This text was later included in Lévi-Strauss, *Structural Anthropology*, trans. Claire Jacobson (New York: Basic Books, 1974), 167–85; see also Lévi-Strauss, "Le sorcier et sa magie," *Les Temps Modernes* 41 (1949): 3–24.

48. Lévi-Strauss, *Introduction to the Work of Marcel Mauss*, 15.

49. Lévi-Strauss, *Introduction to the Work of Marcel Mauss*, 17, 18.

50. *Translator's note:* This is a very close paraphrasing of Lévi-Strauss; see Lévi-Strauss, *Introduction to the Work of Marcel Mauss*, 18.

51. As one might anticipate, the development of Lévi-Strauss's argument leads to questioning the validity of the notion of "mental illness"; Lévi-Strauss, *Introduction to the Work of Marcel Mauss*, 21 [original emphasis].

52. Lévi-Strauss, *Introduction to the Work of Marcel Mauss*, 19.

53. Lévi-Strauss, *Introduction to the Work of Marcel Mauss*, 22 [original emphasis].

54. Miller, "Suture (Elements of the Logic of the Signifier)," in *Concept and Form*, 1:93.

55. Miller, "Suture," 1:97, 98.

56. Miller, "Suture," 1:97.

57. Miller, "Suture," 1:99.

58. Miller, "Suture," 1:101.

59. Miller, "S'truc dure," *Pas tant: Revue de la "découverte freudienne"* 8–9 (1985): 4–11.

60. Miller, "S'truc dure," 7.

61. Miller, "S'truc dure," 10.

62. Miller, "S'truc dure," 11.

63. Ernesto Laclau, *New Reflections on the Revolution of Our Times* (London: Verso, 1990).

64. Jorge Dotti, "¿Cómo mirar el rostro de la Gorgona? Antagonismo, estructuralismo y decisionismo," *Deus Mortalis* 3 (2004): 456.

65. Lévi-Strauss, *Introduction to the Work of Marcel Mauss*, 18.

66. Lévi-Strauss, *Introduction to the Work of Marcel Mauss*, 63.

67. See Jacques Lacan, "Aggressiveness in Psychoanalysis," in *Écrits: The First Complete Edition in English*, trans. Bruce Fink (New York: W. W. Norton, 2007), 82–101.

68. "That seems to me to be the conclusion that emerges from Dr. J. Lacan's profound study, 'L'Agressivité en psychanalyse,' 1948"; Lévi-Strauss, *Introduction to the Work of Marcel Mauss*, 68n13.

69. Badiou, "(Re)commencement of Dialectical Materialism," 153.

70. "The first *ensemble* or set that is thus constructed, then, is the *list of practices*. Althusser provides several lists, most of them open-ended. The invariant segment of these lists contains: economic practice [. . .]; ideological practice; political practice; and theoretical practice"; Badiou, "(Re)commencement of Dialectical Materialism," 153 [original emphasis]. On this point, see Manuel Cruz, *La crisis del stalinismo: El caso Althusser* (Barcelona: Península, 1977).

71. Althusser, as cited in Badiou, "(Re)commencement of Dialectical Materialism," 154.

72. Badiou, "(Re)commencement of Dialectical Materialism," 154.

73. Althusser as cited in Badiou, "(Re)commencement of Dialectical Materialism," 154 [original emphasis].

74. "The complex whole has the unity of a structure articulated in dominance"; Althusser, as cited in Badiou, "(Re)commencement of Dialectical Materialism," 155.

75. Badiou, "(Re)commencement of Dialectical Materialism," 155 [original emphasis; translator's note in brackets].

76. Althusser, as cited in Badiou, "(Re)commencement of Dialectical Materialism," 155.

77. Badiou, "(Re)commencement of Dialectical Materialism," 155 [original emphasis].

78. The vocabulary Althusser accepts leads to the unfortunate formulation of a "determinate instance in the last instance," the source of many misunderstandings.

79. Badiou, "(Re)commencement of Dialectical Materialism," 155 [original emphasis].

80. Badiou, "(Re)commencement of Dialectical Materialism," 156 [original emphasis].

81. Badiou, "(Re)commencement of Dialectical Materialism," 156 [original emphasis].

82. Badiou, "(Re)commencement of Dialectical Materialism," 156 [original emphasis].

83. Badiou, "(Re)commencement of Dialectical Materialism," 156.

84. Badiou, "(Re)commencement of Dialectical Materialism," 157 [original emphasis].

85. Badiou, "(Re)commencement of Dialectical Materialism," 157 [original emphasis].

86. Badiou, "(Re)commencement of Dialectical Materialism," 157, 158 [original emphasis]. A perhaps supplementary interest in Badiou's exposition is its clearing the way for a theoretical conceptualization that avoids many of the difficulties stemming from the double function of the economic instance-practice. This conceptualization also takes up, as in Badiou, the distinction between determination and domination. But it establishes a prior distinction, interior to the concept of economy and frequently mentioned by Marx, between the *direct production process* (which includes the relations of production) and *circulation* (another "economic" process). Production framed within definite relations of production would be the determining practice, whereas circulation (instance of the whole) could be dominant or not, depending on the type of social formation in question. From this perspective, it would be possible to conserve the definitions of determination and domination proposed by Badiou with one addition: the dominant, qua instance, would establish the hierarchy of efficacies of the other instances, but, conceived as a "practice"—in Badiou's sense of both terms—it would also satisfy the principal condition of reproducing the process of direct production and its specific relations of production. The economistic deviation is an understandable temptation for those who take capitalism as their model, given that circulation is dominant within it. But nothing prohibits other processes of a different nature (political, ideological, etc.) from satisfying the aforementioned condition within other societal

formations. However, this framework did not become popular for the simple reason that critiques of the cliché of instances had already advanced too far for it to be viable to reinstate the classic distinctions between structure and superstructure. It was a case of what has been called the "vanishing mediator."

87. "Jacques-Alain Miller has given an exposé of this problem to which we must refer. [. . .] We will nevertheless try to show elsewhere: (a) that the—extraordinarily clever—use of Frege's construction of number for the purpose of illustrating the problem of structural causality is epistemologically inadequate; (b) that we cannot think the logic of the signifier as such [. . .] without reduplicating the structure *of metaphysics*"; Badiou, "(Re)commencement of Dialectical Materialism," 157n45 [original emphasis].

88. Badiou, "(Re)commencement of Dialectical Materialism," 147n24.

89. *Translator's note:* The heading for this section appears in Spanish as "El sujeto en causa," which deploys an untranslatable play on words. While my translation captures the idea that the subject in question is the question of the subject, de Ípola conveys this idea with the Spanish phrase *en causa* (normally *poner en causa/poner en cuestión*), alluding to the relationship between subject and cause as well as to the prior section, "Cause [*Causa*] of the Structure."

90. See, in particular, Althusser, "Object of *Capital*," 201–12.

91. Althusser, "Object of *Capital*," 207.

92. Althusser, "Object of *Capital*," 211, 212.

93. Althusser, "Object of *Capital*," 208. By way of a literary reference, this statement is taken up again and further illustrated in "Three Notes on the Theory of Discourses," a text that must be continuously recalled: "Take *Le Rouge et le Noir*. It is an aesthetic discourse. It comprises a series of statements presented in a certain order. [. . .] I maintain that this discourse quite simply *is* the existence of Julien and his 'passion.' We do not have the discourse of *Le Rouge* on the one hand and, on the other, Julien and his passion. Julien's passion, with all its emotional intensity (easily the equal of the intensity of the drives, for what is it if not those very drives, inscribed in a 'discourse' presented by the aesthetic discourse), does not lie behind or even between the lines of this discourse; it is not something other than this discourse, [. . .] it is nothing *but* this discourse itself, it is indiscernible from it"; Althusser, "Three Notes on the Theory of Discourses," in *The Humanist Controversy and Other Writings*, trans. G. M. Goshgarian (London: Verso, 2003), 70, 71.

94. Althusser, "Object of *Capital*," 208.

95. Althusser, *Lire le Capital* (Paris: Presses Universitaires de France, 2008), 646n62 [original emphasis]. [*Translator's note:* This is one of various passages that were eliminated from *Lire le Capital* after the first edition of the text. It does not appear in the existing English translation; however, it can be found in the recent Quadrige Grands Textes edition cited previously, in the section titled "Variantes de la première édition." The original French reads, "C'est pourquoi, *selon le niveau auquel on se place*, on peut dire que la '*Darstellung*' est le concept de la *présence de la structure dans ses effets*, de la modification des effets par l'efficace de la structure présente en ses effets,—ou au contraire que la '*Darstellung*' est le concept de l'*efficace d'une absence*."]

96. Althusser, "Object of *Capital*," 198, 199 [original emphasis].

97. *Translator's note:* As previously mentioned, the English translation of this text is included in the anthology titled *The Humanist Controversy and Other Writings*, and does not appear in the English edition of *Writings on Psychoanalysis*.

98. It is understood that, by the same criteria, the theory of the capitalist mode of production would be a regional theory dependent on the general theory of historical materialism. Althusser refers to this point in a letter to Franca Madonia, but the "Three Notes" focuses on the status of psychoanalysis; see Althusser, *Lettres à Franca (1961–1973)*, ed. François Matheron and Yann Moulier Boutang (Paris: Stock/IMEC, 1998), 114. With the exception of a few brief mentions, historical materialism only indirectly figures in the notes, via the discussion of the concept of ideology.

99. By writing "soon," I am attempting to reconstruct the chronological order of Althusser's reflections, not the sequence of their exposition. The exposition begins with a cover letter, written after the three notes, in which Althusser anticipates the rejection of his prior formulation; Althusser, "Three Notes on the Theory of Discourses," 37, 38.

100. Regarding the aesthetic discourse, Althusser notes that it poses problems too complicated for the theoretical elements available.

101. See Althusser, "Correspondence with Jacques Lacan," in *Writings on Psychoanalysis: Freud and Lacan*, trans. Jeffrey Mehlman (New York: Columbia University Press, 1996), 170–72.

102. *Translator's note:* In the original French, Althusser uses four words to "literally" define *Spaltung: abîme* [abyss], *précipice* [precipice], *manque* [lack], and *béance*, which I have rendered as "gap" rather than "absence" (as it appears in the existing translation). For the original French version, see Althusser, "Trois notes sur la théorie des discours, 1966," in *Écrits sur la psychanalyse: Freud et Lacan*, ed. Olivier Corpet and François Matheron (Paris: Stock/IMEC, 1993), 165. For an example of the English translation of the term *béance* as "gap," see Lacan, *The Four Fundamental Concepts of Psychoanalysis*, trans. Alan Sheridan (New York: W. W. Norton, 1998), 29.

103. Althusser, "Three Notes on the Theory of Discourses," 77, 78 [original emphasis, translation modified].

104. Or rather an "intra-ideological process and progression," or finally an "intra-ideological displacement-progress." [*Translator's note:* See, respectively, Badiou, "Mark and Lack: On Zero," in *Concept and Form*, 1:160; Badiou, "(Re)commencement of Dialectical Materialism," 149n27.]

105. *Translator's note:* De Ípola is referring to a talk that Badiou gave in Vienna and then published in the Spanish-language journal *Acontecimiento* in 1996 before it was published again, two years later, as part of Badiou's book *Abrégé de métapolitique*, translated by Jason Barker into English as *Metapolitics*. I cite the English translation in all subsequent references to Badiou's presentation. For the Spanish version, see Badiou, "¿Cómo pensar la empresa de Louis Althusser?," *Acontecimiento: Revista para pensar la política* 12 (1996): 11–20. For the English translation of the cited passage, see Badiou, *Metapolitics*, trans. Jason Barker (London: Verso, 2006), 58.

106. Badiou, *Metapolitics*, 59.

107. Badiou, *Metapolitics*, 59, 60 [original emphasis].

108. As well as, by the way, the intolerance of certain psychoanalysts that were present.

109. *Translator's note:* For a brief account of this conflictual encounter between Althusser, Lacan, and the members of the Freudian School, see Sherry Turkle, *Psychoanalytic Politics: Jacques Lacan and Freud's French Revolution* (London: Guilford, 1992), 265.

110. Althusser, "From *Capital* to Marx's Philosophy," 17.

111. *Translator's note:* See Lévi-Strauss, "History and Dialectic," in *The Savage Mind* (London: Weidenfeld and Nicolson, 1966), 245–69.

112. *Translator's note:* De Ípola is here referring to the distinction Balibar develops in *Reading Capital* between structuralism's notion of the "combinatory" and the properly Marxist concept of "combination." See translator Ben Brewster's glossary for a concise discussion of this distinction in Althusser, *Reading Capital*, 348.

113. *Translator's note:* De Ípola is paraphrasing Althusser's statement that "we do not find a theory *of the different instances of* the *complex social whole* in Lévi-Strauss"; see Althusser, "On Feuerbach," in *The Humanist Controversy*, 133 [original emphasis].

114. "[T]o think the unity of a determinate ideology unity [. . .] by means of the concept of its *problematic* is to allow the *typical systematic structure* unifying all the elements of the thought to be brought to light, and therefore to discover in this unity a *determinate content* which makes it possible both to conceive the *meaning* of the 'elements' of the ideology concerned—*and to relate this ideology to the problems left or posed to every thinker by the historical period in which he lives*"; Althusser, "On the Young Marx," 67 [original emphasis].

115. A sin of youth. Today Balibar is one of the most brilliant representatives of French philosophy and perhaps the most coherent inheritor of the Althusserian legacy.

116. Balibar, "The Basic Concepts of Historical Materialism," in *Reading Capital*, 253, 264.

117. Balibar, "Basic Concepts of Historical Materialism," 242.

118. Althusser, "Object of *Capital*," 195.

119. Balibar, "Basic Concepts of Historical Materialism," 251.

120. "This *combination*—almost a *combinatory*—that constitutes the actual essence of a determinate mode of production, in which the elements (always the same) are only virtual outside of their linking according to a determinate mode, prompts us, without provisionally examining in more detail the implications (and ambiguities) of this term, to speak here of a *structuralism* that is absolutely strange"; Balibar, *Lire le Capital*, 650n20 [original emphasis]. [*Translator's note:* This is another passage that was eliminated from *Lire le Capital* after the first edition of the text. It does not appear in the existing English translation; however, it can be found in the recent Quadrige Grands Textes edition cited previously in the section titled "Variantes de la première édition."]

121. The philosophy of the last Althusser would use almost identical phrases but would treat them as totally valid.

122. Althusser, "Object of *Capital*," 119, 120.

123. Althusser expressed his reservations toward Lévi-Strauss's thought in a course given in 1966 at the École Normale Supériéure on Marx's *The German Ideology* (or, more precisely, dedicated to presenting and criticizing the thought of Feuerbach). These reservations were analogous to those found in the unpublished note, centering on the supposed absence in Lévi-Strauss of a "theory [. . .] *of* the *complex social whole*" and on a pre-theoretical and aberrant use of the notion of the unconscious; see Althusser, "On Feuerbach," 133, 134 [original emphasis].

124. Jean Pouillon clearly points to this incongruence in Pouillon, "Del lado de Marx," 231–46.

125. Lévi-Strauss, *Mythologiques*, vol. 2, *Du miel aux cendres* (Paris: Plon, 2009), 408.

THREE. **THE TRAPS OF IDEOLOGY**

Epigraph: Étienne Balibar, "The Infinite Contradiction," trans. Jean-Marc Poisson and Jacques Lezra, *Yale French Studies* 88 (1995): 159 [translation modified].

1. Evidence of this can be found in *For Marx* and *Reading Capital*, as well as in his writings on psychoanalysis.

2. *Translator's note*: See Louis Althusser, "Ideology and Ideological State Apparatuses (Notes towards an Investigation)," in *On Ideology* (London: Verso, 2008), 54.

3. *Translator's note*: De Ípola is paraphrasing Lacan's essay on the mirror stage, specifically the phrase "*ligne de fiction* [. . .] *irréductible*," which is worded slightly differently in the English translation: "But the important point is that this form situates the agency known as the ego, prior to its social determination, in a fictional direction that will forever remain irreducible for any single individual or, rather, that will only asymptotically approach the subject's becoming, no matter how successful the dialectical syntheses by which he must resolve, as *I*, his discordance with his own reality"; Jacques Lacan, "The Mirror Stage as Formative of the *I* Function as Revealed in Psychoanalytic Experience," in *Écrits: The First Complete Edition in English*, trans. Bruce Fink (New York: W. W. Norton, 2007), 76 [original emphasis]. For the original French, see Lacan, *Écrits* (Paris: Éditions du Seuil, 1966), 94.

4. *Translator's note*: The English translation of this text can be found here: Althusser, "Freud and Lacan," in *Writings on Psychoanalysis: Freud and Lacan*, trans. Jeffrey Mehlman (New York: Columbia University Press, 1996), 7–32.

5. In any event, although governed by the symbolic, the imaginary operation will determine the point of departure that will define the individual subject (*every* individual subject) as indelibly marked by a kind of constitutive and insurmountable illusion.

6. Jacques-Alain Miller, "Fonction de la formation théorique," *Cahiers Marxistes-Léninistes* 1 (1964): 2 [original emphasis].

7. On this point, see Emilio de Ípola, *Ideología y discurso populista* (Buenos Aires: Folios, 1982), 30.

8. For example, "all science would be superfluous if the form of appearance of things directly coincided with their essence," "there is no royal road to science," etc. [*Translator's note*: The first quotation can be found in Karl Marx, *Capital: A Critique of*

Political Economy, trans. David Fernbach (New York: Penguin, 1991), 3:956. The second quotation can be found in Marx, "Preface to the French Edition," in *Capital: A Critique of Political Economy*, trans. Ben Fowkes (New York: Penguin, 1990), 1:104.]

9. *Translator's note:* For the original publication, see Althusser, "Idéologie et Appareils idéologiques d'État (notes pour une recherche)," *La Pensée: Revue du rationalisme moderne* 151 (1970): 3–38.

10. Althusser, "Marxism and Humanism," in *For Marx*, trans. Ben Brewster (London: Verso, 2005), 233, 234 [original emphasis].

11. In the following pages, I return to an old essay of mine that was previously cited, which presents and evaluates Althusser's theses in "Ideology and Ideological State Apparatuses"; see de Ípola, *Ideología y discurso populista*, 27–73.

12. In his posthumously published writings on psychoanalysis, Althusser utilizes these same terms, adding a pinch of humor to them. He recalls the proverbial saying attributed to soldiers who complain that their counterparts must be recruited from the civilian population—soldiers aren't recruited from soldiers—and affirms that "[f]or ideological discourse, there are no civilians, only soldiers, that is, ideological subjects"; Althusser, "Three Notes on the Theory of Discourses," in *The Humanist Controversy and Other Writings*, trans. G. M. Goshgarian (London: Verso, 2003), 55.

13. Althusser, "Ideology and Ideological State Apparatuses," 48 [original emphasis].

14. Althusser, "Ideology and Ideological State Apparatuses," 54 [original emphasis].

15. *Translator's note:* Although de Ípola attributes this passage to Althusser, Jacques Rancière actually wrote it while referring to and paraphrasing Althusser's discussion of ideology and "social cohesion" in the following text: Althusser, "Theory, Theoretical Practice and Theoretical Formation: Ideology and Ideological Struggle," in *Philosophy and the Spontaneous Philosophy of the Scientists*, ed. Gregory Elliott (London: Verso, 2011), 43–67. For the original passage, see Jacques Rancière, "On the Theory of Ideology: Althusser's Politics," in *Althusser's Lesson*, trans. Emiliano Battista (New York: Continuum, 2011), 130.

16. See Althusser, "Sur Brecht et Marx (1968)," in *Écrits philosophiques et politiques* (Paris: Stock/IMEC, 1997), 2:541–58.

17. Althusser, "Ideology and Ideological State Apparatuses," 58.

18. Althusser, "Ideology and Ideological State Apparatuses," 59, 60.

19. *Translator's note:* As mentioned in the previous chapter, the translation of this text is not included in the English edition of *Writings on Psychoanalysis* but rather in an anthology entitled *The Humanist Controversy and Other Writings*.

20. Althusser, "Three Notes on the Theory of Discourses," 51, 52 [original emphasis].

21. Althusser, "Three Notes on the Theory of Discourses," 52 [original emphasis].

22. In a much later text that I will discuss further on, which compiles Fernanda Navarro's interviews with Althusser, the latter accords a more decorous philosophical status to the notion of the individual and, perhaps unknowingly, opens a path capable of filling in the gap that affects the essay on Ideological State Apparatuses. Althusser affirms that "Wittgenstein says it superbly in the *Tractatus: Die Welt ist alles, was der Fall ist*, a superb sentence that is, however, hard to translate. We might try to render it

as follows: 'the world is everything that happens'; or, more literally, 'the world is everything that befalls us' [*tombe dessus*]. There exists yet another translation, which has been proposed by Russell's school: 'the world is everything that is *the case*' [the world is what the case is]. This superb sentence *says everything*, for, in this world, there exists nothing but cases, situations, things that befall us without warning. The thesis that there exist only cases—that is to say, singular individuals wholly distinct from one another—is the basic thesis of nominalism," or what Althusser will go on to characterize as materialism; Althusser, "Philosophy and Marxism," in *Philosophy of the Encounter: Later Writings, 1978–1987*, trans. G. M. Goshgarian (London: Verso, 2006), 265 [original emphasis]. It is nevertheless clear that the term *individual* in this passage is given a much broader sense than in the essay on Ideological State Apparatuses and perhaps cannot be compared.

23. Althusser, "Ideology and Ideological State Apparatuses," 35 [de Ípola's emphasis].

24. Althusser, "Ideology and Ideological State Apparatuses," 58 [original emphasis].

25. Some are proposed only as tendential laws, which permits Althusser (who will appropriate the concept of tendential law, interpreting it in his own way and highlighting its importance) to clarify the categorical character of some of his longtime theoretical positions, as well as—and this is of particular interest—to orient his thought toward new philosophical positions. On this point, see Althusser, "Philosophy and Marxism," 264.

26. In his book *Montesquieu, la politique et l'histoire* (Paris: Presses Universitaires de France, 1959), Althusser shows that the author of *L'esprit de lois* sometimes confused the two concepts of law.

27. *Translator's note:* See, for example, Althusser, "The Object of *Capital*," in *Reading Capital*, trans. Ben Brewster (London: Verso, 2009), 190.

28. Althusser, "Is It Simple to Be a Marxist in Philosophy?," in *Philosophy and the Spontaneous Philosophy of the Scientists*, ed. Gregory Elliott (London: Verso, 2011), 236, 237 [original emphasis].

29. In this sense, Ernesto Laclau shows himself once again to be an excellent reader of Althusser. In his essay "The Death and Resurrection of the Theory of Ideology," Laclau takes up Althusser's statement that "ideology is eternal," leaving aside everything that, in Althusser's own texts, seems to put limits on this statement's validity. He acutely captures the irrelevance of those texts for delimiting the pertinence of the strong statement; see Laclau, "The Death and Resurrection of the Theory of Ideology," *MLN* 112, no. 3 (April 1997): 297–321.

30. Althusser, "Philosophy and Marxism," 280–85 [original italics, de Ípola's underlining, format modified].

31. "[T]he subject needs—in order to be constituted—to identify with an 'other' who is his peer [*semblable*]; he recognizes himself as existing through the existence of the other and through his identification with him. It would seem that ideology here functions as the image of the 'other,' an image that has been brought into conformity, socially and familially [*conformé socialement et familialement*], with what the family/society expects of every individual who comes into the world, beginning in infancy. The child assumes this prefigured image as the only possible way he can exist as a

social subject. This is what confers his individuality upon him. The individual/subject demands that he be recognized as an individuality and a unity, as a 'someone.' But the 'one' (the subject) must be recognized by the 'other.' It seems that one has a psychosocial need to identify with the 'other' in order to recognize oneself as existing"; Althusser, "Philosophy and Marxism," 284. These statements have been said before, but this time they are said in a simpler yet more precise way.

32. Althusser referred to the interviews and the project Navarro had in mind as "a short book (it would run to some 80 pages)"; Althusser, "Correspondence about 'Philosophy and Marxism,'" in *Philosophy of the Encounter*, 238, 239.

33. Althusser, "Philosophy and Marxism," 261, 262.

34. Althusser, "Philosophy and Marxism," 280. The dialectic is likewise called into question. In a letter to Navarro, Althusser writes: "You say nothing about the dialectic; and, all things considered, I think you are right in this, because long explanations are needed to explain that the dialectic (not only in the form given it by Engels: the science of the laws of motion of matter) is *more than dubious; indeed, it is harmful*, that is, always more or less teleological. If I have the strength, I'll try to show this some day"; Althusser, "Correspondence about 'Philosophy and Marxism,'" 242.

35. Althusser, "Philosophy and Marxism," 266.

36. Althusser, "Philosophy and Marxism," 271.

37. Althusser, "Correspondence about 'Philosophy and Marxism,'" 223.

38. Correct [*justa*] in the sense of "being well adjusted [*justeza*]" (referring to the adequate means for an end) and not in the sense of "justice [*justicia*]"; Althusser, "Philosophy and Marxism," 288. [*Translator's note:* De Ípola exchanges Althusser's French term *juste* for the Spanish word *justa*, which preserves the ambiguity of the original French term better than the English translation of *juste* as "correct." While remaining consistent with the existing English translation, I have included the Spanish in brackets to recover the original ambiguity.]

39. This is a kind of preparatory statement that foreshadows a new characterization of materialism.

40. Althusser, "Philosophy and Marxism," 268.

41. Althusser, "Philosophy and Marxism," 286.

42. Althusser, "Philosophy and Marxism," 257.

43. Althusser, "Philosophy and Marxism," 259.

FOUR. **THE SOLITARY HOUR**

Epigraph: Louis Althusser, "Is It Simple to Be a Marxist in Philosophy?," in *Philosophy and the Spontaneous Philosophy of Scientists*, ed. Gregory Elliott (London: Verso, 2011), 209 [original emphasis].

1. "We are thereby obliged to renounce every teleology of reason, and to conceive the historical relation between a result and its condition of existence as a relation of production, and not of expression, and therefore as what, in a phrase that clashes with the classical system of categories and demands the *replacement* of those categories

themselves, we can call the *necessity of its contingency*"; Althusser, "From *Capital* to Marx's Philosophy," in *Reading Capital*, by Louis Althusser and Étienne Balibar, trans. Ben Brewster (London: Verso, 2009), 48 [original emphasis].

2. For example, in a letter written to Franca Madonia on September 26, 1966, Althusser uses the noun *prise* twice in reference to the theory of the ideological, playing perhaps with the two meanings of the word: *prise* in the sense of taking form and also in the sense of *donner prise* or *to facilitate* [*facilitar*], *to clear the path* [*franquear el camino*]. See Althusser, *Lettres à Franca (1961–1973)*, ed. François Matheron and Yann Moulier Boutang (Paris: Stock/IMEC, 1998), 729. [*Translator's note:* In Spanish translations of Althusser's work, the notion of *prise* typically appears as some variation of the phrase *tomar consistencia* or of the verb *prender*, which I have rendered as "takes form" and "takes," respectively. English translations exhibit other variations as well, including "crystallization," "takes hold," and "the take," depending on the context. These variations can be found throughout Althusser's later writings.]

3. Althusser repeatedly used the term *interstices* to describe aspects of his philosophical endeavor; see, for example, Althusser, "Correspondence about 'Philosophy and Marxism,'" and "Philosophy and Marxism," in *Philosophy of the Encounter: Later Writings, 1978–1987*, trans. G. M. Goshgarian (London: Verso, 2006), 244, 245, 271.

4. In his last writings, the names of Machiavelli and Spinoza were mentioned with the same frequency as those of Marx and Engels, if not more often. Something similar occurred with Antonio Gramsci's name. Althusser's harsh objections directed toward Gramsci in *For Marx* and *Reading Capital* gave way to a gradual convergence with the author of the *Quaderni*.

5. If the ups and downs of history completely alter or disrupt a structure—something that is always possible—this can only be a product of the intervention of "the irreducible contingency without which we could not even conceive of necessity." But this irreducible contingency cannot, for Lévi-Strauss, be the object of science; see Claude Lévi-Strauss, *Mythologiques*, vol. 2, *Du miel aux cendres* (Paris: Plon, 2009), 408; see also Lévi-Strauss, "History and Dialectic," in *The Savage Mind* (London: Weidenfeld and Nicolson, 1966), 245–69.

6. "We can only discover fundamental and essential properties when considering objects that have been simplified considerably by distance. What happens in ethnology is a bit like what happens in astronomy. It is thanks to that remoteness of the celestial bodies that we are condemned to discovering only their fundamental properties, which are astronomy's object of study. If encountering celestial bodies entailed considerably less distance, a celestial geology would exist, perhaps a celestial botany or celestial zoology, but, as a science, there would be no astronomy"; Lévi-Strauss, in "Estructura vs. Historia: Reportaje a Levi Strauss," by Elise Veron and Gilles Lapougue, *Zona Erógena* 4 (1990): 4.

7. *Translator's note:* See Althusser, "Marx dans ses limites (1978)," in *Écrits philosophiques et politiques*, ed. François Matheron (Paris: Stock/IMEC, 1994), 1:357–524. The English translation can be found here: Althusser, "Marx in His Limits," in *Philosophy of the Encounter*, 7–162.

8. Among the disastrous consequences of Marxism-Leninism's failures, Althusser

briefly mentions the failure of the Euro-communist experience, but he does not pause to consider the reasons for this failure.

9. Miguel Vatter, "Althusser and Machiavelli: Politics after the Critique of Marx," *Multitudes: Revue politique, artistique, philosophique* 13 (2013): http://www.multitudes.net/Althusser-and-Machiavelli-Politics/.

10. Vatter, "Althusser and Machiavelli: Politics after the Critique of Marx."

11. *Translator's note:* See Althusser, "Reply to John Lewis," in *On Ideology* (London: Verso, 2008), 61–139.

12. Consider, for example, this passage: "The state, ideology, the Party, the theoretical and political persona in the workers' movement: these are all among Marx's 'absolute limits,' which we have to assess if we are to think seriously about them"; Althusser, "Marx in His Limits," 53, 54.

13. For example, Althusser defends the arbitrary and illegal measures adopted by Lenin in 1918, writing, "I do not say this in order to criticize the statesman Lenin for dissolving the Constituent Assembly without due process of law, for outlawing and prosecuting the Social Revolutionaries, or for banning all political parties except the Bolshevik Party, and so on. Lenin suspended the constitution and governed by decree rather than by voted laws, but he had serious reasons for doing so in a period in which the power of the soviets was under attack from foreign powers that were, inside the borders of the USSR itself, aiding and abetting the forces of the far Right, who had cast all restraint to the winds and were perpetrating unspeakable barbarities"; Althusser, "Marx in His Limits," 87.

14. Althusser, "Le marxisme comme théorie 'finie,'" in *Solitude de Machiavel et autres textes*, ed. Yves Sintomer (Paris: Presses Universitaires de France, 1998), 286. [*Translator's note:* For the Italian version, see Althusser, "Il marxismo come teoria 'finita,'" in *Discutere lo Stato: Posizioni a confronto su una tesi di Louis Althusser* (Bari: De Donato, 1978), 7–21.]

15. Montaigne, as cited in Oscar Terán, *De utopias, catástrofes y esperanzas: Un camino intelectual* (Buenos Aires: Siglo XXI, 2006), 60.

16. Even though already at this point the topic of instances generated for Althusser more doubts than certainties.

17. See Althusser, *The Future Lasts Forever: A Memoir*, trans. Richard Veasey (New York: New Press, 1993), 148.

18. *Translator's note: Machiavelli and Us* and "Machiavelli's Solitude" can both be found in English translation in the following text: Althusser, *Machiavelli and Us*, trans. Gregory Elliott (London: Verso, 2000). To my knowledge, the handwritten text "Machiavel, philosophe" has not yet been published, although it is mentioned in François Matheron's editorial note to *Machiavelli and Us*, viii. The text is held here: Althusser, "Machiavel, philosophe" (Saint-Germain-la-Blanche-Herbe: Fonds Louis Althusser, IMEC), IME, CALT2, A29–06.07. See, finally, Althusser, *Politique et Histoire, de Machiavel à Marx; Cours à l'École normale supérieure, 1955–1972*, ed. François Matheron (Paris: Éditions du Seuil, 2006).

19. *Translator's note:* See Althusser, "Machiavelli's Solitude," trans. Ben Brewster, *Economy and Society* 17, no. 4 (1988): 468–79.

20. *Translator's note:* See Althusser, "Solitude de Machiavel," *Futur antérieur* 1 (spring 1990): 26–40.

21. *Translator's note:* See Althusser, "The Underground Current of the Materialism of the Encounter," in *Philosophy of the Encounter*, 163–207.

22. The titles of these writings included "On Analysis," "On History," "Portrait of the Materialist Philosophy," and "Machiavelli, Philosopher." [*Translator's note:* See Althusser, "Portrait of the Materialist Philosopher," *Philosophy of the Encounter*, 290, 291. To my knowledge, the other texts listed have not yet been published. They are held here: Althusser, "Sur l'analyse" (Saint-Germain-la-Blanche-Herbe, France: Fonds Louis Althusser, IMEC), ALT2, A29–06.11; Althusser, "Sur l'histoire" (Saint-Germain-la-Blanche-Herbe, France: Fonds Louis Althusser, IMEC), ALT2, A29–06.06; Althusser, "Machiavel, philosophe," (Saint-Germain-la-Blanche-Herbe, France: Fonds Louis Althusser, IMEC), ALT2, A29–06.07.]

23. Except for a subsection in the following text: Althusser, "Elements of Self-Criticism," in *Essays in Self-Criticism*, trans. Grahame Lock (London: NLB, 1976), 132–41.

24. *Translator's note:* See Benedict de Spinoza, "The *Ethics*," in *A Spinoza Reader*, ed. Edwin Curley (Princeton, NJ: Princeton University Press, 1994), 142.

25. See Althusser, "On Theoretical Work: Difficulties and Resources," in *Philosophy and the Spontaneous Philosophy of the Scientists*, ed. Gregory Elliott (London: Verso, 2011), 43–67.

26. "*Le vide d'une distance prise* [*the void of a distance taken*]"; Althusser, *Lénine et la philosophie* (Paris: François Maspero, 1969), 51. [*Translator's note:* The English version of this passage renders *vide* as "emptiness" rather than "void," which works well in this passage but makes it difficult for the reader to appreciate how the passage resonates with later writings where *vide* is frequently translated as "void"; see Althusser, "Lenin and Philosophy," in *Lenin and Philosophy and Other Essays*, trans. Ben Brewster (New York: Monthly Review Press, 2001), 38.]

27. Althusser does not neglect to mention that this point is luminously clarified in Claude Lefort's book *Machiavelli in the Making*, trans. Michael B. Smith (Evanston, IL: Northwestern University Press, 2012).

28. This presentation was given in 1978 and later published in German in an anthology of Althusser's writings: Althusser, "Die Einsamkeit Machiavellis," in *Schriften*, Band 2, *Machiavelli, Montesquieu, Rousseau-Zur politischen Philosophie der Neuzeit* (Berlin: Argument, 1987), 2–350. It remained unavailable in French until 1990.

29. Althusser, "Machiavelli's Solitude," 117 [original emphasis].

30. Althusser, "Machiavelli's Solitude," 121 [original emphasis].

31. *Translator's note:* In the English translation of Althusser's *Machiavelli and Us*, Machiavelli's thesis appears with some variation as the following: "It is necessary to be *alone* to found a new republic or completely reform it"; see Althusser, *Machiavelli and Us*, 64 [original emphasis].

32. *Translator's note:* See Karl Marx, *Capital: A Critique of Political Economy*, trans. Ben Fowkes (New York: Penguin, 1990), 1:873–942.

33. Althusser, "Machiavelli's Solitude," 125.

34. It is known that Marx's doctoral dissertation addressed the following subject: "Difference between the Democritean and Epicurean Philosophy of Nature." It is also worth referring to Marx's early, posthumously collected writings on Epicurean, Skeptic, and Stoic philosophy; see Marx and Frederick Engels, *Karl Marx and Frederick Engels Collected Works*, vol. 1, *Marx: 1835–1843* (New York: International Publishers, 1975).

35. *Translator's note:* This is Lucretius as paraphrased in Ilya Prigogine and Isabelle Stengears, *Order Out of Chaos* (New York: Bantam, 1984), 141.

36. Althusser, "Philosophy and Marxism," 260.

37. *Translator's note:* In the previous two paragraphs, de Ípola is closely paraphrasing Althusser, "The Underground Current of the Materialism of the Encounter," 169, 170.

38. Perhaps it will clarify things to suggest that it is like the unforeseen invasion of a realm (call it "alpha") by something that comes from another, heterogeneous realm (call it "beta"). An actual event in Argentina that took place half a century ago could perhaps serve as an illustration of this point. I am referring to General Eduardo Ávalos's ardent refusal, as the leader of the army, to repress the workers marching toward the Plaza de Mayo on October 17, 1945. Both the political scientist Robert Potash and the sociologist Juan Carlos Torre have referred to this event. Ávalos refuses to repress the workers not because of political reasons stemming from the sociohistorical register but rather because of the disturbing memory of a repression in which he participated just two years prior. Something from a different, psychological realm, something, as they say colloquially, coming from "another galaxy," intrudes upon and invades the sociohistorical plane via rough terrain not yet explored. And with some luck, it changes everything: everything changes [*cambia todo: el todo cambia*]. For more on this point, see Emilio de Ípola, "El hecho peronista," in *La Argentina en el siglo XX*, ed. Carlos Altamirano (Buenos Aires: Ariel, 1999), 325–32.

39. *Translator's note:* See Althusser, "Philosophy and Marxism," 265.

40. Althusser is close to Max Weber on this point, perhaps without realizing it.

41. It would not be improper to surmise that this was a very sad and foolish swerve.

42. *Translator's note:* See Georg Lúkacs, *History and Class Consciousness: Studies in Marxist Dialectics* (Cambridge, MA: MIT Press, 1999).

43. Marx, "The Eighteenth Brumaire of Louis Bonaparte," in *Karl Marx and Frederick Engels Collected Works*, vol. 11, *Marx and Engels: 1851–1853* (New York: International Publishers, 1979), 103.

44. See, for example, Althusser, "Reply to John Lewis," in *On Ideology* (London: Verso, 2008), 80, 81. Althusser refers back to the *Communist Manifesto* on this point.

45. Althusser, "Reply to John Lewis," 79 [original emphasis].

46. Althusser, "Reply to John Lewis," 79, 80 [original emphasis].

47. Althusser, "Reply to John Lewis," 82 [original emphasis]. As this argument develops, Althusser insists on the primacy of relations over entities, in this case of the class struggle over classes. It is one of his preferred formulations of the period.

48. Althusser, "Reply to John Lewis," 83. Althusser adds in a footnote, "I put this idea forward in a study called 'Marx and Lenin before Hegel' (February 1968), pub-

lished with *Lenin and Philosophy*, Maspero, Paris, 1972. For more details, see below the *Remark on the Category: 'Process without a Subject or Goal(s)'*"; Althusser, "Reply to John Lewis," 83. [*Translator's note:* The English translation of the first part of this study can be found here: Althusser, "Marx's Relation to Hegel," in *Politics and History: Montesquieu, Rousseau, Marx*, trans. Ben Brewster (London: Verso, 2007), 161–86. The second part can be found here: Althusser, "Lenin before Hegel," in *Lenin and Philosophy and Other Essays*, 71–83. For the original French, see Althusser, *Lénine et la philosophie suivi de Marx et Lénine devant Hegel* (Paris: François Maspero, 1972).]

49. Alain Badiou, *Metapolitics*, trans. Jason Barker (London: Verso, 2012), 65.

50. *Translator's note:* As previously mentioned, de Ípola is referring to a talk that Badiou gave in Vienna in 1996 that would later be included in Badiou's book *Metapolitics*.

51. Badiou, *Metapolitics*, 61.

52. Badiou, *Metapolitics*, 62.

53. For Badiou, moreover, an *object* is also lacking, since politics is not a science.

54. Badiou, *Metapolitics*, 64 [original emphasis].

55. Badiou, *Metapolitics*, 66.

56. As is to be expected, Marxism and today's Althusserianism—or at least some of its representatives—will immediately build a wide range of terminological barricades to put obstacles in the way of this approach. I recognize that terminology can be important when it refers back to real theoretical problems but not when it is brandished as a weapon to impede solving a problem.

57. Daniel Cefaï and Joseph Issac, *L'héritage du pragmatism: Conflits d'urbanité et épreuves de civisme* (La Tour-d'Aigues, France: Éditions de l'Aube, 2002), 52.

58. Emilio de Ípola, "Un recorrido de la acción colectiva: El conflicto en la Facultad de Ciencias Sociales," in *El Etorno retorno: Acción y sistema en la teoría social contemporánea*, ed. Emilio de Ípola (Buenos Aires: Biblos, 2004), 187.

59. Francisco Naishtat, *Ética política de la acción colectiva* (La Plata, Argentina: Universidad Nacional de la Plata, 2000), 6.

60. *Translator's note:* See Jean-Paul Sartre, *Critique of Dialectical Reason*, vol. 1, trans. Alan Sheridan-Smith (London: Verso, 2004).

61. I have emphasized this point in chapter 3 of the following work: de Ípola, "Acción, Decisión, Sujeto," in *Metáforas de la política* (Rosario, Argentina: Homo Sapiens, 2001), 67–84.

62. Regarding this point, my current opinion differs slightly from what I argued in the foreword to Naishtat's book; see Francisco Naishtat, *Problemas filosóficos en la acción individual y colectiva: Una perspectiva pragmática* (Buenos Aires: Prometeo, 2005), 17. This change of opinion does not, of course, imply a critique of Naishtat's rigorous work. I would add that if the latter employs the term *subject*, he gives it an entirely novel meaning, completely foreign from its traditional sense.

63. See Claudia Hilb, ed., *El resplandor de lo público: En torno a Hannah Arendt* (Caracas: Nueva Sociedad, 1994).

CONCLUSION

Epigraph: Jacques Derrida, "Text Read at Louis Althusser's Funeral," in *The Work of Mourning*, ed. Pascale-Anne Brault and Michael Naas (Chicago: University of Chicago Press, 2001), 116.

1. This is the case at least in his earliest writings, in which transgressive formulations seemed to slip past his reasoning as his pen moved across the page, almost as if Althusser did not notice how these formulations introduced new meanings, foreign to his explicit argument.

2. As well as French Marxism. On this point, see the beautiful and relevant work of Étienne Balibar, "The Non-Contemporaneity of Althusser," in *The Althusserian Legacy*, ed. E. Ann Kaplan and Michael Sprinker (London: Verso, 1993), 1–16.

3. *Translator's note:* Throughout this book, de Ípola uses religious imagery and Christian terminology to describe Althusserianism and its followers. Here, for example, he alludes to the division of the Christian church into the Church Militant (Christians on Earth), the Church Triumphant (Christians in Heaven), and the Church Penitent or the Church Suffering (Christians in Purgatory).

4. In my opinion, Jacques Rancière is one of today's greatest exponents of French philosophical and political thought. He is also the thinker with whom I feel most closely aligned philosophically. That said, the critiques to which I refer—quite celebrated at the time by Althusser's adversaries—when revisited today, with thirty years of distance, show to what degree Rancière was trying—unsuccessfully—to cut the umbilical cord that connected him to his mentor, which leads me to view him, as much as he may not like to hear it, as Althusser's heir. An unruly and exceedingly gifted heir, but an heir all the same. His text "Sobre la teoría de la ideología," first published in Spanish, as well as his book *La leçon d'Althusser*, share with Althusser his correct answers and on occasion even perfect his mistakes. Accordingly, the discrepancies that he expressed with such vehemence in the text published in Argentina appear today as easy to integrate into the Althusserian problematic. With a touch of perfidy, I would add that, in the aforementioned book, Rancière points out, also with perfidy, that Althusser's party, the French Communist Party, grants him the freedom to "cite Mao in prefaces for Latin American publications." Yet Rancière, like a good disciple, does the very same thing: his first essay that is critical of Althusser was published in early 1970 in an Argentine publication. French audiences were only able to read that text in their mother tongue in 1974, as an appendix to Rancière's book. As for *La leçon d'Althusser*, the disarming objection that Rancière directs at Althusser applies to his book, as well. *The site of its enunciation refutes point for point the enunciated*: from the deplorable "authority" of an imaginary Maoism and an imaginary China, tailor-made to gratify the illusions of a Parisian intellectual, no criticism can be taken seriously. On this point, see Rancière, "Sobre la teoría de la ideología (La política de Athusser)," in *Lectura de Althusser*, ed. Saúl Karsz (Buenos Aires: Editorial Galerna, 1970), 319–57; see also Rancière, *La leçon d'Althusser* (Paris: Gallimard, 1974). [*Translator's note:* Both texts can be found in English translation here: Rancière, *Althusser's Lesson*, trans. Emiliano Battista (New York: Continuum, 2011).]

5. Largely due to his no less prolonged periods of depression and hospitalization in psychiatric institutions.

6. *Translator's note:* See Marta Harnecker, *Los conceptos elementales del materialismo histórico* (Buenos Aires: Siglo XXI, 1974).

7. I have sought to demonstrate in another text that those abrupt changes are typical of the functioning and transformation of ideologies; see chapter 3 of de Ípola, *Las cosas del creer: Creencia, lazo social y comunidad política* (Buenos Aires: Ariel, 1987).

8. Over time this repudiation was gradually watered down to the point of disappearing. In those years, we had other disappointments to face.

9. *Translator's note:* De Ípola is referring to the Abbaye d'Ardenne at *L'Institut Mémoires de l'édition contemporaine* (IMEC) in Saint-Germain-la-Blanche-Herbe, France where Althusser's papers are currently held.

10. A clarification should be included here: efforts to make the discussion clear and, I must admit, certain excessively Cartesian tics in my writing may have on occasion given the reader the sensation that Althusser's "esoteric" philosophy is to be conceived as altogether separate and autonomous from his "exoteric" philosophy, despite my reiterated cautioning against this reading. In any event, I believe that I have emphasized the necessity of not making that separation in the development of my argument and have illustrated, moreover, modes of relating the "esoteric" and the "exoteric." My initial intuition, which, as I indicated in the previous paragraph, perceived a cumbersome knot of the old and the new, was in the end not so entirely incorrect.

11. In this case, it is my opinion that Althusser's influence was minor and more diffuse than he himself had believed. Althusser's belief in part stemmed from the success of Marta Harnecker's manual, *Los conceptos elementales del materialismo histórico*. In reality, what enjoyed great prestige in Latin America, especially since the mid-1960s, was a confused mix of the Régis Debray of *Revolución en la revolución* and some of Althusser's texts. Althusser maintained a close friendship with Debray. Though distressed by the arrest and detention of his friend in Bolivia, Althusser nonetheless never concealed the profound differences between them. [*Translator's note:* Along with the previously cited text by Harnecker, see Debray, *Revolution in the Revolution? Armed Struggle and Political Struggle in Latin America*, trans. Bobbye Ortiz (New York: Grove Press, 1967).]

12. Incidentally, it is worth calling attention to the fact that an appreciable number of today's most prestigious French philosophers had been disciples of Althusser and of Jacques Derrida. It does not surprise me that Derrida made explicit his friendship with Althusser and the value that he saw in Althusser, even confessing, as if in passing, to his secret complicity with Althusser's work; see Derrida and Élisabeth Roudinesco, *De quoi demain . . . dialogue* (Paris: Flammarion, 2001), 169–73. I will return to this point in what follows.

13. In effect, Bidet's work is a sort of excessive and commandeering repetition of the enterprise of reinventing historical materialism that Althusser initiated. It could be said in Bidet's defense that the hasty support that Althusser extended to him in the 1980s transformed him from a usurping heir into a sort of official, but hardly credible,

dauphin, something akin to the Last Emperor of China. In addition to directing the *Actuel Marx Confrontation* collection (Presses Universitaires de France), Bidet is the author or coauthor of a great number of books, essays, and communiqués, but the mere capacity to work, combined with dogmatism veiled by only apparent acts of renewal, is no substitute for talent.

14. Derrida, "Text Read at Louis Althusser's Funeral," 149.

BIBLIOGRAPHY

Althusser, Louis. "Avertissement aux lecteurs du Livre I du 'Capital.'" In *Le Capital: Livre 1*, by Karl Marx, 5–30. Paris: Garnier-Flammarion, 1969. Translated as "Preface to *Capital* Volume 1." In *Lenin and Philosophy and Other Essays*, 45–70.
———. "Comment lire 'Le Capital?'" *L'Humanité* (March 21, 1969). Translated as "How to Read Marx's 'Capital.'" *Marxism Today* (1969): 302–5.
———. "Contradiction and Overdetermination." In *For Marx*, 87–128.
———. "Correspondence about 'Philosophy and Marxism.'" In *Philosophy of the Encounter: Later Writings, 1978–1987*, 208–50.
———. "Correspondence with Jacques Lacan." In *Writings on Psychoanalysis: Freud and Lacan*, 145–74.
———. "Du côté de la philosophie (cinquième Cours de philosophie pour scientifiques) (1967)." In *Écrits philosophiques et politiques*, 2:255–98.
———. *Écrits philosophiques et politiques*. Vol. 1. Edited by François Matheron. Paris: Stock/IMEC, 1994.
———. *Écrits philosophiques et politiques*. Vol. 2. Edited by François Matheron. Paris: Stock/IMEC, 1995.
———. *Écrits sur la psychanalyse*. Edited by Olivier Corpet and François Matheron. Paris: Stock/IMEC, 1993. Translated by Jeffrey Mehlman as *Writings on Psychoanalysis: Freud and Lacan*. New York: Columbia University Press, 1996.
———. "Elements of Self-Criticism." In *Essays in Self-Criticism*, translated by Grahame Lock, 132–41. London: NLB, 1976.
———. "Freud and Lacan." In *Writings on Psychoanalysis: Freud and Lacan*, 7–32.
———. "From *Capital* to Marx's Philosophy." In *Reading Capital*, 11–76.
———. *The Humanist Controversy*. Translated by G. M. Goshgarian. London: Verso, 2003.

———. "Idéologie et Appareils idéologiques d'État (notes pour une recherche)." *La Pensée: Revue du rationalisme moderne* 151 (1970): 3–38. Translated as "Ideology and Ideological State Apparatuses (Notes towards an Investigation)." In *On Ideology*, 1–60.

———. "Il marxismo como teoria 'finita.'" In *Discutere lo Stato: Posizioni a confronto su una tesi di Louis Althusser*, 7–21. Bari: De Donato, 1978. Published in French as "Le marxisme comme théorie 'finie.'" In *Solitude de Machiavel et autres textes*, edited by Yves Sintomer, 281–94. Paris: Presses Universitaires de France, 1998.

———. "Is It Simple to Be a Marxist in Philosophy?" In *Philosophy and the Spontaneous Philosophy of the Scientists*, 203–40.

———. *L'avenir dure longtemps, suivi de Les Faits. Autobiographies*. Edited by Olivier Corpet and Yann Moulier Boutang. Paris: Stock/IMEC, 1992. Translated by Richard Veasey as *The Future Lasts Forever: A Memoir*. New York: New Press, 1993.

———. "Lenin before Hegel." In *Lenin and Philosophy and Other Essays*, 71–83.

———. *Lénine et la philosophie*. Paris: François Maspero, 1969. Translated by Ben Brewster as *Lenin and Philosophy and Other Essays*. New York: Monthly Review Press, 2001.

———. *Lénine et la philosophie suivi de Marx et Lénine devant Hegel*. Paris: François Maspero, 1972.

———. "Letter to Jean Lacroix (1949–1950)." In *The Spectre of Hegel: Early Writings*, translated by G. M. Goshgarian, 207–44. London: Verso, 2014.

———. *Lettres à Franca (1961–1973)*. Edited by François Matheron and Yann Moulier Boutang. Paris: Stock/IMEC, 1998.

———. "Machiavel et nous (1972–1986)." In *Écrits philosophiques et politiques*, 2:39–168.

———. "Machiavel, philosophe." Unpublished text. Saint-Germain-la-Blanche-Herbe: Fonds Louis Althusser, IMEC, ALT2, A29-06.07.

———. *Machiavelli and Us*. Translated by Gregory Elliott. Edited by François Matheron. London: Verso, 1999.

———. "Marx dans ses limites (1978)." In *Écrits philosophiques et politiques*, 1:357–524. Translated as "Marx in His Limits." In *Philosophy of the Encounter: Later Writings, 1978–1987*, 7–162.

———. "Marxism and Humanism." In *For Marx*, 219–48.

———. "Marx's Relation to Hegel." In *Politics and History: Montesquieu, Rousseau, Marx*, 161–86.

———. *Montesquieu, la politique et l'histoire*. Paris: Presses Universitaires de France, 1959.

———. "The Object of *Capital*." In *Reading Capital*, 77–222.

———. "On Feuerbach." In *The Humanist Controversy and Other Writings*, 85–154.

———. *On Ideology*. London: Verso, 2008.

———. "On the Materialist Dialectic." In *For Marx*, 161–218.

———. "On the Young Marx." In *For Marx*, 49–86.

———. "On Theoretical Work: Difficulties and Resources." In *Philosophy and the Spontaneous Philosophy of the Scientists*, 43–67.

———. "Philosophy and Marxism." In *Philosophy of the Encounter: Later Writings, 1978–1987*, 251–89.

———. *Philosophy and the Spontaneous Philosophy of the Scientists*. Edited by Gregory Elliott. London: Verso, 2011.

———. *Philosophy of the Encounter: Later Writings, 1978–1987*. Translated by G. M. Goshgarian. London: Verso, 2006.

———. *Politics and History: Montesquieu, Rousseau, Marx*. Translated by Ben Brewster. London: Verso, 2007.

———. *Politique et Histoire, de Machiavel à Marx; Cours à l'École normale supérieure, 1955–1972*. Edited by François Matheron. Paris: Éditions du Seuil, 2006.

———. "Portrait of the Materialist Philosopher." In *Philosophy of the Encounter: Later Writings, 1978–1987*, 290–92.

———. *Positions*. Paris: Éditions sociales, 1976.

———. *Pour Marx*. Paris: La Découverte, 2005. Translated by Ben Brewster as *For Marx*. London: Verso, 2005.

———. Preface to *Los conceptos elementales del materialismo histórico*, by Marta Harnecker, 2nd ed., xi–xvi. Buenos Aires: Siglo XXI, 1971. Reprinted in French as "Marxisme et lutte de classe." In *Positions*, 71–78. Translated by Patrick Lyons as "Marxism-Leninism and the Class Struggle." *Theoretical Review* 3 (1978): 17–20.

———. "Reply to John Lewis." In *On Ideology*, 61–139.

———. "Solitude de Machiavel." *Futur antérieur* 1 (spring 1990): 26–40. Translated by Ben Brewster as "Machiavelli's Solitude." *Economy and Society* 17, no. 4 (November 1988): 468–79. Reprinted in *Machiavelli and Us*, 115–30. Published in German as "Die Einsamkeit Machiavellis." In *Schriften, Band 2, Machiavelli, Montesquieu, Rousseau-Zur politischen Philosophie der Neuzeit*, 11–29. Berlin: Argument, 1987.

———. "Sur Brecht et Marx (1968)." In *Écrits philosophiques et politiques*, 2:541–58.

———. "Sur l'analyse." Unpublished text. Saint-Germain-la-Blanche-Herbe, France: Fonds Louis Althusser, IMEC, ALT2, A29–06.11.

———. "Sur la pensée marxiste." *Futur antérieur: Sur Althusser: Passages* (1993): 11–29. Translated by Asad Haider and Salar Mohandesi as "On Marxist Thought." *Viewpoint Magazine*, September 12, 2012. https://viewpointmag.com/2012/09/12/on-marxist-thought/.

———. "Sur le jeune Marx (Questions de théorie)." *La Pensée: Revue du rationalisme moderne* 96 (1961): 3–26.

———. "Sur l'histoire." Unpublished text. Fonds Louis Althusser, Saint-Germain-la-Blanche-Herbe, France: IMEC, ALT2, A29–06.06.

———. *Sur la reproduction*. Paris: Presses Universitaires de France, 2011.

———. "Theory, Theoretical Practice and Theoretical Formation: Ideology and Ideological Struggle." In *Philosophy and the Spontaneous Philosophy of the Scientists*, 1–42.

———. "Trois notes sur la théorie des discours, 1966." In *Écrits sur la psychanalyse*, 111–70. Translated as "Three Notes on the Theory of Discourses." In *The Humanist Controversy and Other Writings*, 33–84.

———. "The Underground Current of the Materialism of the Encounter." In *Philosophy of the Encounter: Later Writings, 1978–1987*, 163–207.

Althusser, Louis, Étienne Balibar, Roger Establet, Pierre Macherey, and Jacques Rancière. *Lire le Capital*. Paris: Presses Universitaires de France, 2008.

Althusser, Louis, and Étienne Balibar. *Reading Capital*. Translated by Ben Brewster. London: Verso, 2009.

Badiou, Alain. "¿Cómo pensar la empresa de Louis Althusser?" *Acontecimiento: Revista para pensar la política* 12 (1996): 11–20.

———. "Mark and Lack: On Zero." In *Concept and Form*. Vol. 1, *Key Texts from the "Cahiers pour l'Analyse*," 159–85.

———. *Metapolitics*. Translated by Jason Barker. London: Verso, 2006.

———. "Le (Re)commencement du matérialisme dialectique." *Critique* 240 (1967): 438–67. Translated by Bruno Bosteels as "The (Re)commencement of Dialectical Materialism." In *The Adventure of French Philosophy*, 133–70. London: Verso, 2012.

Badiou, Alain, and Bruno Bosteels. "Posmaoísmo: Un diálogo con Alain Badiou." *Acontecimiento: Revista para pensar la política* 24–25 (2003): 45–78. Published in English as "Can Change Be Thought?" In *Badiou and Politics*, by Bruno Bosteels, 289–317. Durham, NC: Duke University Press, 2011.

Balibar, Étienne. "Althusser's Object." Translated by Margaret Cohen and Bruce Robbins. *Social Text* 39 (1994): 157–88.

———. *Citizen Subject: Foundations for Philosophical Anthropology*. Translated by Steven Miller. New York: Fordham University Press, 2017.

———. "Eschatology versus Teleology: The Suspended Dialogue between Derrida and Althusser." In *Derrida and the Time of the Political*, edited by Pheng Cheah and Suzanne Guerlac, 57–73. Durham, NC: Duke University Press, 2009.

———. "The Infinite Contradiction." Translated by Jean-Marc Poisson and Jacques Lezra. *Yale French Studies* 88 (1995): 142–64.

———. "The Non-Contemporaneity of Althusser." In *The Althusserian Legacy*, edited by E. Ann Kaplan and Michael Sprinker, 1–16. London: Verso, 1993.

———. Preface to *Althusser, L'adieu infini*, by Emilio de Ípola, vii–xxi. Paris: Presses Universitaires de France, 2012.

———. Preface to *Sur la reproduction*, by Louis Althusser, 7–18.

———. "Une rencontre en Romagne." Introduction to *Machiavelli et nous*, by Louis Althusser, 9–30. Paris: Tallendier, 2009.

Boutang, Yann Moulier. *Louis Althusser: Une biographie*. Paris: Grasset, 1992.

Butler, Judith. *The Psychic Life of Power: Theories in Subjection*. Stanford, CA: Stanford University Press, 1997.

Cefaï, Daniel, and Joseph Issac. *L'héritage du pragmatism: Conflits d'urbanité et épreuves de civisme*. La Tour-d'Aigues, France: Éditions de l'Aube, 2002.

Cruz, Manuel. *La crisis del stalinismo: El caso Althusser*. Barcelona: Península, 1977.

Debray, Régis. *Revolution in the Revolution? Armed Struggle and Political Struggle in Latin America*. Translated by Bobbye Ortiz. New York: Grove, 1967.

Deleuze, Gilles, and Félix Guattari. *Anti-Oedipus: Capitalism and Schizophrenia*. Translated by Robert Hurley, Mark Seem, and Helen R. Lane. Minneapolis: University of Minnesota Press, 1983.

Derrida, Jacques. "The Law of Genre." In *Acts of Literature*, edited by Derek Attridge, 221–52. London: Routledge, 1992.

———. "Text Read at Louis Althusser's Funeral." In *The Work of Mourning*, edited by Pascale-Anne Brault and Michael Naas, 111–18. Chicago: University of Chicago Press, 2001.

Derrida, Jacques, and Élisabeth Roudinesco. *De quoi demain . . . dialogue*. Paris: Flammarion, 2001.

Dotti, Jorge. "¿Cómo mirar el rostro de la Gorgona? Antagonismo, estructuralismo y decisionismo." *Deus Mortalis* 3 (2004): 451–516.

Fornillo, Bruno, and Alejandro Lezama. *Releer Althusser*. Buenos Aires: Parusia, 2003.

Giner, Salvador. "Intenciones humanas, estructuras sociales: Para una lógica situacional." In *Acción humana*, edited by Manuel Cruz, 21–126. Barcelona: Ariel, 1997.

Hallward, Peter, and Knox Peden, eds. *Concept and Form*. Vol. 1, *Key Texts from the "Cahiers pour l'Analyse."* London: Verso, 2012.

———. *Concept and Form*. Vol. 2, *Interviews and Essays on the "Cahiers pour l'Analyse."* London: Verso, 2012.

Harnecker, Marta. *Los conceptos elementales del materialismo histórico*. Buenos Aires: Siglo XXI, 1971.

Hartley, L. P. *The Go-Between*. New York: New York Review of Books, 2002.

Hegel, G. W. F. *Phenomenology of Spirit*. Translated by A. V. Miller. Oxford: Oxford University Press, 1977.

Hilb, Claudia, ed. *El resplandor de lo público: En torno a Hannah Arendt*. Caracas: Nueva Sociedad, 1994.

———. *Leo Strauss: El arte de leer; Una lectura de la interpretación straussiana de Maquiavelo, Hobbes, Locke y Spinoza*. Buenos Aires: Fondo de Cultura Económica, 2005.

Ípola, Emilio de. "Acción, Decisión, Sujeto." In *Metáforas de la política*, 67–84. Rosario, Argentina: Homo Sapiens, 2001.

———. *Althusser, el infinito adiós*. Buenos Aires: Siglo XXI, 2007. Translated by Marie Bardet as *Althusser, l'adieu infini*. Paris: Presses Universitaires de France, 2012.

———. *Las cosas del creer: Creencia, lazo social y comunidad política*. Buenos Aires: Ariel, 1987.

———. "El hecho peronista." In *La Argentina en el siglo XX*, edited by Carlos Altamirano, 325–32. Buenos Aires: Ariel, 1999.

———. *Ideología y discurso populista*. Buenos Aires: Folios, 1982.

———. "Un recorrido de la acción colectiva: El conflicto en la Facultad de Ciencias Sociales." In *El Eterno retorno: Acción y sistema en la teoría social contemporánea*, edited by Emilio de Ípola, 187–222. Buenos Aires: Biblos, 2004.

Karsz, Saúl, ed. *Lectura de Althusser*. Buenos Aires: Editorial Galerna, 1970.

Lacan, Jacques. "Aggressiveness in Psychoanalysis." In *Écrits: The First Complete Edition in English*, 82–101.

———. *Écrits*. Paris: Éditions du Seuil, 1966. Translated by Bruce Fink as *Écrits: The First Complete Edition in English*. New York: W. W. Norton, 2007.

———. *The Four Fundamental Concepts of Psychoanalysis*. Translated by Alan Sheridan. New York: W. W. Norton, 1998.

———. "The Mirror Stage as Formative of the *I* Function as Revealed in Psychoanalytic Experience." In *Écrits: The First Complete Edition in English*, 75–81.

Laclau, Ernesto. "The Death and Resurrection of the Theory of Ideology." MLN 112, no. 3 (April 1997): 297–321.

———. *New Reflections on the Revolution of Our Times*. London: Verso, 1990.

Laplanche, Jean, and Serge Leclaire. "The Unconscious: A Psychoanalytic Study." Translated by Patrick Coleman. *Yale French Studies* 48 (1972): 118–75.

Laplanche, Jean, and Jean-Bertrand Pontalis. *The Language of Psychoanalysis*. Translated by Donald Nicholson-Smith. New York: W. W. Norton, 1974.

Lefort, Claude. *Machiavelli in the Making*. Translated by Michael B. Smith. Evanston, IL: Northwestern University Press, 2012.

Leibniz, G. W. *Theodicy: Essays on the Goodness of God, the Freedom of Man and the Origin of Evil*. Translated by E. M. Huggard. La Salle, IL: Open Court, 1985.

Lévi-Strauss, Claude. "History and Dialectic." In *The Savage Mind*, 245–69.

———. "Introduction à l'oeuvre de Marcel Mauss." In *Sociologie et anthropologie*, by Marcel Mauss, ix–lii. Paris: Presses Universitaires de France, 1950. Translated by Felicity Baker as *Introduction to the Work of Marcel Mauss*. London: Routledge and Kegan Paul, 1987.

———. *Mythologiques*. Vol. 2, *Du miel aux cendres*. Paris: Plon, 2009.

———. "Le sorcier et sa magie." *Les Temps Modernes* 41 (1949): 3–24.

———. *The Savage Mind*. London: Weidenfeld and Nicolson, 1966.

———. *Structural Anthropology*. Translated by Claire Jacobson. New York: Basic Books, 1974.

Lúkacs, Georg. *History and Class Consciousness: Studies in Marxist Dialectics*. Cambridge, MA: MIT Press, 1999.

Lyotard, Jean-François. *Dérive à partir de Marx et Freud*. Paris: Editions Galilée, 1994. Translated as *Driftworks*. New York: Semiotext(e), 1984.

Maniglier, Patrice, ed. *Le Moment philosophique des années 1960 en France*. Paris: Presses Universitaires de France, 2011.

Marx, Karl. *Capital: A Critique of Political Economy*. Vol. 1. Translated by Ben Fowkes. New York: Penguin, 1990.

———. *Capital: A Critique of Political Economy*. Vol. 3. Translated by David Fernbach. New York: Penguin, 1991.

———. "The Eighteenth Brumaire of Louis Bonaparte." In *Karl Marx and Frederick Engels Collected Works*. Vol. 11, *Marx and Engels: 1851–1853*, 99–197. New York: International Publishers, 1979.

———. "Preface to the French Edition." In *Capital: A Critique of Political Economy*, 1:104.

Marx, Karl, and Frederick Engels. "Introduction: Production, Consumption, Distribution, Exchange (Circulation)." In *Karl Marx and Frederick Engels Collected Works*. Vol. 28, *Marx: 1857–1861*, 17–48. New York: International Publishers, 1986.

———. *Karl Marx and Frederick Engels Collected Works*. Vol. 1, *Marx: 1835–1843*. New York: International Publishers, 1975.

Mauss, Marcel. *A General Theory of Magic*. New York: Routledge, 1972.

———. *The Gift: The Form and Reason for Exchange in Archaic Societies*. Translated by W. D. Halls. New York: W. W. Norton, 1990.

Miller, Jacques-Alain. "Action of the Structure." In *Concept and Form*. Vol. 1, *Key Texts from the "Cahiers pour l'Analyse*," 69–84.

———. "Fonction de la formation théorique." *Cahiers Marxistes-Léninistes* 1 (1964): 1–3.

———. "S'truc dure." *Pas tant: Revue de la "découverte freudienne"* 8/9 (1985): 4–11.

———. "Suture (Elements of the Logic of the Signifier)." In *Concept and Form*. Vol. 1, *Key Texts from the "Cahiers pour l'Analyse*," 91–102.

Milner, Jean-Claude. *Le périple structural*. Lagrasse: Verdier, 2008.

Naishtat, Francisco. *Ética política de la acción colectiva*. La Plata, Argentina: Universidad Nacional de La Plata, 2000.

———. *Problemas filosóficos en la acción individual y colectiva: Una perspectiva pragmática*. Buenos Aires: Prometeo, 2005.

Onaka, Kazuya. "Pratique et temps: Louis Althusser et les 'courants souterrains du matérialisme.'" PhD diss., University of Paris X, Nanterre, 2003.

Pommier, Gérard. *Louis du néant: La mélancolie d'Althusser*. Paris: Aubier, 1998.

Pouillon, Jean. "Del lado de Marx." In *Lectura de Althusser*, 231–46.

Prigogine, Ilya, and Isabelle Stengears. *Order out of Chaos*. New York: Bantam, 1984.

Rancière, Jacques. *La leçon d'Althusser*. Paris: Gallimard, 1974. Translated by Emiliano Battista as *Althusser's Lesson*. New York: Continuum, 2011.

———. "La scène du texte." In *Politique et philosophie dans l'oeuvre de Louis Althusser*, edited by Sylvain Lazarus, 47–67. Paris: Presses Universitaires de France, 1993.

———. "On the Theory of Ideology: Althusser's Politics." In *Althusser's Lesson*, 125–54.

———. "Sobre la teoría de la ideología (La política de Athusser)." In *Lectura de Althusser*, 319–57.

Rozitchner, Léon. "La tragedia del althusserianismo teórico." *El Ojo Mocho* 17 (2003): 43–50.

Sartre, Jean-Paul. *Critique of Dialectical Reason*. Vol. 1. Translated by Alan Sheridan-Smith. London: Verso, 2004.

Spinoza, Baruch. *Political Treatise*. Translated by Samuel Shirley. Indianapolis: Hackett, 2000.

———. "The *Ethics*." In *A Spinoza Reader*, edited by Edwin Curley, 85–265. Princeton, NJ: Princeton University Press, 1994.

Strauss, Leo. *Persecution and the Art of Writing*. Chicago: University of Chicago Press, 1988.

Terán, Oscar. *De utopías, catástrofes y esperanzas: Un camino intelectual*. Buenos Aires: Siglo XXI, 2006.

Thompson, E. P. "Eighteenth-Century English Society: Class Struggle without Class?" *Social History* 3, no. 2 (1978): 133–65.

Turkle, Sherry. *Psychoanalytic Politics: Jacques Lacan and Freud's French Revolution.* London: Guilford, 1992.

Vatter, Miguel. "Althusser and Machiavelli: Politics after the Critique of Marx." *Multitudes: Revue politique, artistique, philosophique* 13 (2013). http://www.multitudes.net/Althusser-and-Machiavelli-Politics/.

Verstraeten, Pierre. "Lévi-Strauss ou la tentation du néant." *Les Temps Modernes* 206 (July 1963): 66–109.

Veron, Elise, and Gilles Lapougue. "Estructura vs. Historia: Reportaje a Levi Strauss." *Zona Erógena* 4 (1990): 1–8.

INDEX

Abrégé de métapolitique (Badiou), 126n105
Absolute Subject, 69. *See also* Subject
action, 18, 46, 66, 76, 97–102
"Action of the Structure" (Miller), 46, 121n29
"Aggressiveness in Psychoanalysis" (Lacan), 50
alienation, xxi, xxii, 30
Allende, Salvador, xiv
Althusser, Louis: Badiou and, 46, 56–58, 99–101, 111n5; Balibar and, 59–60, 107, 111; class and, xxiii, 7, 70, 73, 75, 85, 97–98, 135n47; classic, xiv, 4, 8, 27, 87, 92, 100–107, 114n2, 137n1; declared project and, 12–14, 22, 75; determination and, 37, 51; encounter and, xxii, 94–95, 104, 117n3; esoteric project and, 62, 82, 104, 138n10; exoteric project and, 25, 118n18, 138n10; French influence of, 15–19, 24–25, 31, 35, 120n9, 121n18; governance and, 31–33; history and, xxi, 59, 61, 85, 97, 118n17; humanism and, 65, 96; ideology and, xviii, 26, 35, 64–67, 70–80, 95, 129n15; Italian influence of, 86, 90, 105, 113n18; Lacan and, xx, 26, 56–59, 65–66, 72, 95, 118n15, 119n21; "last Althusser" and, xviii, xxii, 1–7, 12, 15, 23–27, 33, 84, 93–96; Latin America and, xiv, 16, 104–5, 107, 111, 112n7, 121n18, 138n11; Lévi-Strauss and, xv–xviii, 18–22, 46, 59–62, 84, 122n36, 128n123; Machiavelli and, 88–95; Marxism and, xiv–xviii, 3–7, 11, 24, 31–35, 58, 61, 81–87, 92–96, 104–5, 135n56; materialism and, xxii, 53, 62, 130n22, 131n34, 138n13; overdetermination and, 36–39, 54; philosophy and, 25–26, 29, 76, 80–81, 83, 87, 99–100, 118n10, 132n3; politics and, xxiii, 5, 34, 61, 80, 84–85, 96, 113n18; posthumous, 1–7, 27, 33, 84, 89, 106, 113n16, 114n1; production and, xx, xxi, 36; psychoanalysis and, 106, 129n12; science and, 19, 32; structuralism and, xv, xvii, xxii, 54, 62–63, 83–84; subjectivity and, xx, 32, 54–59, 67, 77, 96–98, 100, 130n31; subterranean, xvi, 10, 13–14, 22–23, 27, 87; theory and, xvi, xix, 7. *See also* French Communist Party; Marx, Karl; Marxism; revolution; structuralism
Althusserianism: classic, 26–27, 29, 87, 100, 114n2; ideology in, 66–68; Lévi-Strauss and, 18–19; Marx and, 20, 105, 136n56; structuralism and, 23, 39–40, 46, 59, 62, 73
Anderson, Perry, 15
antihumanism, 21, 96, 98. *See also* humanism
Aragon, Louis, 20
Aron, Raymond, 16–17, 87
atoms, xxii, 93–95
Austin, J. L., 101
Ávalos, Eduardo, 135n38

Bachelard, Gaston, xix, 21, 81
Badiou, Alain, xxii–xxiv, 2–4, 40–46, 50–61, 98–101, 107, 115n5, 124n86
Balibar, Étienne, xiii–xxiv, 2, 25, 64, 107, 127n112, 127n115, 127n120, 137n2
Barthes, Roland, 30, 60
becoming, 44, 74, 86, 94, 128n3
Bidet, Jacques, 2, 107, 138n13
Borges, Jorge Luis, xiv
Borgia, César, 90, 119n28
Bosteels, Bruno, 115n5
Boutang, Yann Moulier, 117n8
Butler, Judith, 113n15

Cahiers maxistes-léninistes, 30
Cahiers pour l'analyse, 30
Canguilhem, Georges, 21
Capital (Marx), 40, 73, 92, 98, 116n22, 119n27, 128n8
capitalism, xx, xxiii, 40, 74, 92, 113n17, 126n98. *See also* class; economy; Marx, Karl; Marxism; production
Castro, Fidel, xiv
causality, xvi, 39–40, 46–54, 60–64, 95, 121n29, 122n33, 125n87
Cefaï, Daniel, xxiv, 100
class, xxiii, 7, 20, 70, 72–73, 80, 90–91, 96–97. *See also* capitalism; economy; masses; proletariat
classic Althusser, 4, 8, 27, 65, 87, 100–103, 107, 114n2, 137n1. *See also* Althusser, Louis
clinamen, xxii, 83, 94–95. *See also* Epicurus; Lucretius; swerve
collectives, 98–101
communism, xx, 16, 29, 85–86, 132n8
Comte, Auguste, 11
Conein, Bernard, 67
Congress of Argenteuil (1966), 20
conjuncture, xvii, xxii, 51–52, 57, 83, 88, 93
"Contradiction and Overdetermination" (Althusser), 17, 37–38
Contribution to the Critique of Political Economy (Marx), 30, 37, 113n17
"Course on Philosophy for Scientists" (Althusser), 25–27, 84

Critique of Dialectical Reason (Sartre), xvi, 59, 62, 101
Cultural Revolution, 21

Darstellung, 54, 125n95
"Death and Resurrection of the Theory of Ideology, The" (Laclau), 130n29
Debray, Régis, xiv, 138n11
decision, 99–102
"Dérive à partir de Marx et Freud" (Lyotard), 111n6
Derrida, Jacques, 20, 83, 93, 108, 138n12
De Sanctis, Francesco, 89
Descartes, René, 11
despotism, 32–33, 90
determination, 34, 37, 40, 52–53, 65. *See also* structuralism
Discourses (Machiavelli), 91–92
dispositif, 19, 67, 75, 79, 100
Dotti, Jorge, 49

École Normale Supérieure, 16, 25, 84, 128n123
Economic and Philosophic Manuscripts of 1844 (Marx), 33
economy, xxiii, 39–40, 52–53, 57, 124n86. *See also* capitalism; class
Écrits (Lacan), 20
Écrits philosophiques et politiques (Althusser), 11
Eighteenth Brumaire of Louis Bonaparte, The (Marx), 96
encounter, xxii, xxiii, 28, 93–95, 104, 113n20
Engels, Friedrich, 7, 30, 37, 83, 93, 100, 105
Epicurus, xxii, 93–94. *See also* clinamen; Lucretius; swerve
"Estructura vs. Historia: Reportaje a Levi Strauss" (Veron and Lapougue), 132n6

Feuerbach, Ludwig, xx, 128n123
Fondation Althusser, 3
For Marx (Althusser), xiii, 15–16, 23, 30, 50, 59, 67
Foucault, Michel, 20–21, 30, 60, 93, 96
Frege, Gottlob, xix, 46–47

150 Index

French Communist Party, 16–17, 19, 24–25, 31, 120n9, 121n18, 137n4. *See also* Althusser, Louis; Marx, Karl
Freud, Sigmund, xvi, xvii, 6, 56, 65, 73
"Freud and Lacan" (Althusser), 65
Freudian School of Paris, 58
Freudian slip, xvi, xviii
Futur antérieur (journal), 87
Future Lasts Forever, The (Althusser), 3, 5, 115n15

Gadet, Françoise, 67
Garaudy, Roger, 16, 18, 35, 117n8
German Ideology, The (Marx), 34, 85
Gift, The (Mauss), 41
Giner, Salvador, 4, 115n7
Goldmann, Lucien, 18
Gramsci, Antonio, xvii, 89, 91, 119n28, 132n4
Guevara, Che, xiv
Guilhaumou, Jacques, 67

hailing, 68. *See also* interpellation
Harnecker, Marta, 105, 112n7, 138n11
Haroche, Claudine, 67
Hegel, G. W. F., xix, xx, xxii, 23, 34–35, 81, 89
Henry, Pierre, 67
history, xxiii, 74, 95. *See also* ideology; materialism; structuralism
History and Class Consciousness (Lukács), 96
humanism, xvii, 16, 30, 65. *See also* antihumanism
Husserl, Edmund, xix

Ideological State Apparatuses (ISAs), 67, 69–70, 72, 75, 78
ideology: Althusser and, 55, 64, 79, 95, 113n16; class and, 69–71, 73, 75–77; science and, 19, 26–27, 30, 34–35; structuralism and, 40, 60, 68–69, 127n114; subjectivity and, 64–65, 67, 69, 71–72, 97; *Träger* and, 54, 65, 71–74. *See also* history; knowledge; materialism
"Ideology and Ideological State Apparatuses" (Althusser), 27
Imaginary, 48

Institut mémoires de l'édition contemporaine (IMEC), xiv, 3, 8
interpellation, xix–xxi, 67–69, 71–72, 76, 78–79, 113n18
Introduction to the Work of Marcel Mauss (Lévi-Strauss), 19, 40–41, 43, 48–50, 53, 122n43

Kant, Immanuel, xix
Kautsky, Karl, 19, 65, 112n13
knowledge, xvii–xviii, xix, 42, 65, 98. *See also* Subject; subjectivity

Lacan, Jacques, xv, xvii, 6, 19–21, 46–61, 65, 118n15, 119n21, 128n3
Laclau, Ernesto, 2, 83, 130n29
Lacroix, Jean, 116n19
La leçon d'Althusser (Rancière), 137n4
La Pensée, 27
Laplanche, Jean, 6, 38–39, 116n20
Lapougue, Gilles, 132n6
last Althusser, xviii, xxii, 1–7, 12, 15, 23–27, 33, 84, 93–96. *See also* Althusser, Louis
Leclaire, Serge, 6, 116n20
Lefebvre, Henri, 18
Lefort, Claude, 89, 134n27
Leibniz, Gottfried Wilhelm, xxi
Lenin, Vladimir, xix, xxiii, 7, 17, 19, 36, 105, 119n28, 133n13
Les Temps Modernes, 43, 121n18
Lettres à Franca (Althusser), 5
Lévi-Strauss, Claude, xv–xviii, 18–22, 30, 40–53, 59–60, 62, 84, 122n38, 128n123
"Lévi-Strauss ou la tentation du néant" (Verstraeten), 121n18
Lewis, John, 96–97
Lire le Capital (Althusser), 125n95, 127n120
Los conceptos elementales del materialismo histórico (Harnecker), 112n7
Lucretius, xxii, 93. *See also* clinamen; Epicurus; swerve
Lukács, Georg, xvii, xx, 96
Lyotard, Jean-François, 111n6

Macherey, Pierre, 25, 107
Machiavelli, Niccolò, 11–12, 87–95, 119n28

Index 151

"Machiavelli, Philosopher" (Althusser), 87
Machiavelli and Us (Althusser), xv, xxiii, xxiv, 87, 89, 134n31
Machiavelli in the Making (Lefort), 89, 134n27
"Machiavelli's Solitude" (Althusser), 87–88, 91–92
Madonia, Franca, 10–12, 126n98, 132n2
Maldidier, Denise, 67
mana, 43, 46
Maoism, 21, 115n5, 137n4
Mao Tse-Tung, 17, 21, 36, 105
Marx, Karl: Althusser and, xiv–xviii, xxiv, 3–7, 24, 54–61, 74, 81–93, 96–100, 105; history and, xiv, xv, 24; philosophy and, 30, 135n34; production and, 36, 124n86; structuralism and, 72–74. *See also* Althusser, Louis; capitalism; French Communist Party; structuralism
"Marx in His Limits" (Althusser), 84–85, 133nn12–13
Marxism: Althusser and, xiv–xviii, 3, 33–34, 58, 84, 86, 104–5, 136n56; history and, 57, 59–60, 85; humanism and, 21, 30; ideology and, 33–34, 52, 65; Latin America and, 104–5; Lenin and, 36, 61, 85, 97; philosophy and, 23–24, 30, 81; politics and, 17–21, 34, 36, 86, 102, 112n13; post-Marxism and, 23. *See also* Althusser, Louis; capitalism
Marxism and "Primitive" Societies (Terray), 61
masses, xxiii, 45, 96–97. *See also* class
materialism: aleatory, xxii, 33, 80, 96, 113n20; dialectical, xix, 24, 52–53, 81; historical, 23, 51, 53, 61, 73, 81, 83, 138n13. *See also* history; ideology
Mauss, Marcel, 41, 44–45, 122n37
mental illness, 44–45
Merleau-Ponty, Maurice, 89
militant, 5, 19–21, 26, 89, 99, 105, 137n3
Miller, Jacques-Alain, xv, 19, 46–50, 53–54, 62, 65, 121n29, 125n87
Milner, Jean-Claude, xvii
Montaigne, 86, 133n15
Montesquieu, 8, 31–33, 64
Montesquieu, la politique et l'histoire (Althusser), 10, 31, 82, 130n26
Mury, Gilbert, 18, 35

Naishtat, Francisco, xxii, xxiv, 100–101, 114n21, 136n62
Navarro, Fernanda, 75–77, 88, 129n22, 131n34
Newton, Isaac, 32
"Non-Contemporaneity of Althusser, The" (Balibar), 137n2

"Object of *Capital*, The" (Althusser), 39, 60–61, 125n93
October Revolution, 36, 38
Onaka, Kazuya, 113n20
"On Contradiction" (Althusser), 36
"On the Materialist Dialectic" (Althusser), 17, 19, 39
"On the Young Marx" (Althusser), 33
orenda, 43, 46
overdetermination, 36–39. *See also* structuralism

Paris Commune of 1871, 36
Pêcheux, Michel, 67
perception, 65, 99
Persecution and the Art of Writing (Strauss), 112n12
"Philosophy and Marxism" (Althusser), 131n34
Philosophy and the Spontaneous Philosophy of the Scientists (Elliot), 129n15
Philosophy of the Encounter (Althusser), 130n22
Plato, xix, 6
Politique et Histoire, de Machiavel à Marx (Althusser), 87
Pommier, Gérard, 6
Pontalis, Jean-Bertrand, 38–39
Positions (Althusser), 5
posthumous Althusser, 1–7, 27, 33, 84, 89, 106, 113n16, 114n1. *See also specific works*
post-Marxism, 23
Potash, Robert, 135n38
primitive accumulation, 92
Prince, The (Machiavelli), 89–91
problematic, xvi, xviii, 13, 22, 34–38, 55, 60–62, 83–84, 118n16
production, 36, 51, 60, 65, 85, 124n86, 126n98. *See also* capitalism; structuralism

152 Index

proletariat, 96, 98. *See also* class
Psychic Life of Power, The (Butler), 113n15
psychoanalysis, 6, 27, 38–44, 53–55, 59–61, 106, 129n12. *See also* Freud, Sigmund; Lacan, Jacques

Rancière, Jacques, 2, 17, 23, 54, 107, 114n4, 117n9, 120n4, 137n4
Reading Capital (Althusser), xv, xvi, 15–16, 23, 30, 50, 54, 59–60, 82
Real, 46–48, 58
"(Re)commencement of Dialectical Materialism, The" (Badiou), 40, 50, 111n5, 123n70, 124n86
Regnault, François, 25
religion, 31–32, 69, 122n32, 137n3
"Reply to John Lewis" (Althusser), 98, 135n48
revolution, xx, 21, 39, 77–78, 84, 97–98. *See also* Althusser, Louis
Revolution in the Revolution (Debray), xiv, 138n11
Robin, Régine, 67
Rousseau, Jean-Jacques, 83, 89, 117n1
Rozitchner, León, 115n15
Russell, Bertrand, 95, 130n22
Russian Revolution, 36, 38

Sarte, Jean-Paul, xv, xvi, xxii, xxiii, 11, 18, 62, 96, 101
Savage Mind, The (Lévi-Strauss), xvi
science, xix, 20, 30, 32, 42, 73, 75
seriality, 101
shamanism, 43–45, 48–50
signification, 19, 21, 41–43, 46, 49–50, 122n38. *See also* structuralism
"Sobre la teoría de la ideología" (Rancière), 137n4
socialism, 20
society, xvii, 41, 45, 69
sociology, xxii–xxiii, 3, 48, 100–102, 106
"Sorcerer and His Magic, The" (Lévi-Strauss), 43, 48
Soviet Union, 16, 29; Twentieth Congress of the Communist Party, 33
Spinoza, Baruch, xix, 83, 88–89, 93, 113n14

Spirit of Laws, The (Montesquieu), 32
Stalin, Joseph, 16, 81, 85, 99
State, 27, 37, 67–75, 78, 85–92, 113n16
Strauss, Leo, 112n12, 118n18
"S'truc dure" (Miller), 48–49, 62
Structural Anthropology (Lévi-Strauss), 19, 48, 61
structuralism: Althusser and, 18–22, 60–63, 83; causality, 39–40, 62; determination and, 38–39, 49–54, 101, 127n120; Lévi-Strauss and, xvi, xvii, 59–61, 84, 132n5. *See also* Althusser, Louis; determination; history; overdetermination; production
Subject, 21, 46–49, 53–59, 65–79, 115n15, 125n89, 130n31. *See also* knowledge
subjectivity, xvii, xx, 48–49, 56, 78–79, 95–102. *See also* knowledge
superstructure, 37, 71
Sur la reproduction (Althusser), 113n16
suture, 46–48
"Suture" (Miller), 46
swerve, xxii, 74, 93, 95, 98. *See also* clinamen; Epicurus; Lucretius
Symbolic, 48
symbolism, 42–44, 46, 128n5
symptomatic reading, xvi, 6–7, 16, 62, 70, 103
synecdoche, 50

teleology, 131n1
Terán, Oscar, 4, 86, 115n12
Terray, Emmanuel, 61
"Theory, Theoretical Practice and Theoretical Formation: Ideology and Ideological Struggle" (Rancière), 129n15
"Theses on Feuerbach" (Marx), 34
Thompson, E. P., 114n24
"Three Notes on the Theory of Discourses" (Althusser), 27, 55, 71, 98, 119n25, 125n93
Torre, Juan Carlos, 135n38
Trotskyists, 21

"Unconscious: A Psychoanalytic Study, The" (Laplanche and Leclaire), 6, 116n20
"Underground Current of the Materialism of the Encounter, The" (Althusser), 87, 95

Vatter, Miguel, 85
Veron, Elise, 132n6
Verstraeten, Pierre, 121n18
Vorstellung, 54

Weber, Max, 135n40
What Is to Be Done? (Lenin), 19, 112n13

Wittgenstein, Ludwig, 95, 101
Writings on Psychoanalysis (Althusser), 27, 55, 71

Žižek, Slavoj, 2